# India's War Heroes

# INDIA'S WAR HEROES

S.K. Sharma

PRASHANT PUBLISHING HOUSE
DELHI-110094

*Published by :*
**Prashant Publishing House**
C-34, 28 Foota Road, Gali-3,
West Karwal Nagar, Delhi-110094
Phone : 011-22963970, Mob. : 9810396373
e-mail.: prashantpublishinghouse@gmail.com

**India's War Heroes**
Reserved
*First Published 2018*

**ISBN** 978-81-938012-1-5



---

**PRINTED IN INDIA**
Published by Mr. R.K. Jha M/s Prashant Publishing House and Published at H.S. Offset House Press, Delhi.

# Contents

# Preface

Take a look at India's history and you'll realise that we have never attacked a country first. Unfortunately, we have been subjected to war on a number of occasions. India's armed forces have kept the invaders out and in the process, many brave sons of the soil have had to make the ultimate sacrifice to keep the country safe.

Hamid joined the army in December 1954, and was posted to the 4th Battalion of the Grenadiers regiment. During the Sino-Indian War, his battalion participated in the battle of Namka Chu against the People's Liberation Army. During the Indo-Pakistani War of 1965, the 4 Grenadiers battalion was entrusted with a vital position before the village of Chima on the Khem Karan–Bhikhiwind line. At the Battle of Asal Uttar on 9–10 September 1965, Hamid destroyed six Pakistani tanks and was killed during an engagement with a seventh.

Cariappa was promoted to the substantive rank of lieutenant-colonel on 17 July 1946. The same year, he was promoted to Brigadier of the Frontier Brigade Group. It was during this time that Colonel Ayub Khan - later Field Marshal and President of Pakistan, 1962-1969 - served under him. In 1947, Cariappa was the first Indian who was selected to undergo a training course at Imperial Defence College, Camberly, UK on the higher directions of war. During the traumatic period of partition, he handled the division of the Indian Army and sharing of its assets between Pakistan and India, in a most amicable, just and orderly manner. He was then the Indian officer in charge of overseeing the transition.

Field Marshal Sam Hormusji Framji Jamshedji Manekshaw is, without a doubt, the most popular and colourful military leader in India. Having led the nation to its first decisive victory in 1971, "Sam Bahadur", as he is popularly known, became a household word. He was India's first Field Marshal, and remains, even today, the most admired and idolised of our Army Chiefs. He has a charismatic personality, and it is impossible not to feel overawed in his presence. Vigour, dash and elan - he has them all, the typical signs of a great soldier. However, if there is one attribute which can be called his hall mark, it is his ready wit, and sense of humour. Anecdotes about Sam abound, and one always keeps hearing new ones, even now, more than thirty years after he has quit active service.

This is a reference book. All the matter is just compiled and edited in nature, taken from the various sources which are in public domain.

This is a major work of historical research. It will be indispensable to historians and sociologists, as well as to students and the Indian army.

—*Editor*

# 1

# Abdul Hamid: Hero of Indo-Pak War 1965

Company Quartermaster Havildar Abdul Hamid, PVC (1 July 1933 – 10 September 1965), was an Indian Army soldier who posthumously received India's highest military decoration, the Param Vir Chakra, for his actions during the Indo-Pakistani War of 1965.

Hamid joined the army in December 1954, and was posted to the 4th Battalion of the Grenadiers regiment. During the Sino-Indian War, his battalion participated in the battle of Namka Chu against the People's Liberation Army. During the Indo-Pakistani War of 1965, the 4 Grenadiers battalion was entrusted with a vital position before the village of Chima on the Khem Karan–Bhikhiwind line. At the Battle of Asal Uttar on 9–10 September 1965, Hamid destroyed six Pakistani tanks and was killed during an engagement with a seventh.

1965! A year of unprecedented turmoil in Indo-Pak history. In April that year, a minor border dispute in the Rann of Kutch area had resulted in limited scale conflicts between the armies of India & Pakistan.

Due to superior armaments & training that it received from the US, the Pakistan Army dominated the skirmishes in the Rann area and made some territorial gains. India on the other hand was recovering from a disastrous war with China and still licking her wounds. Though the modernization of its military was underway, it was still to gather steam. India was at its most vulnerable position in1965.

This emboldened the Pakistanis and set in motion a chain of events that would lead to the Second Kashmir War of 1965.

Meanwhile, much before any of these events,in 1933, a Tailor named Mohammad Usman and his wife were blessed with a baby boy after many years of marriage in Dhamupur, District Ghazipur UP of pre-partition India. The grateful parents decided to name the boy Abdul Hamid.

Abdul Hamid had an unremarkable journey to adolescence, and was trained by his Father in the craft of Tailoring. However when a childhood friend successfully enlisted in the Army, this set young Abdul thinking. He had dreams of his own. He wanted to travel the world and see far off places, instead of being confined to his village for his entire life. The stories narrated by his friend in the Army, instilled a new found passion to serve his country. He would dream of scenarios in which he envisioned himself performing some brave act or the other and that his entire village celebrated him as a Hero.

All his plans for valour and chivalry crash landed when his idea was shot down by his rattled parents. They were not ready to send their only son off to serve in the Army. To make matters worse, he was soon married off to a Girl of his mother's choice, with the hope that wedlock will drive out all such 'crazy notions' from his head. However, young Abdul had other plans and he made it clear to young Rasoolan (his bride) on the very first night of his marriage that he intended to enlist in the Army and that nothing, not even marriage, could make him change his mind.

To his utter surprise, he found that his wife was actually supportive of his plans. With the support of his wife, but against the wishes of his parents, Abdul Hamid applied for and was enlisted into the Grenadiers infantry regiment as Army enrolment number 239885 on 27 December 1954.

He was later posted in the 4th Battalion of the regiment where he served all his service life. During the Sino-Indian War of 1962, Hamid's battalion was part of 7th Infantry Brigade commanded by Brigadier John Dalvi, and participated in the battle of Namka Chu against the Chinese. Surrounded and cut off, the battalion had made a fighting breakaway into Bhutan by foot and then to Misamari. Abdul was the only survivor of his Platoon who made his way back to the camp, and nearly died trying.

Though this experience served to wash away any shred of Romanticism that was left in his heart, the awards and citations that he received for his grit and determination further emboldened his resolve to continue his career with the Army. He was awarded with the Raksha Medal, Sainya Seva Medal and the Samar Seva Medal.

Rising steadily through the ranks, Abdul Hamid was promoted and being the most experienced and best 105mm recoil-less rifle shot in the battalion, he was entrusted with the NCO command of battalion's recoil-less rifle platoon.

In May 1965 following the mood of jubilation in Pakistan because of the Rann-of-Kutch episode, Ayub Khan was advised by his trusted advisers to launch "Operation Gibraltar"; a military master plan that envisaged capturing Kashmir by launching armed soldiers and militiamen, dressed as locals into Indian held Kashmir. The immediate objective of such a move was to intice the local Muslim population to revolt against India, finally forcing India to abandon Kashmir.

Operation Gibraltar was set into motion in the first week of August 1965, as soldiers from the Pakistani infantry infiltrated the border in small teams of twos and threes, dressed in local Kashmiri attire, till their numbers eventually swelled to almost 9000, or roughly, a size of an entire Division.

India was caught unawares, but soon the news started pouring in from the valley that Armed Intruders from across the border were wreaking havoc. India countered them by bringing in additional troops. However it was soon clear to the Indian leadership that if they kept the war confined to Kashmir, the state will soon be lost. In order to relieve pressure on its defensive lines in J&K, the Indian Army also launched attacks on the logistical bases of the insurgents in POK, and opened up another front in the plains of Punjab.

The Pakistani Army was left with little choice but to break their defensive lines and charge forward, and they did so at a massive scale in what was to be called as Operation Grand Slam. Pakistan's invading force, consisting of the 1st Armoured Division and 11th Infantry Division, crossed the International Border and captured the Indian town of Khem Karan.

The enemy outmatched us 6:1 in the particular theatre of operations and enjoyed overall technological superiority in Armour. The freshly supplied American M-48 "Patton" Tank was the pride and joy of the Pakistan Army, of which they had around 350 in numbers. Facing them on the Indian side were WWII era Tanks such as Chieftains & Shermans and a few dozen AMX light Tanks, which belonged more in the Museum than on the battlefield.

Considering the gravity of the situation, General-Officer-Commanding of the Indian 4th Mountain Division, Maj. Gen. Gurbaksh Singh immediately ordered the division to fall back and assume a horseshoe shaped defensive position with Assal Uttar as its focal point.

As per the new defence tactics, the 4 Grenadiers occupied a vital area in the vicinity of Chima village on the Khem Karan-Bhikhiwind road. It was made clear to the defending company that a firm hold on this area was vital to the defence of the entire theatre.

On the night of September the 8th, the enemy made repeated attacks on Indian positions but was frustrated in all the attempts. The most serious threat, however, developed when the enemy attacked with a regiment of Patton tanks at 08:00 hours on September 10th. The attack was preceded by intense shelling that littered the entire area in and around India positions with shrapnel and unexploded shells. By 09:00 hours, the enemy tanks had penetrated the forward company positions. At this critical juncture, Abdul Hamid was commanding an M-

40 recoil-less gun detachment. Seeing the gravity of the situation, he moved out to a flank with his gun mounted on a jeep. Intense enemy shelling and tank fire did not deter him.

From his new position, he knocked out the leading enemy tank with accurate fire. Then he changed his position and knocked out another enemy tank. By this time the enemy who had spotted his position brought down concentrated machine gun and high explosive fire on him. He continued to fire on one enemy Tank after another, using the natural camouflage of Sugarcane fields, constantly changing his position.

This forced the Pakistani Commander to order his tanks to spread out, further weakening their tactical position. Though this allowed several Tanks to be knocked out by Indian Jawans armed with Bazookas, Abdul Hamid eventually ran out of luck when his RCL Jeep came face to face with an enemy Tank. He was knocked out by an enemy shell, but not before he had managed to knock out as many as 7 Patton tanks!

This had a considerable debilitating effect on the morale of the enemy and in the decisive Battle of Assal-Uttar, the entire Pakistani Armored Division was decimated and around 100 Pakistani tanks mostly Pattons were lost to Indian fire.

Ayub Khan's evil plan to snatch away Kashmir was buried in the sugarcane fields of Punjab !

For his supreme sacrifice and unmatched valour, Abdul Hamid was honoured with the highest war time gallantry award - the Param Vir Chakra, posthumously received by his wife Rasoolan Bibi from Dr. Sarvepalli Radhakrishnan, then President of India during the 1966 Republic Day Parade.

The residents of Asal Uttar operate a dispensary, library and school in the village named after Abdul Hamid. In his memory, a mausoleum was constructed on his grave by the 4th Grenadiers at Asal Uttar and each year a "mela" is held there on the date of his martyrdom.

Company Quartermaster Havildar Abdul Hamid, PVC (1 July 1933 – 10 September 1965) was a soldier in the 4th Battalion, The Grenadiers of the Indian Army, who died in the

Khem Karan sector during the Indo-Pakistani War of 1965 in the Battle of Asal Uttar, and was the posthumous recipient of the Republic of India's highest military decoration, the Param Vir Chakra.

## EARLY LIFE

Abdul Hamid was born in a Muslim family at Dhamupur village of Ghazipur District ofUttar Pradesh on 1 July 1933, the son of Mohammad Usman

## Army

Abdul Hamid was enrolled into The Grenadiers infantry regiment as army number 239885 on 27 December 1954. He was later posted in the 4th Battalion of the regiment where he served all his service life. During his service, Abdul Hamid served with his battalion in Agra, Amritsar, Jammu & Kashmir, Delhi, NEFA and Ramgarh. During the Sino-Indian War of 1962, Hamid's battalion was part of 7th Infantry Brigadecommanded by Brigadier John Dalvi, and participated in the battle of Namka Chu against the Chinese. Surrounded and cut off, the battalion had made a fighting breakaway into Bhutan by foot and then to Misamari. A young officer, 2 Lt GVP Rao had been awarded a posthumous Maha Vir Chakra, the highest gallantry medal received by the battalion since Independence till Hamid's own award eclipsed it.

Abdul Hamid was born on 1 July 1933 in Dhamupur village of district Ghazipur in Uttar Pradesh to Sakina Begum and Mohammad Usman, who had three more boys and two girls. Abdul's father was a tailor by profession and Abdul would often help him stitch clothes before he decided to join the Army.

Hamid was 20 years old when he was recruited at Varanasi into the Army. After undergoing his training at the Grenadiers Regimental Centre at Nasirabad, he was posted to 4 Grenadiers in 1955. Initially, he served in a rifle company and was then posted to a recoilless platoon. He fought in the '62 war in Thang La, then in the North-East Frontier Province, as part of the 7 Mountain Brigade, 4 Mountain Division.

After ceasefire was declared his unit moved to Ambala where Abdul was appointed Company Quarter Master Havildar (CQMH) of an administration company. Nevertheless, being the best shot with the 106 mm recoilless rifle, the battalion commander wanted him back as NCO of the rifle platoon.

In 1965, when war broke out between India and Pakistan, Abdul Hamid had already completed ten years of service in the Indian army and was serving in the 4th Grenadiers. The news came that the enemy had attacked Aknoor in Jammu with the goal of cutting off communication and supply routes to the Indian forces on the border of Jammu and Kashmir.

As Hamid's battalion, the 4th Grenadiers occupied a vital area near Chima village on the road to Punjab's Khem Karan sector, they were given the job of holding the enemy near the village of Asal Uttar. Firm hold of this area was essential for the Indian plan of defence and so the 4th Grenadiers was ordered to move forward and to collect their 106 RCL guns from the nearest ordnance depot. Hamid was one of the non-commissioned instructors. Due to absence of anti-tank detachment commanders, he was told to take over an antitank detachment.

On September 8, the enemy made repeated attacks on the Grenadiers' position, but was repulsed each time. The most serious assault came when the enemy advanced with a regiment of Patton tanks. So intense was the attack that a shell littered every yard of ground occupied by the Indian battalion. Hamid was in command of a recoilless gun detachment. He moved out to a flank with his gun mounted on a jeep.

The moment the tanks came within shooting distance, Hamid fired and watched the trajectory of the shell as it hit its targets. The tank he hit went up in flames in front of his eyes while the remaining two are again abandoned by the enemy soldiers.

By the end of the day, Hamid had destroyed two tanks, while four had been abandoned. He then called army engineers and asked them to immediately lay out anti-tank mines in the area. The next morning he was back at his recoilless gun, even as his battalion faced an air attack from Pakistani Sabre jets. By the end of the day, Hamid had shot down two more tanks.

At 0800 hours on September 10, 1965, a battalion of Pakistani Patton tanks attacked the holding area of the 4th Grenadier positions. The Indian soldiers came under intense artillery bombardment but didn't respond. Within an hour, the Pakistanis had penetrated forward Indian positions. The situation grew grim. In the melee, Hamid spotted six Pakistani tanks heading towards his men. He didn't think twice, hopped on to his jeep which had a gun mounted on it and rushed towards the tanks to flank them.

Intense enemy firing did nothing to deter him. Using the the tall cotton crop growing in the fields to camoufalge his position, Hamid knocked out the leading tank with accurate fire. Then changing position, he disabled two more. By now the enemy had spotted him and employed machine guns and explosives to bring him down. As he hit another enemy tank, he was mortally wounded by a high explosive shell.

Throughout this blistering attack, Hamid had singlehandedly managed to destroy a total of eight enemy tanks, many more than what an armoured formation could take on. His unparalleled bravery and determination inspired his comrades to put up a gallant fight and to beat back the heavy tank assault by the enemy. Approximately 97 Pakistani tanks were destroyed or abandoned during this battle. The enemy was routed and they never made it past Khem Karan.

Abdul Hamid did not live to see the next day or share in the joy of victory that came after three days of intense fighting. A citation had been sent on September 9, 1965, crediting him for destroying four tanks but nobody knew that Hamid would again blow up three more tanks the very next day. As the citation was already sent, it gives him credit for destroying four tanks. He had, in fact, destroyed eight. For his selflessness, dogged determination and raw courage in the face of the enemy, Hamid was posthumously awarded independent India's highest wartime gallantry award, Param Vir Chakra.

Buried at the battlefield, Hamid lies in a modest grave at Asal Uttar today. A brick-red roadside plaque with the words 'memorial of CQMH (Company Quarter Master Havildar) Abdul Hamid' announces its location. Inside a walled-in area of a little over an acre of land, a pathway lined by shrubs and trees leads to the actual memorial that houses his grave. An inscription on a tablet solemnly attests to his having given his life defending his motherland.

And so he lives on — in war trophies that stand in Army cantonments across India, in the sugarcane fields where he beat back intruders, in a memorial park in a village and in the proud reminiscences of a dearly-loved daughter. Interestingly, few people know that the renown social activist Anna Hazare was a comrade of Abdul Hamid during the war. His assignment was to carry firearms and bombs to the border!

## INDO-PAK WAR

After five years of service in the anti-tank section Abdul Hamid had recently been promoted and given charge of quartermaster stores of his company. As he was the best 106mm recoilless rifle shot in the battalion, he was reverted to his former charge as NCO commanding the battalion's recoilless rifle platoon.

In the Lahore sector of operations, 4 Mountain Division of India, having been rebuffed in its advance to the Ichhogil by the Pakistani counter-offensive, fell back to the Khem Kharan area. In the new defence plan of the Division, 4 Grenadiers, along with three other battalions of the division formed a defence line between Assal Uttar and Chima villages on the Khem Karan-Bhikhiwind-Amritsar road and the Patti axis. 4 Grenadiers was on the northern flank in general area of Chima village while other battalions were to the south ending with its sister battalion, 7 Grenadiers, in Asal Uttar village itself.

Earlier the battalion had captured its objective on the Ichhogil canal but being outflanked by the Pakistani counter-offensive was ordered back to new positions. It had already been in combat for more than 24 hours when it began digging trenches and weapon pits in its defensive positions. The battalion defended area was covered with cotton and sugarcane fields and the battalion was able to camouflage its location, using ploughed fields for field of fire. The 106mm recoilless guns were deployed along the Khem Karan-Amritsar road. On 8 September, the enemy made repeated probing attacks on the 4th Grenadiers position. The battalions recoilless weapons and automatics were effectively sited by Hamid's company officers, Lt H. R. Jahnu and 2Lt V. K. Vaid. That afternoon Abdul Hamid destroyed two Patton tanks, the commander of one of which asked Hamid for directions just before Hamid destroyed the tank.

On 10 September 1965 at 0800 hours, a battalion of Pakistani armour supported by Patton tanks attacked the 4th Grenadier positions but was unable to locate the battalion's defences. The attack preceded by intense artillery bombardment to soften the target and to garner a heavy fire in an attempt to draw Indian response. By 0900 hours, the enemy tanks had penetrated the forward company positions. In the melee, Hamid saw a group of Pattons heading towards his battalion defences. Seeing the gravity of the situation, he moved out to a flank with his gun mounted on a jeep. Intense enemy shelling and tank fire did not deter him. He fired continuously knocking out three Pattons one after another but was killed by tank fire from the fourth before he could engage it.

Successful actions by Indian armour, artillery and infantry anti-tank actions, such as those of Abdul Hamid, tarnished the reputation of theM48 Patton and after the 1965 war, the M48 was largely replaced by the M60. India set up a war memorial named "Patton Nagar" ("Patton Town") in Khemkaran District, where the captured Pakistani Patton tanks are displayed.

## Indo-Pakistani Air War of 1965

The Indo-Pakistani War of 1965 saw the Indian and Pakistani Air Forces engaged in large-scale aerial combat against each other for the first time since the Partition in 1947. The war took place during the course of September 1965 and saw both air forces conduct defensive and offensive operations over Indian and Pakistani airspace. Both countries made contradictory claims regarding the number of losses that they suffered and the number of planes that they claimed to have shot down. Indian losses have been placed at between 59 and 110, while Pakistani losses were between 18 and 43.

## Background

The war began in early August 1965 and initially the fighting was confined mainly to the ground. Later, however, as the war progressed, the war took on another dimension as the two sides began air operations against each other. Although the two forces had previously taken part in the First Kashmir War which had occurred shortly after Partition, that engagement had been limited in scale compared to the 1965 conflict and the air operations that both sides had undertaken were limited and largely confined to interdiction and other strategic purposes such as re-supply and troop transport operations. Although there had been one incident where Indian fighter aircraft intercepted a Pakistani transport, there had been no significant air-to-air combat. During the 1965 conflict, however, the PAF flew a total 2,364 sorties while the IAF flew 3,937 sorties.

All out War erupted between India and Pakistan, and during the vicious 17 day conflict PAF flew defensive CAPs over its own bases, offensive counter air missions against Indian airfields, and close-support and interdiction sorties, causing significant damage.

## Main Battle

The aerial phase of the war began on 1 September 1965 when the Indian Air Force (IAF) responded to an urgent call for air strikes against the Pakistani Army, which had launched an attack known as Operation Grand Slam. The IAF's 45 Sqn was tasked to carry out Close air Support missions in support of Indian troops. The squadron had recently been moved from Pune to Pathankot, after a merger of No 220 Sqn into it, under the command of Sqn. Ldr. S.K. "Marshal" Dhar. Three missions of four aircraft each were tasked, with the first wave taking off at 1719 hours. These strafed Pakistani positions and attacked Pakistani tanks and ground targets, though a lot of damage from "friendly fire" was also reported later on. The Indian aircraft were intercepted by two Pakistan Air Force (PAF) F-86 Sabres, flown by S/L Sarfraz Rafiqui of No 5 Sqn and F/L Imtiaz Bhatti of No 15 Sqn. In the ensuing dogfight four IAF Vampires were lost, one from the first wave and three from the second. After this, the IAF immediately withdrew about 130 Vampires, together with over 50 Ouragons, from front-line service.

On 2 September, both sides flew in support of their ground forces, however no major aerial engagement was observed.

The next day witnessed an aerial combat of two Sabres of No 11 Squadron and four Gnats of No 27 Sqn from Akhnur. The Sabres were augmented by an F-104. In the course of action, one Sabre was severely damaged, though its pilot managed to land safely. Later on, one of the Gnats landed at Pasrur Airfield, resulting in the capture of the aircraft.

On 4 September, an F-86 Sabre was lost. The PAF claimed the cause to be friendly ground fire while the IAF claimed to have shot it down.

Rafiqui was shot down over Halwara on 6 September, while Bhatti ended the war with 34 combat missions to his credit, the maximum combat missions flown by any pilot during the war.

During the conflict, the Pakistani F-86 Sabre Flying Ace, Muhammad Mahmood Alam shot down seven Indian aircraft including claims of two as 'probable'. Five Hawker Hunter aircraft were shot down in one minute, of which four were brought down in 30 seconds.

On September 6, the Indian Army crossed the border at Lahore to relieve pressure on the Chamb Jaurian sector. On the evening of the same day, the PAF responded with attacks on Indian airfields at Pathankot, Adampur and Halwara. The attack on Pathankot was successful, while the attacks on

Adampur and Halwara were failures. The IAF lost almost ten aircraft on the ground at Pathankot. The Adampur strike turned back before even reaching Adampur while at Halwara two of the three attacking raiders were shot down for the loss of two Indian Hunters in air combat. Both the Indian pilots survived as they ejected over their base, whereas the intruding Pakistani pilots were killed in action. This included the ace Squadron Leader Sarfaraz Rafiqui who had shot down two Vampires on 1 September. Before being shot down, Rafiqui is credited with shooting down the first of the Hunters. He was later posthumously awarded the Sitara-e-Jurat for the Chamb action and the Hilal-i-Jurat for the Halwara action.

On 7 September 1965 the PAF parachuted 135 Special Services Group (SSG) para commandos at three Indian airfields (Halwara, Pathankot and Adampur). The daring attempt proved to be an "unmitigated disaster". Only ten commandos were able to return to Pakistan, the rest were taken as prisoners of war (including one of the Commanders of the operations, Major Khalid Butt). At Halwara and Adampur these troops landed in residential areas where the villagers caught and handed them over to police.

Also on 7 September the IAF mounted 33 sorties against the heavily guarded PAF airfield complex at Sargodha. The IAF lost two Mysteres and three Hunters due to the defence mounted by the PAF's local squadrons. One of the Indian Hunter pilots, who ejected near Sargodha, was made POW and released after the war. One of the crippled Mysteres flying solo got involved in a dogfight with an F-104 Starfighter and each somehow shot the other down; the Pakistani pilot safely ejected, while the Indian pilot, Squadron Leader Ajamada B. Devayya, was killed. Squadron Leader Devayya was awarded the Maha Vir Chakra for his bravery 23 years later, after his feat was revealed by an author appointed by the PAF to write its official history of the 1965 war.

The seventh of September also marked the day when the PAF attacked IAF airfields in the Eastern Sector. During the PAF's raid on Kalaikunda, Indian pilot Flight Lieutenant A T

Cooke engaged four Pakistani Sabres, shooting down one while flying at tree-top height and making another a write off in the process.

The war lessened in intensity after 8 September, with occasional clashes between the IAF and the PAF. Both air forces now changed their doctrine from air interdictions to ground attack and concentrated their efforts on knocking out soft skin targets and supply lines, such as wagons carrying ammunition; and armoured vehicles. During the conflict IAFEnglish Electric Canberras raided a few of the Pakistani bases. On 10 September one Mystere was downed by anti-aircraft fire in Pakistan but the pilot ejected safely.

On September 13 one PAF F-86 Sabre was downed while attacking a train near Gurdaspur and the pilot was killed. In another encounter the same day between PAF Sabres from Sargodha and IAF Gnats from No. 2 Squadron, an Indian Gnat was shot down by a PAF F-86 Sabre flown by Flt Lt Yusaf Ali Khan although the Indian pilot managed to eject safely. The other Gnat was engaged and damaged in air combat by Flt Lt Imtiaz Bhatti.

The experienced pilot somehow managed to return to base, where according to All India Radio the Gnat's pilot later died of wounds sustained during the combat. He was said to have brought his damaged aircraft back to base and to have died during landing. His funeral was attended by the Indian President.

Yusaf Ali Khan was credited with a kill whereas, Imtiaz Bhatti was credited with damaging the IAF Gnat despite the later confirmation that the pilot died of wounds and the Gnat crashed during its landing attempt. Later in the night of 13/14 September, Indian Canberras undertook the deepest penetration of Pakistani airspace of the war, attacking Pakistani bases around Peshawar and Kohat. Rather than bombing the Peshawer runway, however, IAF bombers mistook the mall road in Peshawer as the runway and dropped their bombs there instead. The PAF admits that the IAF came very close to annihilating its entire fleet of B-57 bombers.

The Canberras were intercepted by a Pakistani F-104 near Lahore but they managed to evade the Starfighter and return home safely. They also had an encounter with F-86 Sabres, one of which fired at the Canberras, which sustained some damage. A Pakistani F-86 Sabre also crashed while conducting an evasive maneuvere in an attempt to escape pursuit, from an escorting Gnat as it tried to defend the Canberra bombers; the PAF pilot was killed. The Gnat pilot, W/C Singh, was later credited with an aerial victory for this incident near Amritsar. Later, one Pakistani B-57 was shot down by anti-aircraft fire over Adampur, although both of its crew managed to eject safely and remained POWs.

On 15 September the PAF employed a number of its Lockheed C-130 Hercules transport aircraft as bombers, which proved unsuccessful; two of them were shot down by the IAF. The following day, one IAF Hunter and a PAF F-86 Sabre were shot down over Halwara. The IAF pilot was killed in the encounter, although the Pakistani pilot ejected and spent the rest of the war as a POW. A Pakistani Cessna was also shot down that day, as well as an Auster observation aircraft. On 18 September a Sabre was shot down by a Gnat over Amritsar; the matter was reported by the Collector, who had witnessed the entire dogfight. The same day a Pakistani Sabre shot down a civilian Indian aircraft even after the civilian plane indicated its identity, the PAF pilot assuming it to be a reconnaissance mission. Years later, the PAF pilot wrote a letter to the Indian pilot's daughter to apologize for shooting down the aircraft. The aircraft had been carrying the then Gujarat Chief Minister Balwant Rai and his family.

On 19 September a Gnat and two Sabres were downed over Chawinda. One of the Sabres that were shot down was credited to Squadron Leader Denzil Keelor, the brother of Trevor Keelor, who was credited with the first Indian aerial victory of the war. The following day, another two Hunters and an F-86 Sabre were lost over Kasur, Pakistan.

At one stage the IAF was operating 200 air missions simultaneously. IAF Folland Gnats of Nos 9 and 23 squadrons played a significant role in major air battles. On 21 September IAF Canberras carried out a daring daylight strike into Pakistan against the radar complex in Badin. The raid proved to be successful. Under the command of Wing Commander Peter Wilson, six Canberras from No. 16 Squadron took off from Agra, over 1,000 km from Bladin and proceeded towards the radar complex at low level. About 80 miles (130 km) short of the target, one Canberra climbed to an altitude of 10,000 feet in order to act as a decoy, before returning to base. The other five Canberras continued on towards the target. The flight then separated and four of the aircraft approached the target in two sections, each two minutes apart, at low level; before climbing to 7,000 feet from where they carried out bombing runs, dropping approximately 10,000 lbs of explosives. Wilson then approached from the south at an altitude of just 30 feet firing a salvo of 68mm rockets at the radar dome.

On the same day a PAF F-104 intercepted a Canberra bomber on its way back from Sargodha and shot it down, while one Hunter pilot who was the son of Chief of the Indian Army was shot down by anti-aircraft fire; he ejected and was taken POW. The ceasefire was declared on the night of September 22, 1965.

## Outcome

There are conflicting claims by either side on this issue. Pakistani sources suggest that Indian losses were in the range of 59–110 and Pakistani losses were around 18–43. Recent works have, however, attempted to move beyond the raw statistics of the number of losses each side incurred, arguing that in terms of aircraft lost to sorties flown, the Indian Air Force's attrition rate (1.5%) was lower than the Pakistani attrition rate (1.82%). Arguably this indicates that had the war continued, the PAF would have found it increasingly difficult to sustain operations at the same level. Nevertheless, a similar argument can be made about the IAF also, although it did have a significant size advantage that might have proved telling if the war had been prolonged.

Another factor which makes it difficult to determine the outcome of the 1965 air war is the issue of aircraft lost in the air in air-to-air combat or to ground fire as opposed to aircraft lost on the ground due to bombing. Indian sources claimed that a large number of Indian aircraft losses occurred on the ground during the attacks on Kalaikkunda and Pathankot—up to 60 per cent by some accounts

## Learning the Lessons

Much of the lessons of the 1965 war lead India to refine tactics which proved decisive in the 1971 war. Pakistani forces failed to take account of the extent to which they had relied on two factors which the IAF could not take for granted-complete ground based defensive radar coverage and an adequate supply of air-to-air missiles. Much effort was expended in India to remedy these deficiencies before 1971.

With Soviet aid, India established a modern early warning radar system, including the recently introduced 'Fansong-E' low-level radar, linked with SA-2 'Guideline' surface-to-air missiles and a large number of AA guns. By December 1971 the IAF comprised a total of 36 squadrons (of which 10 were deployed in the Bengal sector) with some 650 combat aircraft.

Moreover, the 1965 war resulted in the USA imposing a 10 year arms embargo on both sides. This had no effect, on India, which had always looked to Britain, France and even Russia for arms, but was disastrous for Pakistan, which was forced to acquire 90 obsolete second hand Sabre via Iran, a mere 28 Mirage IIIs from France and 74 maintenance intensive Shenyang F-6s. It was unable to replace losses among its (already weak) force of B-57s, or to acquire a modern interceptor in realistic numbers.

## 1965: RESILIENCE IN WAR, DEFTNESS IN DIPLOMACY

'Stalemate', 'futile', 'forgotten' — the descriptions of the 1965 War between Indiaand Pakistan often do injustice to its profound impact on the history of the Indian subcontinent. The war of 1965 altered the fates of both the countries and began the new 'Great Game' in Asia. One of its biggest outcomes was the sealing of the China-Pakistan entente and New Delhi's realisation of a two-front strategic threat, with a heightened risk of collusion between its two neighbours.

The war of 1965 was a test for the political leadership of Prime Minister Lal Bahadur Shastri, who was still finding his feet post his predecessor Jawaharlal Nehru's death. He was under intense scrutiny from the international community as India was still recovering from the scars of 1962, while also battling an acute food crisis. The National Conference leader Sheikh Abdullah's mission to find a solution to the Kashmir crisis was aborted after Nehru's death and historians believe Pakistan felt emboldened to strike for the 'cause' of Kashmir, sensing India was at its most vulnerable.

## Four-phase plan

The blueprint was in the form of a four-phase plan: a probing encounter to check the Indian response in the Rann of Kutch; an engineered uprising in Kashmir via infiltrators (Operation Gibraltar); followed by a sophisticated Patton tank assault in Punjab aimed at cutting of Jammu and Kashmir; and finally, the, capture of Amritsar and many parts of the Indian territory, to be exchanged for Kashmir.

General Mohammed Musa, the then Pakistani Army Chief, has recorded in his book My Version, "the Kashmir Cell, a highly secretive group put together by the Pakistani Army in early 1964, directly reporting to the President, had by now concluded that 'it was time for Pakistan to take some overt action' for reviving the Kashmir issue and "defreezing", what from Pakistan's point of view was a dishearteningly quiet and stable situation in Kashmir."

Altaf Gauhar, the then Pakistan Minister of Information and Broadcasting and author of the biography Ayub Khan: Pakistan's First Military Ruler, tells that "Ayub's judgement" was over-ridden with the "prejudice" that "the Hindu has no stomach for a fight" and this "turned to belief, if not a military doctrine, which had the decisive effect on the course of events."

While surprised at first, India fought back. In this war, fought between August and September 1965, India captured 1,920 sq. km of Pakistani territory while Pakistan captured 550 sq. km of Indian territory, as per the government records. Officially declared inconclusive, the war results ultimately did favour India.

Fifty years on, there is still a lot left to be understood on the intense diplomatic manoeuvring that New Delhi undertook to emerge on the right side of history.Most prominent among this is how India managed Chinese moves, aimed at pushing Pakistan's case both during the war and negotiations in the United Nations Security Council (UNSC), patterns which ironically are followed till date.

Since 1962, Pakistan referring to its special friendship with China while dealing with India. First, Foreign Minister Zulfikar Ali Bhutto, in the National Assembly in 1963, and later, President Ayub, alluded to this: "If we are attacked by India, then that means, India is on the move and wants to expand. We assume that other Asiatic [sic] powers, especially China would take notice." (as noted by J.W. Garver in his book Protracted Contest: Sino Indian Rivalry in the Twentieth Century.)

Pakistan's strengthened relationship with China had caught the attention of the world powers at the height of the Cold War. After concluding a border agreement with China in March 1963, through which it handed over disputed territories in Jammu and Kashmir to China, Islamabad had openly began to court Beijing.

Gauhar's memoirs of Ayub recount a series of hectic diplomatic consultations between Pakistan and China in the lead up to 1965. First, Chinese Premier Zhou Enlai had made a state visit to Pakistan in February 1964. He then laid out the red carpet for Ayub in March 1965. Zhou Enlai later returned to Pakistan in June 1965 and there was speculation, writes Gauhar, that it was the Chinese tactics of guerrilla warfare that were deployed by Pakistan in the attack on Kashmir.

Both the U.S. and Russia were concerned of Pakistan falling into China's lap, which Pakistan used to its advantage. Interestingly, after being stumped by India's attack on Lahore on September 1 and worried following reports of dwindling supplies of ammunition on the battlefield post the American embargo on arms supply to both India and Pakistan; an exasperated Ayub, recalls Gauhar, reportedly said at an emergency cabinet meet: "The Americans have let us down, but they are afraid of Chinese involvement [...]. Our best card is the China card. We have to decide at what stage the Chinese aid needs to be obtained. Our dealings with China should be frank and above board"

The Chinese were only too happy to come to Pakistan's rescue if one looks at the details that emerge from the records of Gauhar as also from the war diaries of the then Indian Defence Minister Y.B. Chavan ( 1965 War: The Inside Story, by R.D. Pradhan). They outline that Chinese Foreign Minister, Marshal Chen Yi, had already met with Foreign Minister Zulfikar Ali Bhutto in Karachi on September 4, 1965 and assured Pakistan support against "India's armed provocation in Kashmir". China followed this up with a statement on September 7 which said, "The Indian government probably believes that since it has the backing of the U.S. imperialists and modern revisionists, it can bully its neighbours, defy public opinion and do whatever it likes," records Gauhar.

According to Chavan's war diaries, China had previously, on August 27, accused the Indian Army of committing acts of aggression on the border of Sikkim and Tibet in July and August, accusations that were rejected by India.

By September 8, it renewed these accusations claiming, "India must bear responsibility of all consequences arriving therefrom," which India again rejected and called for a neutral and independent observer to visit the China border and look at these complaints.

On September 17, notes Chavan, the Chinese again upped the ante, dismissing India's offer as "pretentious" and sending a fresh note accusing India of "maintaining 56 military installations on the Tibetan side of the Sikkim-Tibet border and demanding their dismantling within two days or face grave consequences."

C.P. Srivastava, author of the biography Lal Bahadur Shastri: A Life of Truth in Politics, notes that by now Prime Minister Shastri had calculated that "China was unlikely to launch an attack like 1962 because they had no immediate objective of their own to achieve" and "would not risk a war with the U.S." or "draw USSR into the South Asia". India had already sought the offices of the U.S. and USSR to help tackle an impending attack from China. So, Srivastava argues that, with these calculations in mind Shastri reiterated India's offer of joint inspection to assuage Chinese complaints. He conveyed on the floor of the Parliament that he hoped "China would not take advantage of the present situation and attack India." He, however, stood his ground in while assuring the country his countrymen that in case of an attack from China, India was prepared to fight back.

## Sino-Pak. joint manoeuvring

While the Chinese ultimatum was set to expire at midnight on September 19, Chavan's notes indicate that the Chinese had already begun moving their troops towards the Sikkim border on September 18 , with reports of firing in Nathu La reaching New Delhi.

In a new move, they extended their deadline of dismantling of military structures by 72 hours, knowing that a UNSC resolution demanding a ceasefire would be tabled by September 20 and that continuing the pressure on India would bolster Pakistan's case, says Chavan.

It was later revealed that China was pushing Ayub Khan to continue the Indo-Pak. war. Gauhar says Ayub, who flew to Beijing for a secret meeting on September 19-20, was assured by Zhou Enlai of continued support "for as long as necessary" and told "but you must keep fighting even if you have to withdraw to the hills." Gauhar records that it was now that However, it had become "clear to Ayub and Bhutto that if

Pakistan wanted full Chinese support it had to be prepared for a long war and the loss of important cities like Lahore," which they were not prepared for. It was this realisation that led to Pakistan accepting the ceasefire proposed by the UNSC on September 22 1965 ending hostilities and making way for the Tashkent Agreement.

In retrospect, 1965 was a watershed event for the subcontinent. For India, it banished the ghosts of 1962, and proved to be a litmus test for its capabilities both on the battlefront and the diplomatic chessboard. The war also established that the China-Pakistan entente was now a reality India will have to live with and battle, both militarily and politically, for years to come.

## HOSTILITIES OF 1965

In early 1965, relations between India and Pakistan were strained again because of their conflicting claims over the Rann of Kutch at the southern end of the international boundary. The situation steadily deteriorated during the summer of 1965, and, in August, military hostilities between India and Pakistan erupted on a large scale along the ceasefire line in Kashmir. In his report15 of 3 September 1965, the Secretary-General stressed that the ceasefire agreement of 27 July 1949 had collapsed and that a return to mutual observance of it by India and Pakistan would afford the most favourable climate in which to seek a resolution of political differences.

On 4 September 1965, the Security Council, by resolution 209 (1965), called for a ceasefire and asked the two Governments to cooperate fully with UNMOGIP in its task of supervising the observance of the ceasefire.

Two days later, the Council adopted resolution 210 (1965), by which it requested the Secretary-General "to exert every possible effort to give effect to the present resolution and to resolution 209 (1965), to take all measures possible to strengthen the United Nations Military Observer Group in India and Pakistan, and to keep the Council promptly and currently informed on the implementation of the resolutions and on the situation in the area".

From 7 to 16 September, the Secretary-General visited the subcontinent in pursuit of the mandate given to him by the Security Council.

In his report of 16 September to the Council, he noted that both sides had expressed their desire for a cessation of hostilities, but that each side had posed conditions which made the acceptance of a ceasefire very difficult for the other.

In those circumstances, the Secretary-General suggested that the Security Council might take a number of steps: first, it might order the two Governments, pursuant to Article 40 of the United Nations Charter, to desist from further military action; second, it might consider what assistance it could provide in ensuring the observance of the ceasefire and the withdrawal of all military personnel by both sides; and, third, it could request the two Heads of Government to meet in a country friendly to both in order to discuss the situation and the problems underlying it, as a first step in resolving the outstanding differences between their two countries.

On 20 September, after the hostilities had spread to the international border between India and West Pakistan, the Council adopted resolution 211 (1965), by which it demanded that a ceasefire take effect at 0700 hours GMT on 22 September 1965 and called for a subsequent withdrawal of all armed personnel to the positions held before 5 August. The Council also requested the Secretary-General to provide the necessary assistance to ensure supervision of the ceasefire and the withdrawal of all armed personnel.

## Establishment of UNIPOM

In Kashmir, the supervision called for by the Security Council was exercised by the established machinery of UNMOGIP. For this purpose, its observer strength was increased to a total of 102 from the same contributing countries as before.

Since the hostilities extended beyond the Kashmir ceasefire line, the Secretary-General decided to set up an administrative adjunct of UNMOGIP, the United Nations India-Pakistan Observation Mission (UNIPOM), as a temporary measure for the sole purpose of supervising the ceasefire along the India-Pakistan border outside the State of Jammu and Kashmir.

The function of UNIPOM was primarily to observe and report on breaches of the ceasefire as called for by the Security Council. In cases of breaches, the observers were to do all they could to persuade the local commanders to restore the ceasefire, but they had no authority or power to order a cessation of firing. Ninety observers were assigned to UNIPOM.

The Mission was closely coordinated both administratively and operationally with UNMOGIP. The Chief Military Observer of UNMOGIP, General Nimmo, was initially also placed in charge of UNIPOM. After the arrival of the newly appointed Chief Officer of UNIPOM, Major-General B.F. Macdonald (Canada) in October 1965, General Nimmo was asked by the Secretary-General to exercise oversight functions with regard to both operations.

## Further Security Council action

On 27 September 1965, after learning that the ceasefire was not holding, the Security Council adopted resolution 214 (1965), by which it demanded that the parties urgently honour their commitments to the Council to observe the ceasefire, and called upon them to withdraw all armed personnel as necessary steps in the full implementation of resolution 211 (1965).

As ceasefire violations continued to occur and there were no prospects for the withdrawal of troops, the Security Council met again in November and adopted resolution 215 (1965) of 5 November.

By this decision, the Council called upon the Governments of India and Pakistan to instruct their armed personnel to cooperate with the United Nations and cease all military activity.

The Security Council further demanded the prompt and unconditional execution of the proposal already agreed to in principle by India and Pakistan that their representatives meet with a representative of the Secretary-General to formulate an agreed plan and schedule of withdrawals. In this connection, the Secretary-General, after consultation with the parties, appointed Brigadier-General Tulio Marambio (Chile) as his representative on withdrawals.

On 15 December, the Secretary-General reported that the two parties directly involved, India and Pakistan, had informed him of their desire that the United Nations should continue its observer function after 22 December 1965, which was the end of the first three months of the ceasefire demanded by the Security Council in its resolution 211 (1965) of 20 September 1965.

In the circumstances, the Secretary-General indicated his intention to continue the United Nations activities relating to the ceasefire and withdrawal provisions of the resolution by continuing UNIPOM for a second period of three months and maintaining the added strength of the Military Observer Group.

## Tashkent agreement

On 10 January 1966, the Prime Minister of India and the President of Pakistan, who had met in Tashkent at the invitation of the Chairman of the Council of Ministers of the Soviet Union, announced their agreement that the withdrawal of all armed personnel of both sides to the positions they had held prior to 5 August 1965 should be completed by 25 February 1966 and that both sides should observe the terms of the ceasefire on the ceasefire line.

The principles of a plan and schedule of withdrawals were subsequently agreed upon by military representatives of India and Pakistan, who had held meetings for that purpose since 3 January 1966 at Lahore and Amritsar under the auspices of General Marambio, the Secretary-General's representative on withdrawals. The plan for disengagement and withdrawal was agreed upon by the military commanders of the Indian and Pakistan armies in New Delhi on 22 January.

At a joint meeting on 25 January, under the auspices of the Secretary-General's representative, the parties agreed upon the ground rules for the implementation of the disengagement and withdrawal plan. The plan was to be implemented in two stages and the good offices of UNMOGIP and UNIPOM were to be requested to ensure that the action agreed upon was fully implemented. In the event of disagreement between the parties, the decision of General Marambio would be final and binding on both sides. The good offices of UNMOGIP and UNIPOM were similarly requested for the implementation of the second stage of the agreement, as were the good offices of the Secretary-General's representative with regard to withdrawals of troops.

### Termination of UNIPOM

On 26 February 1966, the Secretary-General reported that the withdrawal of the troops by India and Pakistan had been completed on schedule on 25 February, and that the withdrawal provisions of the Security Council's resolutions had thus been fulfilled by the two parties. With regard to withdrawals, the responsibilities of the Secretary-General's representative came to an end on 28 February, and his mission ceased on that date.

As planned, UNIPOM was terminated on 22 March 1966 and the 59 additional observers appointed in September 1965 to the Military Observer Group were gradually withdrawn.

## MILITARY AWARDS

### Param Vir Chakra Citation

The Param Vir Chakra citation on the Official Indian Army Website reads as follows:

**CITATION**

**COMPANY QUARTERMASTER HAVILDAR ABDUL HAMID**

**4 GRENADIERS (NO 2639985)**

At 0800 hours on 10 September 1965 Pakistan forces launched an attack with a regiment of Patton tanks on a vital area ahead of village Cheema on the Bhikkiwind road in the

Khem Karan Sector. Intense artillery shelling preceded the attack. The enemy tanks penetrated the forward position by 0900 hours.

Realising the grave situation, Company Quartermaster Havildar Abdul Hamid who was commander of a RCL gun detachment moved out to a flanking position with his gun mounted on a jeep, under intense enemy shelling and tank fire. Taking an advantageous position, he knocked out the leading enemy tank and then swiftly changing his position, he sent another tank up in flames. By this time the enemy tanks in the area spotted him and brought his jeep under concentrated machine-gun and high explosive fire. Undeterred, Company Quartermaster Havildar Abdul Hamid kept on firing on yet another enemy tank with his recoilless gun. While doing so, he was mortally wounded by an enemy high explosive shell.

Havildar Abdul Hamid's brave action inspired his comrades to put up a gallant fight and to beat back the heavy tank assault by the enemy. His complete disregard for his personal safety during the operation and his sustained acts of bravery in the face of constant enemy fire were a shining example not only to his unit but also to the whole division and were in the highest traditions of the Indian Army.

The award was announced on 16 September 1965, less than a week after the battle that cost his life. The award was presented to his spouse, Rasoolan Bibi by Sarvepalli Radhakrishnan, then President of India during the 1966 Republic Day Parade.

## Legacy

In his memory, a mausoleum was constructed on his grave by the 4th Grenadiers at Asal Uttar and each year a "mela" is organised on the date of his martyrdom. The residents of Asal Uttar have named and operate a dispensary, library and school in the village. In his honour, theArmy Postal Service issued a special cover on 10 September 1979.

In the 1988 Television serial *Param Vir Chakra* by Chetan Anand, Abdul Hamid is played by actor Naseeruddin Shah.

A pictorial postage stamp of value Rs 3 was issued by India Post on 28 January 2000 as part of a set of five postage stamps on gallantry award winners. The stamp had Abdul Hamid's bust on it along with an illustration of a jeep with recoilless rifle.

Hamid's widow, Rasoolan Bibi had met President of India Pratibha Patil in Lucknow in 2008 with a number of requests including creation of a military recruitment center in his village, converting Hamid's home in Dullapur into a memorial, observing the day of his martyrdom as an occasion at the national level and help for her grandchildren to get government employment.

A memorial to Abdul Hamid was constructed in his home village of Dhamupur but later fell into neglect. The memorial was renovated in 2011 by the Flags of Honour Foundation on Hamid's 46th death anniversary. The renovation included the installation of a new statue of him, repair and painting of gates and boundary and improvement of the garden. Indian Member of Parliament Rajeev Chandrasekhar, founder of Flags of Honour, spoke on the occasion.

## VEER ABDUL HAMID: GHAZIPUR WARRIOR

Company Quarter Master Havildar Abdul Hamid (July 1, 1933 – September 10, 1965) was a soldier in the 4 Grenadiers, Indian Army, who died in theKhem Karan sector during the Indo-Pakistani War of 1965, and was the posthumous recipient of the Republic of India's highest military decoration, theParam Vir Chakra. The award was announced on 16 September 1965, less than a week after the battle that cost his life. During the India-Pakistan war Vir Abdul Hamid had blasted several tanks of the enemy country. For his bravery, Hamid was awarded posthumously with the country's highest military decoration Pram Vir Chakra.. The award was announced on 16 September 1965, less than a week after the battle that cost his life..The award was presented to his spouse, Shrimati Rasoolan Bibi by Dr Sarvepalli Radhakrishnan, then President of India during the 1966 Republic Day Parade.

The Param Vir Chakra is awarded for most conspicuous bravery or some daring or pre-eminent act of valour or self sacrifice, in the presence of the enemy, whether on land, at sea, or in the air. The decoration may be awarded posthumously. Abdul Hamid was born in a Muslim Darzi family at Dhamupur village ofGhazipur District of Uttar Pradesh on July 1, 1933, the son of Mohammad Usman, who was also a wrestler.

He was enrolled in the 4 Grenadiers on 27 December 1954. In the 1988 Television serial *Param Vir Chakra* by Chetan Anand, Abdul Hamid is played by actor Naseeruddin Shah.

The Vice President, Shri Mohd. Hamid Ansari releasing a book entitled "Veer Abdul Hamid" authored by Shri Syed Ahsan Ali, in the Presence of Smt. Rasoolan Bi, widow of Late Shri Abdul Hamid, (Paramvir Chakra recipient), in New Delhi on September 08, 2009. Photo Division Ministry of I & B Government of India.

**Citation**

The citation for the *Param Vir Chakra* awarded to him reads:

**COMPANY QUARTER MASTER HAVILDAR ABDUL HAMID**

**4 GRENADIERS (NO 2639985)**

*At 0800 hours on 10 September 1965 Pakistan forces launched an attack with a regiment of Patton tanks on a vital area ahead of village Cheema on the Bhikkiwind road in the Khem Karam Sector. Intense artillery shelling preceded the attack. The enemy tanks penetrated the forward position by 0900 hours. Realising the grave situation, Company Quarter Master Havildar Abdul Hamid who was commander of an RCL gun detachment moved out to a flanking position with his gun mounted on a Jeep, under intense enemy shelling and tank fire. Taking an advantageous position, he knocked out the leading enemy tank and then swiftly changing his position, he sent another tank up in flames. By this time the enemy tanks in the area spotted him and brought his jeep under concentrated machine-gun and high explosive fire. Undeterred, Company Quarter Master Havildar Abdul Hamid kept on firing on yet another enemy tank with his recoilless gun. While doing so, he was mortally wounded by an enemy high explosive shell.*

*Havildar Abdul Hamid's brave action inspired his comrades to put up a gallant fight and to beat back the heavy tank assault by the enemy. His complete disregard for his personal safety during the operation and his sustained acts of bravery in the face of constant enemy fire were a shining example not only to his unit but also to the whole division and were in the highest traditions of the Indian Army.*

## LEGACY

In his memory, a mausoleum was constructed on his grave by the 4th Grenadiers at Asal Uttar and each year a "mela" is organised on the date of his martyrdom. The residents of Asal Uttar have named and operate a dispensary, library and school in the village. In his honour, the Army Postal Service issued a special cover on 10 September 1979.

A pictorial postage stamp of value Rs 3 was issued by India Post on 28 January 2000 as part of a set of five postage stamps on gallantry award winners. The stamp had Abdul Hamid's bust on it along with an illustration of a jeep with recoilless rifle.

Hamid's widow, Rasoolan Bibi had met President of India Pratibha Patil in Lucknow in 2008 with a number of requests including creation of a military recruitment center in his village, converting Hamid's home in Dullapur into a memorial, observing the day of his martyrdom as an occasion at the national level and help for her grandchildren to get government employment.

A memorial to Abdul Hamid was constructed in his home village of Dhamupur but later fell into neglect. The memorial was renovated in 2011 by the Flags of Honour Foundation for the 46th death anniversary of the award winner.

The renovation included the installation of a new statue of the martyr, repair and painting of gates and boundary and improvement of the garden. Indian Member of Parliament Rajeev Chandrasekhar, founder of Flags of Honour, spoke on the occasion. The tank battles of 1965 form part of military history as the most intense armored battles between the end of World War II and the 1991 Gulf War.

Close to a thousand tanks, on both sides, took part in the pitched battles and offensives. At the start of the war, Indian strength was limited to one armored division and one independent armoured brigade, along with six armoured regiments supporting infantry divisions. Pakistan had two armored divisions, with the then very modern M-48 Patton tanks. India had an equivalent tank in the Centurion, but their strength was limited to only four armored regiments.

## Patton Nagar

Near the Bhikhiwind village, a strip of land was called Patton Nagar for a short while in 1965 It was here that more than 60 tanks of the Pakistani army were displayed at the end of the September India-Pakistan conflict.

The Pakistan Army tanks were captured at the Battle of Asal Uttar by India's 4 Mountain Division and it became a memorial to the Pakistani tanks being bogged down in the marshes during the 1965 War. The tanks were displayed for some time after which they were shipped to various cantonments and army establishments in India for display as war trophies.

## 97 tanks captured at Assal Uttar

The Indian Army managed to capture 97 Pakistani tanks as a result of the botched assault by the 1 Armoured Division of the Pakistan Army at the Battle of Assal Uttar on 10 September 1965.Six Pakistani Armoured Regiments took part in the battle, namely the 19 Lancers (Patton), 12 Cavalry (Chaffee), 24 Cavalry (Patton) 4 Cavalry (Patton), 5 Horse (Patton) and 6 Lancers (Patton).

The Indian forces in the field that day consisted of three Armoured regiments with tanks of varying quality, the Deccan Horse (Shermans), 3 Cavalry(Centurion) and the 8 Cavalry (AMX- The battle was so fierce and intense that at the end of the war, the Pakistani 1st Armored division had lost about 97 tanks in destroyed/damaged or intact condition. This included 72 Patton tanks and 25 Chaffees and Shermans. 32 of the 97 tanks, including 28 Pattons, were in running condition. The Indian 4th division lost 32 tanks, mostly Sherman tanks, fifteen of which were captured by the Pakistan Army.

## Khemkaran

The 1965 Indo-Pakistani War was witness to the largest tank battle in military history since World War II. This battle led to the creation of Patton Nagar (or Patton City) at the site of the battle viz., Khemkaran. This is because many Patton tanks fielded by the Pakistani forces were either captured or destroyed at the scene.

Guru Tegh Bahadur Sahib (1621-1675) Ninth Sikh Prophet visited Khem Karan and Stayed here a local Built a Well in Memory of Guru Sahib a Old Building Gurdwara Stood here which in 1965 during the Indo-Pak war The Pakistani Army Captured Khem Karan Town The Locals Fled. The Pakistani Army damaged The Historic Gurdwara Much Damage was done to it it was when the Indian Army Arrived and After a battle the Indian Army won the battle Pushing the Pakistani Army out from this Area that the Sikhs Repaired the Gurdwara and Renovated it again. Before the partition Khem Karan used to be in Lahore District During the Partition it was Given to Amritsar Sahib to East Punjab (India).

## Indo Pak War (1965)

The tank battles of 1965 form part of military history as the most intense armored battles between the end of World War II and the 1991 Gulf War. Close to a thousand tanks, on both sides, took part in the pitched battles and offensives. At the start of the war, Indian strength was limited to one armored division and one independent armored brigade, along with six armored regiments supporting infantry divisions. Pakistan had two armored divisions, with the then very modern M-48 Patton tanks. India had an equivalent tank in the Centurion, but their strength was limited to only four armored regiments.

# 2

# Field Marshal Kodandera Madappa Cariappa

Field Marshal Kodandera "Kipper" Madappa Cariappa, OBE (28 January 1899 – 15 May 1993) was the first Indian Commander-in-Chief (C-in-C) of the Indian Army. He led Indian forces on the Western Front during the Indo-Pakistani War of 1947. He is one of only two Indian Army officers to hold the five-star rank of field marshal; the other being Field Marshal Sam Manekshaw.[1] He was appointed commander-in-chief of the Indian Army in 1949.

His distinguished military career spanned almost three decades. Born on 28 January 1899, in Madikeri, Kodagu, Cariappa joined the British Indian Army shortly after the end of World War I, and was commissioned as a temporary second lieutenant into the 2/88 Carnatic Infantry. He was transferred between multiple regiments early in his career before settling on 1/7 Rajputs, which became his permanent regiment.

He was the first Indian military officer to attend the Staff College, Quetta, the first Indian to command a battalion, and was also one of the first two Indians selected to undergo training at the Imperial Defence College, Camberley, UK. He served in various staff capacities at various unit and command headquarters (HQ) and also at the General HQ, New Delhi. Before taking over as the C-in-C of the Indian Army, Cariappa served as the commander of the Indian Army's Eastern and Western Commands.

Kodandera Madappa Cariappa was, for generations of Indians, the epitome of military leadership. As the country's first Indian Commander-in-Chief of the Army, he laid the foundations of the modern Indian Army.

Kipper, as he was affectionately called, was a 'pucca' sahib, even more than the British themselves. Though many Indians considered him a WOG (Westernised Oriental Gentleman), he was fiercely patriotic. Known for his iron discipline, integrity and forthright views, Kipper had many admirers. However, what he was known for best was his love for the Indian soldier, or 'jawan'. No wonder, the troops loved and worshipped him. For a military leader, there can be no greater approbation.

Kipper was born on 28 January 1900, at Madikeri (Mercara), in Kodavu (Coorg), a small state on the Western coast of South India. It is a picturesque region, known for its coffee plantations, and is inhabited by the Kodagas (Coorgs), a warlike race. Cariappa came from a family of prosperous farmers, belonging to the Kodandera clan. His father, Madappa, was an official in the revenue department, who lived in a house called Lime Cottage, in Madikeri. Madappa had four sons, Aiyanna, Cariappa, Nanjappa and Bopaiah, and two daughters, the eldest being Bollu. After his schooling at the Centre School in Madikeri, Cariappa joined the Presidency College in Madras, in 1917. While at the College, he came to know that Indians were being selected for commissions in the Indian Army, and would be trained in India.

The British Government had decided to open a Temporary School for Indian Cadets (TSIC), for the duration of the War, at the Daly College, in Indore. Candidates were to be selected from families which were loyal to the Crown, and had displayed zeal in recruitment of soldiers for the War. The age limit was fixed as 25 years, and there was to be a written test, followed by an interview. The period of training was not to exceed one year, at the end of which the cadets would be granted temporary King's Commissions. As an incentive, it was stated that these officers would be eligible for confirmation as permanent commissioned officers, after the end of the War. The first batch was to have 50 cadets, with another of the same size to follow after six months.

Cariappa had always aspired to become a soldier, and decided to apply. Of the 50 vacancies, only one was allotted to Coorg. Out of seventy candidates who appeared, forty two were finally selected, and granted admission. Cariappa was one of the successful candidates, and on 1 June 1918, joined the TSIC, which was also called the Daly Cadet College, at Indore. At the College, Cariappa performed well. He took keen interest in all activities, and played hockey and cricket. Being shy and reticent by nature, his social interaction with others was limited. This could also be due to the fact that most of the other cadets were from an aristocratic background, and included the sons of the rulers of Indian States such as Jamnagar, Jind, Kapurthala and Baroda. Though he could not match them in wealth and a luxurious life style, Cariappa was able to hold his own in all activities concerned with training. When he passed out, he was placed seventh in overall order of merit.

It was initially planned that the period of training would be only six months. However, after the end of World War I, it was decided to extend the training by one year. Hence, instead of December 1918, as initially planned, the batch passed out on 1 December 1919. 39 cadets passed out, and were granted temporary commissions. Subsequently, vide a Gazette Notification issued on 9 September 1922, 33 were granted permanent commissions, with effect from 17 July 1920 (one died, two were found unsuitable, and three resigned). The date of commission was decided by the War Office in order to make them junior to the batch which had passed out from Sandhurst on 16 July 1920.

In fact, 27 officers had been commissioned into the Indian Army from Sandhurst on 17 December 1919; 104 from Wellington on 29 January 1920; and 57 from Sandhurst on 16 July 1920. By this adjustment of their seniority, the Indian officers became junior to 188 British officers, who had passed out after them. This was done to account for the shortfall in training, as compared to the Sandhurst trained officers, who had undergone two and a half years training, while the Indore batch had spent only 18 months. There were loud protests, from the affected officers, who felt that the decision was discriminatory and unfair.

Some of them even resigned in protest, and were allowed to retire. As it happened, Cariappa's batch was the only one to pass out from Indore, because subsequent batches were trained at Sandhurst. Before this, nine Indians, serving in the Imperial Cadet Corps, who had rendered service during the War, had been granted King's Commissions, in August 1917. These were Zorawar Singh, Kunwar Amar Singh, Aga Kasim Shah, Khan Muhammad Akbar Khan, Malik Mumtaz Muhammad Khan, Kunwar Prithi Singh, Bala Saheb Daphle, Rana Jodha Jung Bahadur, and Kanwar Savai Sinhji. The first batch of Indians to join Sandhurst in January 1919 had five cadets, of which two died and one was withdrawn. The two who passed out from Sandhurst, on 16 July 1920, were Syed Iskander Ali Mirza and Iqbal Ali Beg, but the latter did not join. The sole survivor, Syed Iskander Ali Mirza, did not stay in the Army for long, and was transferred to the political service.

Cariappa's first posting was to the 2nd Battalion, the 88th Carnatic Infantry, then stationed at Bombay. After spending just three months there, he was transferred to 2/125 Napier Rifles, which moved to Mesopotamia in May 1920. After his return to India in June 1922, Cariappa was again transferred, to the 7th Prince of Wales Own Dogra Regiment. The battalion was then located at Khirgi, in Waziristan, and its main task was to keep the Pathan tribesmen under control, and maintain law and order. Within a few months of his arrival, Cariappa had his baptism by fire. He was leading a convoy of twenty lorries, which was ambushed, a few miles outside the post. Cariappa immediately rallied his men, and led an assault against the tribesmen, who were firing from a hill top. The quick reaction resulted in the tribesmen running away from the scene, and the convoy suffered very little damage. By the time reinforcements arrived, Cariappa had the situation well under control.

In 1923, the process of Indianisation began, and two units of Cavalry (7th Light Cavalry and 16th Cavalry), and six of Infantry (2/1 Madras Pioneers, 4/19 Hyderabad, 5/5 Mahratta Light Infantry, 1/7 Rajput, 1/14 Punjab and 2/1 Punjab) were nominated, to which Indian officers were to be posted. In June 1923, Cariappa was transferred to 1st Battalion the 7th Rajput Regiment (Queen Victoria's Own Light Infantry), known in short as 1/7 Rajput (2 QVOLI), which was one of the units thus selected, and this became his parent unit.

The battalion had just moved to Waziristan, and was employed on duties similar to those of his erstwhile unit. Life on the Frontier was monotonous, but not free of danger. The tribesmen were quick to exploit the slightest sign of laxity in vigil, and the frequent skirmishes often resulted in casualties. The North West Frontier was the best training ground for young officers, and Cariappa learned the basics of his profession during the three years he spent there. He developed an excellent eye for ground, and learnt the importance of good administration, which were to stand him in good stead in later years.

In 1925, Cariappa decided to go on a Grand Tour. He had saved enough money, and General HQ in Delhi not only accorded him permission, but arranged for his stay with British units, wherever possible. Cariappa went around the World, and visited Europe, USA, Japan, China and several other countries. He met a large number of soldiers, as well as civilians, of different nationalities, and was able to see for himself, the reason why some of them were far ahead, in many fields. The trip was a great education for him, and he returned a much wiser and better man. The battalion had moved to Fatehgarh in 1925, and for the first time in his career, Cariappa was able to settle down. It was here that he got his nick name, 'Kipper'. It is said that a British officer's wife found his name difficult to pronounce, and started calling him Kipper.

As a young officer, Cariappa took his soldiering seriously. He was a stickler, who lived by the book, and thus rarely got into trouble. There is an interesting anecdote about Mussourie, which was then a popular holiday resort for British officers.

Once, Cariappa applied for a few days leave, to visit the hill station. When his CO heard about it, he told Cariappa to go somewhere else. Cariappa was surprised, and wanted to know the reason. The 'Old Man' (an euphemism in the Army, for the Commanding Officer, or Commander) told him that Mussourie was full of disreputable women, and it was a regimental tradition that bachelors did not visit the place. Cariappa took the advice seriously, and did not go to Mussourie till after he was married, and his son was born.

## ROLE OF K.M. CARIAPPA IN INDIAN ARMY

Kodandera Madappa Cariappa is a legendary name in Indian Army; he was the first and one of the few to have ever occupied the prestigious chair of Field Marshal in armed forces ranking. From an early childhood, after losing his parents, Cariappa was engrossed to make it big in the army and become a jawan.

He was a dedicated student in school and under British administration he had surprisingly excelled in every task he performed, earning admiration wherever he went. As a starting milestone, Cariappa made himself selected as a Commissioned officer under British officers, overlooking several hurdles. With strict perseverance, belief and duty towards his Almighty and British high-rankers, Cariappa slowly and subtly started to move up the Army ranks, performing each duty with pain and care. His choice of missions under severe circumstances and extreme turbulence made everyone wonder about his prowess and to how much he could stretch his limits. Quite obviously, he was promoted after regular intervals and he can be termed as one of the few unusual Indian beings, who maintained a stable rapport with both natives and Britishers. With the historical event of India becoming free from British yoke, Cariappa was commissioned in the newly created Indian Army, which further ushered in a series of eventful sagas, leading to his becoming the top-ranker.

On 15th August 1947, India's Independence Day, K.M. Cariappa wore the insignia of a Major General and occupied his chair as the Deputy Chief of General Staff (Dy CGS) at the Army Headquarters. British Indian Army was wrapped up and Indian Army had finally taken a fresh look. A week earlier, the General Headquarters had once again been re-named as Army Headquarters.

On this great day, soon after the throng of well-wishers left his room, Cariappa felt sad and missed his erstwhile compatriots. The remaining Pakistani officers were to leave India by December 1947. Cariappa also prayed to Goddess Kaveri for the millions of innocent people who had been caught in the whirlwind of communal carnage. Then he informed his father in Madikeri and other friends living in U.K. The dawn of freedom meant so many things to him as he saw the huge responsibilities lying ahead of him. K.M. Cariappa in Indian Army was now to assume responsibilities to take the task further and make it known as a new wing to the world.

As Indian Army Officers were gradually replacing the British, Cariappa heard about his next promotion to the rank of Lieutenant General. He was in England, attending the Commonwealth Conference. On his return, Cariappa relieved Lt. General Sir Francis Tuker at the Eastern Command, Ranchi in November 1947. But within six weeks, he was called back to Delhi as conditions began deteriorating on the Western Border. The remaining Pakistani officers were to leave India by December 1947.

As early as October 1947, Pakistan had started its hostile activities by providing covert logistic support to the tribals. Besides, its regular soldiers were given long leave to fight as 'deserters' and lead the tribals clandestinely. Since Pakistan had launched the offensive, it had all the tactical advantage in choosing the terrain for infiltration beforehand. Its lines of communication were shorter and more secure. On the other hand, India had numerous logistical problems. The mountainous region posed serious difficulties in transporting the medium guns of the artillery. Its wireless messages were often intercepted while the telephone lines were not reliable. The fighting units were strung over hundreds of kilometres far from each other and Delhi was far away from the scene of action. Cariappa's suspicions that some Britishers were leaking army secrets turned out to be true.

A peculiar situation developed as the same set of Britishers, after the Partition, was fighting against each other now. Under these circumstances, Cariappa, leading from the forefront in Indian Army, kept his plans secret from his superior British officer, the C-in-C (Commander-in-Chief), General Roy Bucher. He moved his headquarters to a place near Jammu. Furthermore, he intended to be near his troops.

In the intense war that ensued between the two newly-created countries, the Indian Forces fought valiantly and recaptured many strategic places. During this fierce operation, the list of martyrs and gallantry awards went on increasing and Cariappa kept moving from one post to the other, unmindful of the hail of bullets. Indian Army perhaps never had found such a valiant officer, fearless in the face of pellets. Cariappa truly proved his position and stance, awarded each time by the armed forces organisation.

Knowing the nature of Pathan tribals very well, Cariappa even appealed to their conscience to live and not die for a cause which was not theirs. But this, time, it seems there was little effect on them. As winter set in, the road from Jammu to Srinagar was also blocked by snow, near Bannihal at the higher altitudes.

The Royal Indian Air Force (RIAF) provided close support for the ground forces and struck heavily on Pakistani targets. Some Dakotas, in addition to their normal function of transporting men and material, were modified so as to drop bombs. However, Cariappa's problems increased by mid-1948. Ladakh had to be defended at all costs and he looked at Zoji La, Kargil, Leh, Skardu with great concern. Here, Cariappa, who knew his history well, decided to repeat the performance of Maharaja Ranjit Singh's bold commander Zorawar Singh, who had swept through Ladakh and reached Baltistan through Western Tibet. A battalion crossed the 17,470 ft. Umasi La, romped into Zanskar valley and carried out their operations successfully. The people of Ladakh considered Cariappa as their saviour.

In the annals of military operations, 24th May 1948 was a red-letter day for the RIAF when Air Commodore Mehar Singh DSO, the legendary hawk of the Burma Operations, made history by landing his two-engine Dakota aircraft at Leh airstrip at an altitude of 11,000 feet under very trying conditions. The VIPs on board were none other than the Deputy Chief of the General Staff, Lieutenant General Cariappa and Major General Thimayya. This transport aircraft, though extremely versatile, lacked adequate heating, pressurisation and de-icing facilities. To fly at nearly 25,000 feet over the Western Himalayas, Mehar Singh was careful enough to keep extra oxygen-masks for the VIPS, but Cariappa refused to use it despite hard-breathing.

Their arrival had earlier been radioed and a huge crowd of Ladakhis led by their Head Lama Kushak Bakula greeted Cariappa as they saw the awe-inspiring sight of the messenger from the skies. As Mehar Singh kept the engines running, Cariappa re-assured the people and returned safely by the same aircraft. K.M. Cariappa by this very courteous move had just elevated his position even higher, both practically as well as allegorically. Cariappa's career in Indian Army had to go through such several perilous issues, which he passed with ease, making him reach such a prestigious position as Field Marshal.

While the month of May brought some good tidings from the front-lines, the next month of June turned out to be a month of some wrong political decisions later leading to much slippery moves. Aware of the acutely demoralising effect on the soldiers, Cariappa channelled his protest through General Roy Bucher to Pandit Jawaharlal Nehru. But he was advised to restrain himself. Thimayya and other senior officers exerted pressure on Cariappa to resign. But Cariappa did not waver in his resolve to do what was best for the country and began going around personally inspecting and visiting various forward positions in order to re-instill a spirit of high morale among his soldiers. Apparently, Cariappa had the foresight to visualise the dangerous chain-reaction that was bound to shatter the morale of his battle-weary men in case he yielded to the mental pressure being exerted on him. The consequences would have been catastrophic.

A commander is supposed to remain cool despite provocation and Cariappa had that enormous capacity to face such an acid test. Perhaps, this was one of the most important incidents of Cariappa's life while serving in Indian Army, which elevated him to a much higher pedestal than others.

By merely contemplating the explosive situation of the country in retrospect, one can easily fathom what a blessing it was to have such a towering military leader who could deliver the goods for the nation with such success. Even after his retirement, when Cariappa visited jawans in the Amritsar/ Lahore sector, soon after the 1965 war, the Pakistani soldiers shouted from the other side of the no-man's land that General Cariappa should come over to their side and honour them as well. The 'Grand Old Man' of the Indian Army was only too glad to move over to their positions and enquired about their welfare. Field Marshal Ayub Khan thanked Cariappa for this kind gesture. On the outside, Cariappa was all steel but inside, he was ready to melt at the slightest human warmth.

In course of the 1965 War with Pakistan, a ceasefire came into existence finally. The ground positions held by the two opposing forces came to be called the Line of Control (LoC). This was also the time when the British C-in-C (Commander-in-Chief) in India handed over the charge to General Cariappa, who had been promoted once more in the freshly-formed Indian Army.

The day that dawned on 15th January 1949 fulfilled Cariappa's cherished desire to command the Army which he had so painstakingly nurtured. No doubt, he had fully deserved it. Congratulations began pouring in from everywhere and the event turned his New Delhi residence into a magnificent 'mela', where a medley of people from all walks of life had descended to see their hero.

However, Cariappa's joy was tinged with sorrow. The frenzy of hatred resulting in unnecessary bloodshed had hardly been contained while the gigantic task entrusted to the Army for transporting and rehabilitation of more than ten lakhs of refugees now faced him. Cariappa had set up a military evacuation organisation for this purpose. All this time, Cariappa reminded himself of his father's words that there was a big task before him now. Every significant point in his job was taken up as a milestone by Cariappa while his extensive hold in Indian Army. Fearing nothing and moving forward with the courage of a tiger, Cariappa was a braveheart personified.

## INDIAN FIELD MARSHAL: K.M. CARIAPPA

Kodandera Madappa Cariappa, or K.M. Cariappa was a declared Commissioned officer under British Indian Army. He was a rare example during pre-independent India, when everybody was fighting against British army, only to see them ousted. However, Cariappa made a separate process to rise up and demonstrate to English people that Indians can also ascend from another direction. Since his early life, Cariappa was sublimely interested to become a jawan in armed forces. His wish came true when he became selected in British Army, that too into the King's Commission. From then on, his rise was successfully graphed by British men, as well as Indian well-wishers. His gentle nature, yet rock-solid determination in battlefield made him ascend and ascend to positions even not achieved by British officers serving in Army. Cariappa's legendary and unusual character was slowly coming to light by his clever strategies, because of his fantastic rising under British Indian Army.

Picking up the threads of new wartime assignments, Cariappa found himself in Baghdad once again. This time, he had joined the 10th Indian Division under Major General William Slim who was once his role model. General Headquarters had especially chosen him for this area, as they combined to become a formidable cohesive force at the Command level in the field. Here, in the capacity as DAA & QMG, Cariappa's engagements took him to Syria, Iran and Egypt. Thus was heralded the marvellous ascension of Cariappa under British Army.

A very interesting episode occurred while Cariappa was on the move with the Indian Army, through a small city called Der'azr in Syria. Someone had spread a mischievous rumour in advance in the city that the approaching Indian Army will be molesting their women-folk. The poor Mayor took immediate precautions by ordering that all the women must remain indoors till these soldiers cleared out.

The effect of such an order can easily be fathomed. So, when it became impossible for these wretched women to bear this confinement, the cheerless Mayor gathered his courage and met Cariappa and asked for his permission if he could allow the women to come out of their homes.

Cariappa was shocked at this strange request and enquired why in the first place had they been restricted in such a manner. He was hugely bewildered when he heard the Mayor expressing his fear about the Indian soldiers' assumed misconduct. Cariappa calmly reassured the Mayor and the women were soon on the streets and moving about happily. Not a single one had been harmed.

As an initiation into ascension, Cariappa was awarded the 'Mention-in-Despatches' medal, for his excellent work in this area, which is given for conspicuous gallantry. During this time, he visited the frontlines and saw to it that all needs of the jawans were addressed. In the light of his close liaison, he devised new alternatives with his shrewd planning and thus provided better logistic support. But more than this, his deep love for his men had made him very popular among them. They did not mind his 'stick' of discipline and hard task-mastership. By now, his devotion forced the British Anti-Indian lobby to crumble. He was promoted to the rank of Lieutenant Colonel. It implied an important change in the British way of thinking and brought in a rich harvest of fruits for India vis-a-vis the Indian Army.

Lieutenant General William Slim, who had also been promoted, was among the first to send his warmest congratulations, coming to know of K.M. Cariappa's ascension to a further prestigious post. It was a moving letter, in which he poured lavish praise on Cariappa, saying that there was no one better than him to work with. This letter was received by Cariappa after Slim's forces had retreated from Burma.

As a result of the changes in the army, Cariappa was made the first Indian Commanding Officer (CO) of a Battalion. This meant he was the first Indian to have British officers under him. He had finally succeeded in impressing the Britishers to Indianise the Indian Army, which meant higher promotions not only for himself, but also for other Indian officers. This was an important milestone not only in his ascend towards the top, but also for the Indian Army to move ahead with renewed confidence.

In his race to ascend to the top, Cariappa was given the command of a battalion to be raised on 15th April 1942. This battalion was named as 7th Rajput Machine-gun Battalion. He couldn't ask for more when the orders allowed him a free hand to put his act together at Fatehgarh, with eight British and three Indian officers (KCOs) as his subordinates.

Not outlined but implicit in the orders, were the expectations of the highest level of dynamism, pride and prestige. With the allotment of the new Vickers machine-guns and the Range-Finders which were still in the process of final trials for accuracy, the Battalion was listed as one of the elite formations and Cariappa had to make it fit for 'operational readiness' at the earliest. He took up the job as a challenge and within a span of just one year, this unit lived up to its expectations and could move into the battlefield at just two hours' notice. With Cariappa's ascension in armed forces, came more responsibilities, which he adjusted to the fullest. The Battalion had been thus put through day and night rigorous training sessions. It was nothing less than a miracle. Cariappa had motivated his jawans with the same spirit of self-confidence with which he always faced every challenge.

On 1st April 1943, Lt. Col. Cariappa was a very proud man, as he handed over the charge of this unit to Lt. Col. G.B. McNamara. By this time, this leading formation had undergone further conversions. Major General Frank Messervy, who was later allotted to Pakistan Army, evaluated Cariappa's performance and said that he was fit for Command Formations. As such, K.M. Cariappa's road to ascension was even more polished in the way, with every top ranking official recommending about his excellence.

On being relieved, Cariappa was urgently called to the Headquarters, Eastern Command, Nomkum, Ranchi to plan and provide logistic support for the entire Eastern Region. Here, General Slim's 14th Army was preparing to re-capture Burma from the Japanese. Incidentally, U.S. forces were also thrown in here under the American Lieutenant General Stilwell and this involved extra liaison work for Cariappa.

This was the time when Mahatma Gandhi's Quit India Movement was causing widespread unrest in India after failure of the Cripps Mission. The mounting countrywide protests had put the British Raj in a tight spot. The only silver lining was that in the midst of their despair, the Indian Army did not let them down either inside the country or abroad in Africa or Europe and the recruitment in the Army went on unhampered. This was, of course, not true for Singapore and Malaya where Netaji's INA (Indian National Army) was creating havoc.

By August 1943, i.e., within four months of Cariappa's arrival at Nomkum, a new South East Asia Command (SEAC) was formed under Admiral Louis Mountbatten and the 14th Army became a part of it. In the new set up, Cariappa volunteered to be in the front lines where multi-pronged operations had been launched against the advancing enemy which included amphibian and air assaults. It is interesting to note that the Royal Indian Air Force (RIAF) which had just completed its 10th year on 1st April, 1943 started pounding the Japanese in their air-to-ground and air-to-air combat sorties, while the United States Air Force (USAF) mounted their bombing runs by its Liberator Squadrons. These 4-engine bombers were later inducted in the RIAF.

During this ongoing period of wartime turbulence, Cariappa was awarded the Order of the British Empire (OBE) for his meritorious Staff services. Cariappa's ascension in British Army was furthered in the upcoming days. He was now a Colonel and was recommended for the Field Rank of a Brigadier. He received this promotion on 1st November 1944 and was posted in the Wilcox Committee for a year as a member of the Re-Organisation Committee for the Indian Army.

The situation in the closing years of the 20th century was just a shadow of what it was during the earlier times when Brigadier Cariappa was given the command of the Bannu Frontier Brigade in early 1946. Bannu lies in the heart of the Frontier Province and is well connected by roads and a metre-gauge railway. The deadly guerrilla attacks had turned this area into a 'British graveyard'. This compelled the top-brass to bring back Cariappa here for a second time, after a gap of ten years. A fanatic fakir, Haji Mirza Khan was whipping up religious sentiments of the tribes against the Britishers. Cries of 'Jehad' against these 'infidels' rang out all over this country of desolate mountains. British policy of using brutal force in dealing with these insurgents had not changed much in these ten years. The tribes were baying for blood and fire and sword for these Kafirs. They created devastation on the convoys, camps and garrisons by blowing up bridges, cutting the water-mains and sniping on the sentries guarding the pickets and outlying units.

The increasing number of casualties contributed to an atmosphere of frustration among the soldiers, but the Britishers were in no mood to call it quits. Knowing the nature of the tribal folk, Cariappa decided to tackle the difficult situation of insurgency with his two-pronged policy of compassion and tough operational flexibility. K.M. Cariappa's ascension while in British Indian Army had ensured foolproof planning for war strategies. He established a rapport with Mirza Khan on the one hand but on the other, he adopted a new day-night counter-guerrilla strategy and his troops began paying them back in the same coin. The fortunes of this kind of war change easily.

One day, his sincere efforts to win their hearts bore fruit all of a sudden when he chanced upon a group of Pathan women resting on the roadside with loads of water-pitchers. Cariappa enquired about it and found that these women had to fetch drinking water from a place, many miles away. He was deeply moved.

Returning to his camp, he talked to his jawans and a bore-well was ready in no time, near the village itself. Next week, the same fakir was at Cariappa's door along with a group of armed tribals. They embraced him tightly and addressed him as Khalifa (God's Messenger). That was precisely the day when the tribal insurgency was tamed. But their Khalifa did more than that. Cariappa saw to it that no Hindus or Sikhs of that area were harmed when they left their homes and migrated to India.

Cariappa stayed there for only about a year. He was called to Delhi to preside over one of the court martials of the INA (Indian National Army) prisoners. The fate of these personnel had become a sensitive topic of national dimensions, which clashed with British prestige. Although, on gaining Independence, India treated them as freedom fighters, Cariappa opposed their re-entry into the Army on grounds of principles. Though Cariappa's sublime ascension during British rule was not tinged with anti-Indian sentiment, yet he was quite strict in matters of armed forces rules and regulations, which at times cropped up in clashing views.

In preparation for granting Independence to India, Field Marshal Claude Auchinleck chose Cariappa to attend a course at the Imperial Defence College, U.K. in January 1947. Incidentally, Field Marshal Slim, Cariappa's long-time friend, was the Commandant here. Although Field Marshal Bernard Montgomery had initially expressed his reservations, Cariappa prevailed upon everybody when his views were heard on the partition of India.

By March 1947, the then British Prime Minister, Sir Clement Attlee relieved Field Marshal Wavell and sent Lord Mountbatten to India. Meanwhile, Cariappa's stay at the Imperial Defence College was cut short as the Indian Armed Forces-the Army, Navy and Air Force had to be divided in view of the fast-moving political events in the wake of the partition of the country into India and Pakistan. As the modalities for dividing the Armed Forces were being worked out, Cariappa opposed it vigorously. However, he was not alone in voicing his opposition. Thousands of soldiers became openly sentimental at the prospect of seeing their colleagues going separate ways. Cariappa made desperate attempts to convince both Jawaharlal Nehru and Muhammad Ali Jinnah. He proposed to keep the Army undivided for a period of at least five years. Chakravarti Rajagopalachari liked the proposal. Lord Mountbatten praised Cariappa's bold stand and placed them before Nehru, Jinnah and Liaquat Ali with slight modifications. To make them acceptable, he suggested that the Armed Forces of the two countries may be pooled together. But nobody accepted them. The division of the Armed Forces was termed as-'Reconstitution' of the Indian Armed Forces. K.M. Cariappa's ascension during British Indian Army did not come to much avail when division of army men were considered. Indian government had gained a fresh status free from British supremacy, as such, British regulations were not taken into account. The only consolation for Cariappa was that most of the British officers had opted to remain behind. Their services were badly needed by India.

When the time came for parting, Cariappa presented a souvenir to his Muslim friends which showed two jawans-a Hindu and a Muslim-standing side by side pointing their guns at a common enemy. Then he delivered a moving speech and said, 'Au Revoir'-till we meet again! It is significant to note that he never said 'Good Bye' and the orchestra's notes 'Auld Lang Syne'-The good old days-echoed through the hall of Delhi Gymkhana Club. K.M. Cariappa's ascension never did make him a stricter, who would always look down upon his fellow officers. But, he had in the way, become even more submissive to army rules, governing everyone as his own.

## LAST PHASE OF K.M. CARIAPPA, INDIAN FIELD MARSHAL

Kodandera Madappa Cariappa, or K.M. Cariappa is a luminous example of how a human can reach the top with just determination and discipline. Born into a quite middle class family, Cariappa had since his early days wanted to become a Class-I officer in the British Indian Army. The British Empire was during Cariappa's boyhood times well established in every sphere of living. As such, Indian society was not free from turbulence.

In the midst of all these, Cariappa was silently prepared to get himself selected as a commissioned officer in the King's Commission. British officers were pretty jealous of an Indian native towering above an English soldier. However, K.M. Cariappa was oblivious of such incidents, roaring like a lion in warfront, facing every kind of perilous situations and coming out with ease.

His steep rise in the army ranking, accompanied by the incident of partition of India, post independence made a significant divide in the British Indian Army. Hence was created the Indian Army, with K.M. Cariappa serving at its forefront. With passing years, his army life was coming to a close, after wrapping up issues and battles. Cariappa's last phase were however free from combat hassles and political decisions amidst tribulations. It is known that Cariappa had been through all of this. In addition, he had an abiding faith in God and the blessings of his elders. By the time he reached the top, there was enough tenacity in his grip to hold his flag high.

Approaching the task methodically, he cleared the decks first and then set about fixing the matters which required his immediate attention. He personally trained his domestic staff because his 'Army House' was going to be the meeting-point for VIPs, functions and social gatherings. Already into is last phase, on this great day when Cariappa took charge as Commander-in-Chief, he placed a wreath on Mahatma Gandhi's 'Samadhi' at 8 a.m. Then he started replying to a heap of congratulatory letters. One of the letters had come from Field Marshal Birdwood. Cariappa assured him that the traditional links which had been developed over a long period of history would be maintained by the Indian Army.

Then he proceeded to lay the foundations for its modernisation. Among the issues he tackled first and foremost, included the following:

Transforming the colonial profile of the Army to a national one and ensuring its apolitical image.

Restraining the civilian 'Babudom' in their unimaginative attempts to control the Army.

Amalgamation of the armies of the princely-states into the Indian Army.

Ensuring the continuance of the traditional relationship with the retired or serving British officers who had opted to remain behind.

Rehabilitation of the refugees and the members of the Indian National Army.

In addition, Cariappa streamlined the administrative procedures, formulated new rules and took steps to remove some irritating anomalies in the rank and pay structure of the officers. But, between his work and hectic touring schedule, Cariappa found enough time to attend to the problems of the ex-servicemen whose welfare was very close to his heart. A man like his stature, Cariappa during his last phase in his eventful army career was amiable enough to bring himself down to any measure and assist the common man. This very quality of gentleness and absence of vanity, made Cariappa hold up the supreme rank in Indian Army division and stand out to fulfil his dream. So, by all means, he had projected an unusually strenuous task for himself. However, with his superhuman stamina for hard work, he was able to achieve a remarkable degree of success during his tenure of four years. An Indian Field Marshal perhaps could not have asked for more, with both parties moving towards a smooth administration. Like any other human being, Cariappa also had enough ups and downs in life in order to reach that position into his last phase. In 1950, he was invited to visit Nepal where the king made him an honorary General of the Royal Nepalese Army. Soon thereafter, the President of USA, Harry Truman conferred upon him the 'Order of the Chief Commander of the Legion of Merit'. But at the same time, this period gave him enough tense moments as a blizzard had started building up in the Himalayas. The entry of the Communist China into Tibet made him very apprehensive.

In January, 1951, approximately 11 years before the large-scale Chinese aggression on India, Cariappa's worst fears came true when on an urgent request from the Assam Government, he had to rush a platoon of para-troopers to a place near Rima-Tatu. This timely action stopped the Chinese in their tracks and thus the threat was well contained. Cariappa placed further proposals for taking defensive measure before Prime Minister Jawaharlal Nehru, but the latter was too preoccupied with Kashmir and spurned the proposal.

On completion of his long and fruitful innings, General Cariappa was glad to hand over his C-in-C's (Commander-in-Chief) charge to Lieutenant General Rajindra Singh, in mid-January 1953. K.M. Cariappa's last phase in Indian Army was governed by magnanimous affairs, with loads of nostalgia and recollections to be recounted. The shining path which he had laid out, gave him the honour to be remembered as the 'Father of the Indian Army'. His farewell was marked by unusually touching scenes and a stampede near the New Delhi railway station.

He had hardly settled down in Madikeri when Cariappa was summoned to become India's High Commissioner to Australia and New Zealand. He sailed out in July 1953 and the Governor General who welcomed him was none other than his old friend Field Marshal William Slim. Cariappa's tenure kept him there till April 1956.

By 1971, Cariappa was thoroughly disillusioned with the government's failure to follow up the hard gains of the Indian Army's victory in the Indo-Pak War. Losing this good opportunity to recover its territory in Kashmir made him contest the general elections as an independent candidate from N.E. Bombay. But he had no chance against the corruption prevalent in politics. However, his deep interest in serving the country and the welfare of the ex-servicemen never flagged. Though into a last phase in his terrific career, in which he had seen it all, Cariappa was never lacking in zeal when his country was concerned. Everything would then take a back-seat.

On 14th January, 1986, the then President Zail Singh conferred on Cariappa the rank of Field Marshal for life. He was eighty-seven on that day. After successfully wrapping up every task he was ordained to, Cariappa could make himself proud to have been blessed with such parents who brought him up to live to witness such a day. The Almighty had also showered Cariappa with all his blessings. In fact, just to end Cariappa's last phase in army life with such mere words seems an understatement, for the man had perhaps achieved everything. The entire nation and the media rejoiced at the news. Besides, Cariappa's well-wishers from across the world sent their emotional messages and greetings. But his failing health gave Cariappa just enough time to live up the age of 94 years and a few months. This great Indian soldier passed into history quite peacefully on 15th May 1993.

## POST-RETIREMENT AND DEATH

Cariappa's alliance with the Indian Army was spread over a period of around three decades, during which he had broad experience of staff and command work. After his retirement in 1953, he served as the Indian high commissioner to Australia and New Zealand until 1956. With a view toward ex-servicemen's welfare, Cariappa founded the Indian Ex-Servicemen's League (IESL) in 1964. He was also instrumental in setting up the Directorate of Resettlement (later Directorate General Resettlement), an inter-service organisation under the Department of Ex-servicemen Welfare, Ministry of Defence, that looked after the various issues surrounding the resettlement of retired soldiers, especially those who retired young.

Cariappa took part in the re-organisation of the armed forces in many foreign countries. He was awarded the Legion of Merit in the degree of Chief Commander by the American President Harry S. Truman.

Cariappa also tried his luck in politics after a lot of persuasion from his friends and admirers. In the 1957 general elections, he contested the Lok Sabha seat for North-East Bombay as an independent against Krishna Menon and J.B. Kripalani, but lost.

As a mark of recognition for the commendable service rendered by him to the nation, the Government of India conferred the rank of field marshal on Cariappa on 28 April 1986, at a special investiture ceremony held at Rashtrapati Bhavan, the official home of the president of India.

Cariappa's health began to deteriorate in 1991; he suffered from arthritis and heart problems. He died in his sleep on 15 May 1993, at the Bangalore Command Hospital where he had been receiving treatment for a few years. His mortal remains were cremated in Madikeri two days later. The cremation was attended by the three service chiefs along with Field Marshal Sam Manekshaw. Cariappa's son, Nanda, lit the pyre while the Honour Guard reversed arms.

# 3

# Sam Hormusji Framji Jamshedji Manekshaw

Field Marshal Sam Hormusji Framji Jamshedji Manekshaw, MC (3 April 1914 – 27 June 2008), popularly known as Sam Bahadur ("Sam the Brave"), was the Chief of the Army Staff of the Indian Army during the Indo-Pakistani War of 1971, and the first Indian Army officer to be promoted to the rank of field marshal. His military career spanned four decades and five wars, beginning with service in the British Indian Army in World War II.

Manekshaw joined the first intake of the Indian Military Academy (IMA) in 1932. He was commissioned into the 2nd Battalion, Royal Scots, and later posted to the 4th Battalion, 12th Frontier Force Regiment. In World War II, he was awarded the Military Cross for gallantry. Following the partition of India in 1947, he was reassigned to the 16th Punjab Regiment. Manekshaw was seconded to a planning role during the 1947 Indo-Pakistani War and the Hyderabad crisis, and as a result he never commanded an infantry battalion. He was promoted to the rank of brigadier while serving at the Military Operations Directorate. He became commander of 167th Infantry Brigade in 1952 and served in this position until 1954, when he took over as the Director of Military Training at Army HQ.

After completing the higher command course at the Imperial Defence College, he was appointed General Officer Commanding of the 26th Infantry Division. He also served as the commandant of the Defence Services Staff College. In 1961, Manekshaw made derogatory comments about the political leadership which allowed his opponents to label him as unpatriotic, and he was charged with sedition. After being exonerated in the subsequent court of inquiry, he took command of IV Corps in November 1962. The next year, Manekshaw was promoted to the position of army commander and took over Western Command, transferring in 1964 to the Eastern Command.

Having already commanded troops at division, corps and regional levels, Manekshaw became the eighth chief of the army staff in 1969. Under his command, Indian forces conducted victorious campaigns against Pakistan in the Indo-Pakistani War of 1971, which led to the creation of Bangladesh in December 1971.

He was awarded the Padma Vibhushan and the Padma Bhushan, the second and third highest civilian awards of India.

## CHILDHOOD & EARLY LIFE

- Sam was born to Parsi parents in Amritsar. His father, Hormusji Manekshaw was a doctor. His mother's name was Heerabai and he had three brothers and two sisters.
- Sam's father had been a Captain in the Royal British Army and had come to Amritsar from Bombay where he had started a medical practice and pharmacy.
- He was educated at the Sherwood College in Nainital. He was a brilliant student and achieved a distinction in the School Certificate examination of the Cambridge Board.
- Setting his eyes on becoming a doctor, he asked his father to send him to England to study medicine. His father felt Sam was too young to be on his own and refused to send him until he was older.
- The teenager was upset that his father refused and in rebellion he decided to appear for the entrance examination for enrollment into the Indian Military Academy (IMA).

## EARLY LIFE AND EDUCATION

Manekshaw was born in Amritsar, Punjab to Parsi parents, Hormusji Manekshaw, a doctor, and his wife Heerabai, who moved to Punjab from the small town of Valsad on the Gujaratcoast. After completing his schooling in Punjab and Sherwood College, Nainital, and achieving a distinction in the School Certificate examination of the Cambridge Board at the age of 15, he asked his father to send him to London to become a gynaecologist.

When his father refused to send him until he was older, in an act of rebellion, Manekshaw took the entrance examination for enrollment into the Indian Military Academy (IMA) at Dehradun. He was successful and as a result became part of the first intake of 40 cadets on 1 October 1932. He graduated from the IMA on 4 February 1934 and was commissioned as a second lieutenant in the British Indian Army (which later became the Indian Army after Independence).

After taking over as chief of army staff, at a function on 8 June 1969 to mark the centenary of Sherwood College, Manekshaw recalled that his years at the college had prepared him for war as they had taught him to live alone and independently, to fight without relent, tolerate hunger for long periods and to hate his enemy.

## MILITARY CAREER

Manekshaw's military career spanned four decades, from the British era and World War II, to the three wars against Pakistan and China after India's independence in 1947. He held several regimental, staff and command assignments. Manekshaw went on to become the 8th chief of the army staff, led the Indian Army successfully in a war with Pakistan and become India's first field marshal.

On commissioning, as per the practices of that time, Manekshaw was first attached to the 2nd Battalion, The Royal Scots, a British battalion, and then later posted to the 4th Battalion, 12th Frontier Force Regiment, commonly known as the 54th Sikhs. Immediately after passing out of IMA in 1934, Sam Manekshaw was commissioned as a Second Lieutenant in the British Indian Army. This marked the beginning of his selfless service towards his country. He was first attached to the 2nd Bn The Royal Scots and later to the 4/12 Frontier Force Regiment. It was under this regiment that he was made the company commander of the battalion that fought the famous battle against the Japanese in Myanmar and won. It was this very battle that earned Manekshaw a Military Cross, a recognition that's granted in acknowledgment of "an act or acts of exemplary gallantry during the active operations against the enemy on land to all members, of any rank in the armed forces". After partition, the 4/12 Frontier Force Regiment became a part of the Pakistan army so Manekshaw was transferred to 8th Gurkha Rifles.

The temperament and perspicacity with which Manekshaw handled the planning and administrative issues that had crept up after the country's partition, was remarkable. Shortly after when Pakistan invaded Kashmir; he was made the colonel in charge. The success of the operations of 1947-48 is largely attributed to him for he showed exceptional strategic and battle skills during the military operations. Later in 1962, when India had suffered a defeat in NEFA at the hands of the Chinese, Prime Minister Jawahar Lal Nehru asked Manekshaw to command the retreating Indian forces. The soldiers too, showed immense faith in their commander and successfully checked further intrusion by the Chinese. In the Indo-Pak war of 1965, Manekshaw was made the Company Commander of the eastern command and successfully led India to victory. He, then, went on to become the 8th Chief of Army Staff, succeeding General Kumaramangalam, on June 7, 1969.

The second Indo-Pak war of 1971 again saw the strategic brilliance of Sam into action as he was right in the middle of it all. It is said that there was a difference of opinion between the Prime Minister Indira Gandhi and Manekshaw as to what should be the timing of the military action and that the latter offered to resign from the post if his plans were not accepted.

Indira Gandhi accepted his plans and the result was evident in 93, 000 Pakistani soldiers that were made to surrender in a short span of just 14 days. India had won the war, making it one of the fastest military victories in the history of Indian Military. After four decades of selfless riveted service to the Indian Military and the country itself, Sam Manekshaw retired on 15th June 1973, but not before he was made the first ever Field Marshal.

## WORLD WAR II

During World War II, the then-Captain Manekshaw saw action in Burma in the 1942 campaign on the Sittaung River with the 4/12 Frontier Force Regiment, and had the rare distinction of being honoured for his bravery on the battlefield. During the fighting around Pagoda Hill, a key position on the left of the Sittang bridgehead, he led his company in a counter-attack against the invading Japanese Army and despite suffering 50% casualties the company managed to achieve its objective.

After capturing the hill, Manekshaw was hit by a burst of light machine gun fire and was severely wounded in the stomach. Observing the battle, Major General David Cowan, the then commander of the 17th Infantry Division spotted Manekshaw holding on to life and, having witnessed his valour in the face of stiff resistance, rushed over to him. Fearing that Manekshaw would die, the general pinned his own Military Cross ribbon to Manekshaw saying, "A dead person cannot be awarded a Military Cross." The official recommendation for the MC states that the success of the attack "was largely due to the excellent leadership and bearing of Captain Manekshaw".

This award was made official with the publication of the notification in a supplement to the *London Gazette* on 21 April 1942 (dated 23 April 1942). Manekshaw was evacuated to Rangoon and on arrival was close to death, having been hit by seven bullets in his lungs, liver and kidneys. It was Sher Singh, his orderly, who evacuated him from the battlefield. When the surgeon asked what had happened to him, he replied that he was "kicked by a donkey". Over Manekshaw's protests to treat the other patients, the regimental medical officer, Captain G M Diwan, attended to him.

Having recovered from his wounds, Manekshaw attended the 8th Staff Course at Command and Staff College, Quetta, from 23 August to 22 December 1943. He was then posted as the brigade major of the Razmak Brigade, serving in that post until 22 October 1944 when he was sent to join the 9th Battalion, 12 Frontier Force Regiment in Burma, as part of General William Slim's 14th Army.

Towards the end of World War II, Manekshaw was sent to serve on General Daisy's staff in Indo-China where, after the Japanese surrender, he helped repatriate over 10,000 former prisoners of war (POWs). He then went on a six-month lecture tour to Australia in 1946, and after his return was promoted to the rank of lieutenant-colonel, serving as a first grade staff officer in the Military Operations Directorate.

Upon the Partition of India in 1947, his parent unit – 12th Frontier Force Regiment – became part of the Pakistan Army (rechristenedFrontier Force Regiment), and so Manekshaw was reassigned to the 16th Punjab Regiment, before being posted to the 3rd Battalion, 5th Gorkha Rifles, which he was detailed to command.

The tumultuous events of partition required Manekshaw's retention in army headquarters as a lieutenant colonel in the Military Operations Directorate, though, and because of this he subsequently missed his chance to command an infantry battalion as he was later promoted to brigadier, becoming the first Indian Director of Military Operations. The appointment of Director of Military Operations was upgraded first to major general and later to lieutenant general and is now termed Director General Military Operations.

## Post-independence

While handling the issues relating to Partition in 1947, Manekshaw demonstrated his acumen for planning and administration, and later was able put his battle skills to use during operations in Jammu & Kashmir in 1947–48. After commanding an infantry brigade, he was posted to the Infantry School at Mhow as the school's commandant and also became the colonel of 8 Gorkha Rifles (which became his new regiment, since his original parent regiment, the 12th Frontier Force Regiment, had become part of the new Pakistan Army at partition) and 61st Cavalry.

Manekshaw then commanded a division in Jammu and Kashmir. A stint at the Defence Services Staff College followed where he served as the commandant. It was here that his outspoken frankness got him into trouble with the then Defence Minister, V. K. Krishna Menon. A court of inquiry was ordered against him. The court, presided over by the then-Western Army Commander,Lieutenant General Daulet Singh, exonerated Manekshaw. Before a formal 'no case' could be announced, war with China broke out. Manekshaw was then promoted to lieutenant general and moved to Tezpur to take over IV Corps as its GOC.

A year later, Manekshaw was promoted as army commander and took over the Western Command. In 1964, He moved from Shimla to Calcutta as the GOC-in-C of the Eastern Army. As GOC-in-C, Eastern Command, he successfully responded to an insurgency in Nagaland for which he was later awarded thePadma Bhushan in 1968.

## ARMY CHIEF: INDO-PAKISTANI WAR OF 1971

On 7 June 1969, Manekshaw became the 8th chief of army staff when he succeeded General P P Kumaramangalam. As chief of the army staff, he rendered yeoman service to the nation by forging the Indian Army into an efficient instrument of war. His years of military experience were soon put to the test as India decided to help the Mukti Bahini rebels against West Pakistani forces.

Towards the end of April 1971, Indira Gandhi, who was Prime Minister of India at that time, asked Manekshaw if he was ready to go to war with Pakistan. Manekshaw refused, saying that his single armoured division and two infantry divisions were deployed elsewhere, that only 13 of his 189 tanks were fit to fight, and that they would be competing for rail carriage with the grain harvest at that point of time. He also pointed out that the Himalayan passes would soon open up, with the forthcoming monsoon in East Pakistan, which would result in heavy flooding.

When Indira Gandhi asked the cabinet to leave the room and the chief to stay, he offered to resign. She declined to accept it, but sought his advice. He then said he could guarantee victory if she would allow him to prepare for the conflict on his terms, and set a date for it. These were acceded to by the Prime Minister.

When the Indian Army finally went to war in December that year, under Manekshaw's leadership, it proved victorious against the Pakistan Army. The war, lasting under a fortnight, saw more than 90,000 Pakistani soldiers personnel taken as prisoners of war, and it ended with the unconditional surrender of Pakistan's eastern half, resulting in the birth of Bangladesh as a new nation.

When the Prime minister asked him to go to Dhaka and accept the surrender of Pakistani forces, Manekshaw declined, magnanimously saying that the honour should go to his army commander in the East, Lieutenant General Jagjit Singh Aurora. Time to Award Bharat Ratna to Sam Manekshaw

*16 December is celebrated as 'Vijay Divas' to mark India's greatest military victory in modern times. This article is a tribute to the architect of that great victory, India's greatest soldier of modern times, Field Marshal Sam Manekshaw.*

In a few months from now, on 3rd April 2014, the country will commemorate the 100$^{th}$ birth anniversary of Field Marshal Sam Hormusji Framji Jamshedji Manekshaw, popularly referred to the world over as Sam Manekshaw. His image is one that of larger than life – a charismatic countenance, bravado, inspirational, heroic, humorous, rebellious and defiant towards authority, but surely for the soldiers whom he commanded – just brave, inspiring and one that of immediate connect- a true leader. The image is iconic and of a person the likes of whom rarely walk the earth. There are military leaders and there is Sam Manekshaw.

His achievements - a Military Cross for an act of personal bravery in World War II; actively involved in the planning process of operations in J&K during the 1947 Indo-Pak War while posted in the Military Operations Directorate in Army HQ; in 1962, at the height of the Sino-Indian conflict, he was rushed to take over 4 Corps to stem the advancing Chinese - his famous quote - "There will be no withdrawal without orders – and these orders shall never be issued"; during his tenure as Army Commander Eastern Command, the Naga Insurgency was put down; he was awarded the Padma Bhushan, the third highest civilian award, for distinguished service in the field of civil service in 1968; in June 1969, he took over as the Chief of Army Staff and remained so till January 1973.

His role and contribution to the nation in ensuring a decisive victory for the Indian Army during the 1971 Indo-Pakistan War, leading to the creation of Bangladesh is stuff of legend. In 1972, he was awarded the Padma Vibhushan and on 1st January 1973 the honorary rank of Field Marshal was conferred upon him, a first in the history of Indian military. There remains little doubt that Sam Manekshaw was India's greatest soldier in modern times and arguably, one of the greatest in the history of modern warfare.

Maybe it is time to recall the significance of the Indian victory in the 1971 War to understand what role this great military leader of the country had to play. The 1971 Indo-Pak war was an instance when India took the military initiative, a rare occurrence.

With the Indian military offensive on the anvil, the 1971 campaign was actually triggered by Pakistani pre-emptive air strikes on 3 December 1971. The war concluded two weeks later with the signing of the Instrument of Surrender, in Dhaka on 16 December, making it one of the shortest and most decisive campaigns in the history of warfare.

The 1971 War was the culmination of a long-drawn struggle in erstwhile East Pakistan. A brutal crackdown by the Pakistani military on the night of 25-26th March 1971 saw the persecution of the local people rise to extremely dangerous levels. Soldiers of the East Pakistan Rifles and Regiment, both of which had revolted, students, intellectual, any number of civilians who were considered to be 'Bengali Resistance, were hunted, hounded and massacred, triggering the migration of an estimated 10 million refugees into Indian territory, in what was coined as 'demographic aggression'.

Under these circumstances, India was forced to intervene, both due to her inability to be a bystander in this human cleansing going on in East Pakistan, and growing security concerns of her own given the massive influx of refugees. On the diplomatic front, there did not appear to be much coming out against the atrocities being committed by the Pakistan military in Bangladesh. Therefore, India decided to play an active role and extended support to the Bangladeshi freedom fighters despite opposition from the United States and China. On 3rd December, the Indian Army entered Bangladesh, and in less than a fortnight, ended the war, leading to creation of Bangladesh and India's greatest military victory.

Apart from reducing Pakistan by half and creating a new nation from the ceded portion, the 1971 War can be seen to be the most significant war India has fought in its modern history. For the first time, India displayed its sovereignty in action, by opposing US, China and world opinion in entering the war.

The Indian military comprehensively defeated Pakistan in the East and also significantly in the West. The war also led to a lot of changes in dynamics in the region; it formalised Indo-Soviet ties, cemented the ill-will of Pakistan towards India which continues to this day and served as the start point for the nuclear race in between the two countries. While the Indian policy and all machinations of diplomatic strategy were focused towards its goal of ameliorating the suffering of her East Pakistani neighbour, the strategy would depend mainly on the success of its military campaign, for an early and successful closure of war. When the conflict started in East Pakistan in March 1971, there was pressure from Prime Minister Indira Gandhi on Sam Manekshaw to immediately join the conflict.

However, Sam was firm in refusing to enter into war immediately, choosing rather to wait, prepare and fight a war on his own terms in winter, one amongst other important strategic reasons being to preclude or render difficult Chinese intervention with mountain passes remaining closed during that time.

He was reputed to be an absolute livewire in ensuring preparations for the war – from ensuring the training and employment of the MuktiBahini, exhorting his own army, egging the MoD on various issues related to the war, ensuring the war-fighting wherewithal was in place. But most importantly, when war was joined, Sam would ensure the lightening movement of forces, exploitation of battlefield conditions and seizure of opportunities leading to capitulation of Dhaka. The Indian Army under Sam Manekshaw was set to write history and deliver what the country asked of it.

On and off there has been talk and reportage about whether the Bharat Ratna, the highest civilian award of India, should be conferred upon the late Field Marshal. With the passing away of the Field Marshal in June 2008, there was renewed and vigorous clamour that, if Sam could not be honoured with the award in his lifetime, here was another opportunity to bring the befitting tribute to the great leader. Sadly, we failed to do so then. As the years pass by, we may lose the opportunity to officially recognise the contributions of Field Marshal Manekshaw.

How does a nation honour its greatest military hero? A glimpse into another large democracy into this aspect may help. The highest civilian awards given by the United States of America are the Congressional Gold Medal and the Presidential Medal of Freedom. They are considered to be of the same level, the main difference being that the Presidential Medal of Freedom Medal is awarded by the President of the United States and Congressional Gold Medal is awarded by an Act of Congress.

Both these awards could be given for a singular achievement or lifetime contribution. The Congressional Medal was initially awarded to military leaders; however, with military medals instituted later, this medal was introduced also to recognise achievements in other fields.

The Presidential Medal, too, is used to recognise achievements in various fields. Both these medals recognise military contribution. To show a spread of fields of both the medals: some awardees of the Congressional Gold Medal are - Dr Martin Luther King, Mother Teresa, Pope John Paul, Jesse Owens, Sir Winston Churchill, Joe Lewis, General Norman Schwarzkopf, General Colin Powell and General Douglas MacArthur.

Some recipients of the Presidential Medal of Freedom are Sir Sidney Poitier, Harper Lee, Mohammed Ali, Arthur Rubinstein, Muhammad Yunus, Nelson Mandela, General Peter Pace and General Colin Powell. Mother Teresa has been awarded both these and the Bharat Ratna as well!

The Bharat Ratna is the highest civilian award of the country. Instituted in 1954, it can be awarded to any person without distinction of race, occupation, position or sex in recognition of exceptional service/performance of the highest order in any field of human endeavour.

The awards eligibility criteria was delimited in November 2011, from 'the fields of art, literature, science and public services' to 'exceptional service/performance of the highest order in any field of human endeavor'. The recommendations for Bharat Ratna are made by the Prime Minister to the President. No formal recommendations for this are necessary and the number of annual awards is restricted to a maximum of three in a particular year.

Till today there are 42 awardees of the Bharat Ratna which include, amongst others, Amartya Sen, Lata Mangeshkar, Sachin Tendulkar, MG Ramachandran, Satyajit Ray, JRD Tata and Rajiv Gandhi. So, when drawn in parallel with the USA's awards, (both large democracies) the lists run basically similar, but for the glaring omission recognising military contribution in the Indian award, at least so far. It is clear that the USA honours its military far better than India does. Similar comparisons could be drawn with awards of other countries, but surely this is not an argument to include military contribution as a field of eligibility. The current provisions already cater for it.

Undoubtedly, the Indian Army itself qualifies to be a worthy recipient of this supreme award, the organisation having contributed seminally to preserving the integrity of the nation, both within and outside. Called to meet threats and distresses, the Indian Army has always risen to the occasion. To honour Sam Manekshaw with the award, would be the recognition of the services rendered by the Army. There indeed could be no better way to honour the army than by honouring its greatest icon.

While this is also not an exercise to critique, compare or comment upon the various awardees of the Bharat Ratna with the late Field Marshal, it is doubtless that the stature and aura of Field Marshal Manekshaw will only enhance the quality of this list- a leader who every Indian knows, a leader which the nation requires to continually inspire future generations, a role model. What better tribute can be given than conferring the Bharat Ratna on his 100$^{th}$ Birth Anniversary on Sam Manekshaw, the leader who brought India its greatest military victory of modern times.

## SAM MANEKSHAW, ARCHITECT OF INDIA'S VICTORY OVER PAKISTAN IN 1971 WAR

War lasts many days, many months, and sometimes even years, and sooner it ends the better. Some wars have lasted incredibly longer like the Vietnam War, the Great Northern War, and the Thirty Years War, to name a few.

Rarely do we see that a war involving a million soldiers finish within thirteen days, and this is strangely true for the

India-Pakistan War of 1971. India under General Sam Hormusji Framji Jamshedji Manekshaw (later Field Marshal) fought in the Eastern and the Western theaters defeated the Pakistani Army, and won the first decisive victory after Independence.

Perhaps the situation of 1971 could be best understood by the conversation through Sam's recollection which Sam told in his own breezy way in many interviews.

When Pakistan clamped down East Pakistan, refugees starting pouring down into India, and Mrs. Gandhi held a cabinet meeting at 10 am in the morning. The Foreign Minister, Sardar Swaran Singh, the Defence Minister, Mr. Jagjivan Ram, the Agriculture Minister, Mr. Fakhruddin Ali Ahmed and the Finance Minister, Mr. Yashwant Rao.

I was also ordered to be present. Mrs Gandhi presiding read out messages which she had received from the Chief Ministers of Assam, Tripura, and West Bengal, that hundreds and thousands of refugees are pouring in, and she looked at me and asked, "Chief what are you doing about it?" I said, "Nothing, it has nothing to do with me." Manekshaw asked- "what you want me to do". *She said, "I want you to enter East Pakistan" and I* said, "Do you know that means War?" She said, "I do not mind if it is war". I in my usual stupid way, said, "Prime Minister, have you read the Bible?"And the Foreign Minister, Sardar Swaran Singh (a Punjabi Sikh), in his Punjabi accent said, "What has Bible got to do with this?" and I said, "In the first Book, the First Chapter, the First Paragraph, the First Sentence, God said, 'Let there be light" and there was light. You turn this round and say 'Let there be war' and there will be war. What do you think? Are you ready for a war? Let me tell you – It's 28th April, the Himalayan passes are opening, and if the Chinese gave us an ultimatum, I will have to fight on two fronts". Again Sardar Swaran Singh turned round and in his Punjabi English said, "Will China give ultimatum?" "You are the Foreign Minister. You tell me!"

I have a division in the Assam area, another division in Andhra Pradesh and the Armored Division in the Jhansi-Babina area. I have to bring them all into the concentration area. I will require every railway train, every railway wagon, and every truck to move these people. I turned to the Agriculture Minister, Mr. Fakhruddin Ali Ahmed, We are harvesting in the Punjab, and we are harvesting in Haryana; we are also harvesting in Uttar Pradesh. And you will not be able to move your harvest. If there is a famine in the country afterwards, it will be you to blame, not me." Then I said, "My Armoured Division which is my striking division which should have 197 tanks has only got thirteen tanks which are functioning."

The Finance Minister, Mr. Chawan, a friend of mine, said, "Sam, why only thirteen?"

"Because you are the Finance Minister. I have been asking for money for the last year and a half, and you keep saying there is no money. That is why."

Then I turned to the Prime Minister and said, "Prime Minister, it is the end of April. By the time I am ready to operate, the monsoon will have broken in that East Pakistan area. When it rains, it does not just rain, it pours. Rivers become oceans. If you stand on one bank, you cannot see the other and the whole countryside is flooded. My movement will be confined to roads, the Air Force will not be able to support me. And, if you wish me to enter East Pakistan, I guarantee you a hundred percent defeat."

*"You are the Government", I said "Now give me your orders!"*

I don't know if you have ever seen an angry Prime Minister, I have seen my wife. Then Babu Jagjivan Rao who couldn't call me "Sam", he called me "Shyam" said, "*Shyam maan jao na*". Sam said, "How can I, this is madness". The Prime Minister angry in her face turned round and said, "The cabinet will meet four o'clock in the evening".

Everyone walked out. I being the junior most man was the last to leave. As I was leaving, she said, "Chief, please stay behind?" I looked at her. I said, "Prime Minister, before you open your mouth, would you like me to send you my resignation on grounds of health, mental or physical?"

"Oh, sit down, Sam. Everything you told me the truth?"

*"Yes, it is my job to fight and win, not to lose."* She smiled at me and said, "Sam. You know what I want. When will you be ready?" "I cannot tell you now, Prime Minister, but let me guarantee you this that if you leave me alone, allow me to plan, make my arrangements, and fix a date, I guarantee you a hundred percent victory".

So, Ladies and Gentlemen, as I told you, there is a very thin line between becoming a Field Marshal and being dismissed.

'Fight and win', was not a figure of speech for Sam, he was very particular about it, while addressing the defence college he once remarked, "if you lose no one will remember you, if you will lose don't come back."

In fact Sam was a General with difference and the relationship of mutual trust and respect that he had with Mrs. Gandhi started long way back when Mr. Nehru was the Prime Minister and Indira Gandhi had no official powers, but her authority was enormous. Just after the Sino Indian War Sam had been posted as GOC in Tezpur, and just five days after taking charge Prime Minister Nehru visited the place along with Indira and the Army Chief J N Chaudhuri. Sam reported that his army was advancing, Nehru who have had enough with war expressed his concern and asked the boys to pull back. The Army Chief immediately asked Sam to call the army back, to which Sam revolted saying either he be allowed to deal with the Army unrestricted or he be sent back to Defence Academy. The future 'Iron Lady' obviously didn't like the nasty situation she pointed that given the low morale of the Country and the Army, it demanded deeds of courage to boost the spirits and Sam was exactly doing this, and he may be allowed to go ahead, Sam could little more than thank her.

But before making of the legend of 'Sam Bahadur' as he was fondly known, Sam was son to a very successful doctor in Amritsar. His brothers were sent off to England for further studies and Sam cherished the same dream, waiting patiently to get old enough to sail to England as his father promised. A fifteen year old Sam passed the Senior Cambridge with distinction and reminded his father of the promise, the doctor declined on the ground that Sam was too young to go. With his dreams shattered a furious Sam did not talk to his father for 18 months. In 14th July 1932 Sam had borrowed some money from his mother to appear for the Indian Millitary Academy Examination. Sam scored well; he was sixth in order of merit, the boy who wanted to be a doctor, now marched on to be a soldier, and what a soldier he became! This decision taken out of fury or by love not only became a turning point of his life but also for the Entire Nation.

During the Second World War, in early 1942 Sam was sent to defend Rangoon from the Japanese. The 28 year old Captain faced tremendous gunfire while defending the Sittand Bridge. In the heat of the battle Sam received a volley of nine bullets and fell to the ground, his orderly Mehar Singh carried him on his back to the nearest hospital. Everyone the nurses, and most importantly the doctor had lost all hopes after seeing the wounded body, the doctor asked Sam what had happened, to which the soldier replied, "I was kicked by a mule". 'A lad worth saving', said the doctor, and Sam was saved. While he recovered from the wounds Sam received a letter from his father saying- son, your lungs have been pierced if you smoke you will be a dead man, your intestines and liver have been punctured if you drink you will be dead man. Sam later said he followed all his father's order and he nearly died!

In 1947 when India became independent Sam was a Lieutenant Colonel. A civil war had broken in Kashmir and Maharajah Hari Singh wanted Indian involvement. The Indian Government made it clear to Hari Singh that India will sent in force only when the Maharajah was willing to accede to India. V P Menon the Defence Minister along with Sam was sent in with the document of Accession to obtain Hari Singh's signature and also to assess the situation. They flew in and out of Kashmir rapidly and next day a cabinet meeting was summoned attended by Mountbatten, Pandit Nehru, Baldev Singh, Sardar Patel and others. Sam briefed up the attended pointing that the tribesman were just 9 kilometres from the airfield and if this strip of land was taken, there will be no possibility for sending troops. Sardar Patel was willing to send in troops at once but Nehru had his own thoughts. Nehru talked about the history of Kashmir, the United Nations, among other things, to which an impatient Patel stopped him asking, "Jawahar do you want Kashmir or not?" "Of Course I do", replied Nehru strongly, Patel turned to Sam and said, "you have your orders"!

21st April 1944: Sir Hari Singh Bahadur, the Maharajah of Kashmir and one of India's two representatives at the British War Cabinet inspects civil defence workers in Bermondsey, London.

In 1957 Sam had been promoted to a Major General, and General Thimayya was the Chief of Army staff. Somehow General Thimayya had become sand in the eye of the Defence Minister V P Menon, once in a visit to Sam's division the later asked him what he thought of Gen. Thimayya. Sam replied he was not permitted to think about his Chief. Menon got annoyed and said, "Oh stop your British way of thinking. I can get rid of Thimayya if I want." Sam replied, "You can get rid of him. But then I will get another Chief, and I won't be allowed to think about him too. You know, it is very wrong to ask a Major General what he thinks of the Chief. Tomorrow you will be asking a Brigadier what he thinks of me. This is not done in the Army." In fact Sam always kept politics out of Army.

Sam's success in the Bangladesh war made him so popular that there were rumours that Sam would take over from Mrs. Gandhi. This became so serious that everywhere Sam went this rumour followed him. Even a visiting American diplomat asked Sam, when you are taking over"? Sam replied quickly, "as soon as General Westmoreland takes over in your country".The American ambassador Kenneth Keating was also present he had a big laugh and said, "well done Sam". In the backdrop of these events Sam while in his office received a direct line from Mrs. Gandhi and the following conversation took place.

Mrs. Gandhi asked, "Sam are you very busy"?

Sam: "Prime Minister the Army Chief is always busy, but never too busy to see his Prime Minister".

"Can you come cover?"

"I am having tea Prime Minister".

"No, I will give you good tea, come over".

So Sam went and saw Prime Minister sitting worriedly to his kidney shaped table. Sam asked, "Hello Prime Minister you seem worried".

"I have problems and you are my problem Sam. Everybody is saying you are going to take over", replied Mrs. Gandhi.

Sam was shaken, he went across and "put his nose next to her" and said, "What do you think"?

She said, "You can't". "Oh, you think I am so incompetent", joked Sam. "I didn't mean that Sam, I mean you wouldn't" replied Mrs. Gandhi. "Much better, Prime Minister, much better, I will tell you a little jingle which my daughter when she comes back from Convent recites to me- you mind your own business, I mind my own, you kiss your own sweetheart, I kiss mine, I don't interfere you politically as long as no one interferes with me in the Army." And that extraordinary statement addressed the fear of the Prime Minister.

It was true that Pakistan had lesser chances of war if we consider the numerical superiority of the Indians and the Bangladesh Freedom Fighters. However numerical superiority was not the only thing that matter for Sam, and for that matter he did not underestimate Pakistan. Once war had become inevitable the Indian Government was readying the *Mukti Bahini* with arms, ammunitions, and training. These freedom fighters were used to harass the Pakistani regular troops. Sam's strategy in the Eastern theatre was a multi prong attack, to capture as much as land possible by bypassing the Pakistani strongholds. The Eastern Command was to be headed by Lieutenant General Jagjit Singh Aurora who played a pivotal role in this War. Three Army Corps were to enter East Pakistan,

2 Coprs under Lieutenant General T N Raina from the West, the 4 Corps under General Sagat Singh from the East, 33 Corps under Lieutenant General M L Thapan from the North, and 101 Communitcation Zone Area under Major General Gurbax Singh Gill.

Pakistan opened the war by attacking the Indian airfields on the Western Sector on 3rd December 1971, this operation was code named Operation Chengiz Khan. Mrs. Gandhi shortly after midnight declared that these attacks were a declaration of War against India. The War commenced in short time Pakistan had faced several defeats and at one point there resistance broke down. Sam broadcasted messages calling Pakistan Army to surrender before long-why waste lives? Don't you want to go home and be with your children? Do not lose time; there is no disgrace in laying down arms to a soldier. We will give you the treatment befitting a soldier.

Freedom fighters with captured informer Razakhar, after the Indian Army liberated Jessore in Bangladesh, then part of East Pakistan, circa 1971.

The formal surrender took place on 16th December 1971 at Dhaka, Pakistani troops surrendered their arms, Gen. Niazi handed over his pistol to Gen. Jagjit Singh Aurora. Both generals signed the instrument of surrender, a total of 93,000 soldiers had laid down their weapons. "I had asked Jagjit to take his wife, on the great day, I told him it is a great day for his life", Sam said later. In fact Sam had been very cautious about the behaviour of his troops in Bengal, he had formally said that incidents of rapes and loot will be dealt with court-martial. In his own witty way he said, "Whenever you see a Begum put your hands in your pocket and think of Sam." Sam took utmost care of the prisoners of war, and this was reflected when he visited Lahore after the war. The Governor of Punjab had invited him for a lunch and post lunch the Governor expressed that his staff wanted to meet him. Sam went to meet the men, he found the entire staff lined up, he shook hands, the last man place his '*pugree*' in front of Sam's feet saying, "Sir, it is because of you we were saved. I have five sons who are your prisoners.

They write letters to me. You have given them Quran. They are living in barracks while your men sleep in tents. Now I will never believe anyone who tells me Hindus are bad."

Sam had amazing leadership quality and understanding of situation. In 1971 in a board-room meeting there was a debate on launching pre-emptive strike on Karachi, the Air chief suggested the plan to be cleared from the Defence Minister. Why should we, roared Sam, "once the political decision to wage war has been taken by the Government, we must take responsibility of all military actions ourselves", said he. Sam wrote on leadership, "but to be frightened is one thing, and to show fear is something different." Sam with his tilted hat and dashing look was always the most talked about man, wherever he went on a visit there were stories out of it. Sam was always known to be generous and occasionally he would arrange funds from the Chief's welfare funds towards Army needs. "I just don't know how to say no. Sometimes I thank God for making me a man, and not a woman. Can you imagine my condition if it had been otherwise? I would have been always pregnant", so was Sam Bahadur.

## LEADERSHIP IN THE 21ST CENTURY

Vice President, Ladies and Gentlemen, I am fully conscious of the honour and privilege which is mine to be invited here to address you this evening. The honour is even greater that you should have invited a soldier when you could have invited any number of VVIPs. General Choudhury, I thank you for the very kind words you spoke about me. You have told us all the good things that Field Marshal Cariappa has done. But one big thing that he did, you haven't mentioned. He taught the Indian Army to be completely apolitical. Ours is one country, where soldiers have kept out of politics. I think that was the biggest achievement of Field Marshal Cariappa, the greatest service to this country.

Some years ago, I was invited to a Rotary club function at Madras. It was stated that the youth of this country had not contributed much to the society and they asked me to speak on the subject. I disagreed violently. I said then, and I say now that the youth of this country is confused. It doesn't know why this country is facing all these problems. Wherever they look, they find there are shortages. There is shortage of power and there are power cuts, they can't study and they want to know whose fault it is. They want to join colleges and universities and they are told there is a shortage of seats and they want to know whose fault it is. They look around and they see the dissension amongst politicians and they want to know whose fault it is, not theirs. They want to go abroad for studies and they are told that there is no foreign exchange and they want to know whose fault it is. Wherever they look, they find shortages, corruption, bribery, smuggling and they want to know whose fault it is.

Here was a country, which was considered the brightest jewel in the British crown and they want to know what'd happened to that bright jewel. And nobody gave them any answer. They are no longer fooled with the glib answer that we were under British rule for 200 years and that's why we are in this state. They turn around and say that the British left us four decades ago, what have you done, except making excuses. They say, look at Singapore, look at Malaysia, which too were ruled by the British and look at the progress they have made. They turn around and say look at Japan and look at Germany. They fought a war for four years. Their youth was decimated, they lost, their countries were occupied, their industry was destroyed, portions of the country were taken away, and look what they have achieved. So please stop making excuses and give us an answer. Why? Ladies and gentlemen, I have decided to open my big mouth and say that the answer and the real problem for all our difficulties, all our shortages, etc. is lack of leadership. Mr Vice President don't misunderstand me and gentlemen of the Press don't misquote me. When I turn round and say lack of leadership I do not mean just political leadership.

Books on military leadership What are Generals Made of?, Follow Me-1, Follow Me-II——-I mean lack of leadership in every sphere of this country. Whether it is political, administrative, in industry, in trade unions, in educational institutions, in the law and order, personnel, in our sports organisations and even in the Press, it is lack of leadership. And it is on this subject that I wanted to address you this evening. The Director General of Infantry wanted me to talk about leadership in the 21st century. Ladies and gentlemen, leadership does not change. *The attributes of leadership have come down the years. All that happens is that greater emphasis is placed on certain attributes of leadership as countries advance and technological developments take place.* I do not know whether leaders are born or leaders are made. There is a school of thought, which, says leaders are born. Ladies and gentlemen, we have a population of nine hundred and thirty million people but there is a dearth of leadership. If leaders are not born, can we make leaders? And my answer is yes. Give me a man or a woman with common sense and who is not an idiot and I assure you, you can make a leader out of him or her.

## What are the attributes of leadership?

The primary, the cardinal attribute of leadership is professional knowledge and professional competence. *And you will agree with me, ladies and gentlemen, that you cannot be born with professional knowledge or professional competence. Not even if you are the son of the prime minister, an industrialist or a Field Marshal!* Professional knowledge has to be acquired the hard way. It's a continuous study and you never acquire enough in today's fast moving, competitive, technological world that we are living in. You've got to keep up with your profession, whatever you are in. Doctors, engineers, scientists, all contribute to journals of their profession. They all have contact with their counterparts in other worlds. The problem in India is that as soon as one of us is put in a position of power, he feels that he has the monopoly of the entire knowledge. Those who are responsible for the defence and security of this country, can they cross their hearts and swear that they have ever read a book on strategy, on tactics? On military campaigns, or weapons?

Can they even distinguish between a mortar and a motor, a guerrilla from a gorilla? Professional knowledge and professional competence are the main attributes of leadership. Unless you know, and the men you command know that you know your job, you will never be a leader. Take industry for example. The automobile industry has gone through tremendous technological changes. It's only recently that our industrialists have started thinking and producing a modern car. I want to tell you that unless you have professional knowledge and professional competence, you will never become a leader.

And that takes me to the next attribute of leadership, the ability to think; to make up your mind, to take a decision and accept full responsibility for that decision.Have you ever wondered, why a man doesn't take a decision? Very simple, because he lacks professional knowledge and professional competence or he is afraid that if he takes a decision and goes wrong, he will have to carry the can. Ladies and gentlemen, as a law of average, if you take ten decisions, five should be right. And if you have professional competence and professional knowledge, nine should be right. And the one that is wrong will always be put right by a bright colleague, by an intelligent staff officer or by the gallantry of some soldier. I don't want to give you too many examples of why and when people haven't taken decisions and what has happened. I will give you just one. If the decision had been taken to ensure that the Babri Masjid would not be destroyed, a whole community would not have been antagonised. An act of omission can be corrected but an act of commission cannot be corrected. To do nothing is to do something, which is definitely wrong. When I was the Army Chief, I visited my formation commanders and I asked one of them what he had been doing about some matter. He turned around and said "Sir, I have been thinking, I haven't made up my mind". It is absolutely necessary that a leader must be decisive.

The next attribute of the leadership is absolute honesty and impartiality. we all have our likes and dislikes, but, we must never allow our likes or our dislikes to influence our professional judgment. Those of us, who had the good fortune of commanding hundreds and thousands of men, know this. The leader must be absolutely impartial and honest in dealing with personnel. No man likes to be punished and yet a man will take his punishment if he knows that the punishment awarded to him is similar to the one for a similar crime committed by somebody who has influence, who has the ear of an industrialist, of a minister, of a member of parliament, or the Field Marshal. No man likes to be superseded. And yet, they will accept supersession, if they know they have been superseded by someone better, better qualified under the regulations but not by somebody who is a relative of the minister or by somebody for whom a 'Godman' intervenes. It is vitally important when you are dealing with men that you should be absolutely impartial. We must possess the courage to withstand these pressures.

Moral and physical courage are the next vital attributes, and I do not know which one is more important. While addressing young officers or young policemen, I will put emphasis on physical courage but since I am addressing this gathering, I will lay stress on moral courage. What is moral courage? Moral courage is the ability to distinguish right from wrong and having done so, to say so, irrespective of the consequences to you. A 'Yes man' is a dangerous man. He is a menace. He will go very far. He can become a minister, a secretary or a Field Marshal but he can never become a leader nor, ever be respected. He will be used by his superiors, disliked by his colleagues and despised by his subordinates. So discard the 'Yes man'.

I am going to give you a personal example of moral courage. There is a very thin line between being dismissed and becoming a Field Marshal. In 1971, when Pakistan cracked down in East Pakistan, hundreds and thousands of refugees started pouring into India, into West Bengal, Assam and Tripura. The Prime Minister held a cabinet meeting in her office. The External Affairs Minister, Sardar Swaran Singh, the Agriculture Minister, Mr Fakhruddin Ali Ahmad, the Defence Minister, Babu Jagjivan

Ram, and the Finance Minister, Yashwant Rao Chauhan were present. I was then summoned. A very angry, grim-faced Prime Minister read out the telegrams from the Chief Ministers of West Bengal, Assam and Tripura.

She (Indra Gandhi) then turned around to me and said, "What are you doing about it?"

And I said, "Nothing, it's got nothing to do with me. You didn't consult me when you allowed the BSF, the CRP and RAW to encourage the Pakistanis to revolt. Now that you are in trouble, you come to me. I have a long nose. I know what's happening." I then asked her what she wanted me to do.

She said, "I want you to enter East Pakistan."

And I responded, "That means war!"

She said, "I do not mind if it is war.

"Have you read the Bible?" I queried.

The Foreign Minister, Sardar Swaran Singh asked, "What has the Bible got to do with this?"

I explained, that the first book, the first chapter, the first words, the first sentence God said was, "Let there be light" and there was light. Now you say, "Let there be war" and there will be war, but are you prepared?

I am certainly not. This is the end of April. The Himalayan passes are opening and there can be an attack from China if China gives us an ultimatum.

The Foreign Minister asked, "Will China give an ultimatum?"

And I said, "You are the Foreign Minister, you tell me".

I told them that my armoured division and two of my infantry divisions were away. One in the Jhansi/Babina area, the other in Samba and the third one in Andhra Pradesh and Tamil Nadu. I mentioned that I would require all the road space, all the railway wagons, the entire railway system to move these formations to the operational areas and that harvesting was in progress in the Punjab and UP and they would not be able to move the harvest which would rot; and

I pointed out to the Agriculture Minister that it wouldn't be my responsibility if there were a famine.

Then I said, "My armoured division, which is my big striking force is supposed to have one hundred eighty nine tanks operational. I have got only eleven tanks that are fit to fight."

The Finance Minister, who is a friend of mine asked, "Sam why only eleven?"

So I told him, "Because you are the Finance Minister. I have been asking you for money for over a year and you say you haven't got it!"

And finally I turned around to the Prime Minister and said that the rains were about to start in East Pakistan and when it rains there, it pours and when it pours, the whole countryside is flooded. The snows are melting, the rivers would become like oceans. If you stand on one bank, you cannot see the other. All my movement would be confined to roads. The Air Force, because of climatic conditions would not be able to support me. Now Prime Minister, give me your orders.

The grim Prime Minister with her teeth clenched said, "The Cabinet will meet again at four o-clock". The members of the Cabinet started walking out. I being the junior most was the last to go and as I was leaving, she said, "Chief, will you stay back?" I turned around and said, "Prime Minister, before you open your mouth, may I send you my resignation on grounds of health, mental or physical?"

She said, "Every thing you told me is true". "Yes! It is my job to tell you the truth" I responded, "and it is my job to fight, it is my job to fight to win and I have told you the truth,"

She smiled at me and said, "All right Sam, you know what I want?" I said, "Yes, I know what you want!"

I had the moral courage to tell her the truth. A leader must have moral courage otherwise he will not be respected. I now come to physical courage. Fear, like hunger and sex, is a natural phenomenon and the man who says he is not frightened is a liar. But to be frightened is one thing and to show fear is something quite different. It is when your knees are knocking and your teeth are chattering – that is when the real leader comes out. If you once show fear to your men, you will never have their respect. I could quote you many examples of my own life. I am not a brave man! Please believe me. You have to have physical courage. Never show your fear. How often has a course of a battle, when everything was going wrong, changed because some young officer has picked up a handful of men and changed the situation by his physical courage? How often a poor old Inspector of Police with nothing but a little swagger stick in his hand quelled a riot by showing physical courage?

The other attribute of leadership is loyalty. We all except loyalty but do we give loyalty? Look at things happening around you. The sons of kings, chief ministers and heads of governments have shown disloyalty. Loyalty you must get from your subordinates and also give loyalty to your superiors, colleagues and subordinates.

Men may give you trouble and create problems but a leader must deal with them immediately and sternly. A leader must remember that human beings have human problems, so the leader must have a human touch. Leaders must have the gift of the gab and a sense of humour.

And finally, men and women all over the world like their leader to be a man, to have manly qualities. It is not that only a person who has no vices is a good leader. Look at Caesar or Napoleon, they had vices but they were outstanding leaders.

Since I joined the Army, many changes have taken place; the.303 rifle has been replaced by a new weapon. Horses and mules have been replaced by vehicles and tanks. Signal communications have advanced a great deal. Satellites now give the entire information to the Commanders. But for infantry soldiers, one thing has not changed, and that is their job. Their job is to fight and win. If you lose, you would disgrace your country, your village, your home and your wife. Let your motto be, 'No one provokes me with impunity'. In other words, or in a soldier's language, if your enemy hits you on the chin, black both his eyes and push his teeth down his throat! If you can instil this quality in your men, you will be a great leader. It is —" The leader" that this country lacks at all levels, in all walks of life.

I did not wish to re-iterate leadership traits and qualities from books to this august gathering, but share my perceptions with you in our context. I hope I have been able to do that.

Thank you.

Field Marshal Sam Manekshaw, MC

## HONOURS AND POST-RETIREMENT

For his distinguished service to the country, the President of India awarded Manekshaw a Padma Vibhushan in 1972 and conferred upon him the rank of field marshal, a first, on 1 January 1973. He became one of the only two Indian Army generals to be awarded this prestigious rank; the other being Kodandera Madappa Cariappa who was awarded in 1986. Manekshaw retired from active service a fortnight later on 15 January 1973 after a career of nearly four decades, and settled down with his wife Silloo in Coonoor, the civilian town next to Wellington Military Cantonmentwhere he had served as commandant of the Defence Services Staff College, at an earlier time in his career. Popular with Gurkha soldiers, Nepal fêted Manekshaw as an honorary general of the Nepalese Army in 1972.

In May 2007, Gohar Ayub, son of Pakistani Field Marshal Ayub Khan, claimed that Manekshaw had sold Indian Army secrets to Pakistan during the Indo-Pakistani War of 1965 for 20,000 rupees, but his accusations were dismissed by the Indian defence establishment.

Following his service in the Indian Army, Manekshaw successfully served as an independent director on the board of several companies, and in a few cases, as the chairman.

He was outspoken and hardly politically correct, and when once he was replaced on the board of a company by a man named Naik at the behest of the government, Manekshaw quipped, "This is the first time in history when a *Naik*(corporal) has replaced a field marshal."

## DEATH

Manekshaw died of complications from pneumonia at the Military Hospital in Wellington, Tamil Nadu, on 0030 hours, 27 June 2008 at the age of 94.

He was laid to rest at the Parsi cemetery in Ootacamund(Ooty), Tamil Nadu, with military honours, adjacent to his wife's grave. He was survived by two daughters and three grandchildren.

Reportedly, his last words were "I'm okay!"

That year on 16 December, celebrated each year as "Vijay Diwas" in memory of the victory achieved under Manekshaw's leadership in 1971, a postage stamp depicting Manekshaw in his field marshal's uniform was released by President Pratibha Patil. However, she, the PM or other leaders from the political class did not turn up at his funeral, nor was a national day of mourning declared. In 2014, a granite statue was erected in his honor at Wellington, in the Nilgiris district, close to the Manekshaw Bridge on the Ooty-Coonoor road, which had been named after him in 2009.

# 4

# Rifleman Jaswant Singh : A Hero of the 1962 Indo-China War

Jaswant Singh Rawat (19 August 1941 - 17 November 1962 ) was an Indian rifleman soldier of 4 Garhwal Rifles, Uttarakhand who won the Maha Vir Chakra posthumously at the Battle of Nuranang in the present day Arunachal Pradesh during the 1962 India-China war. He was born on 19 August, 1941 to Shri Guman Singh Rawat, in the village of Baryun, Pauri Garhwal District, Uttarakhand.

The bravery shown by Jaswant Rawat was honoured by building a memorial at the post where he fought the Chinese Army. The post which he held was named "Jaswant Garh". Another honour bestowed upon him is that he continues to serve even after death: he has been awarded promotions as if he is still serving the nation.

Local people in the Tawang area believe that he has become a saint and his spirit protects the area.

The Indian army keeps at least half-a-dozen personnel there to take care of Rawat as if were still alive. He is served tea at 04:30, breakfast at 09:00, and dinner at 19:00 in his private room.

Rifleman(RFN) Jaswant Singh, number 4039009, was serving with the 4th Battalion of the Garhwal Rifles.On 17 November the battalion was subjected to repeated Chinese assaults. A Chinese medium machine gun (MMG) located at a vantage point close to the A company lines was proving to be a dangerous menace. Jaswant, Lance Naik Trilok Singh Negi and RFN Gopal Singh Gusain went after the Chinese MMG and after approaching within 12 metres threw grenades at the bunker and charged it, killing a number of Chinese and capturing the MMG. Jaswant took the MMG and began crawling back towards the Indian lines but he and Trilok were fatally hit by Chinese automatic fire when nearing safety.Gopal Gusain was wounded but managed to drag the MMG into the Indian post. This turned the course of the battle and the Chinese retreated, leaving some 300 dead behind. Jaswant was awarded the Maha Vir Chakra (posthumous) and Trilok and Gopal the Vir Chakra.

A popular and widely-disseminated local story goes as follows : It was the final phase of the Sino-Indian War in November 1962. Even as his company was asked to fall back, Jaswant Singh remained at his post at an altitude of 10,000 feet and held back Chinese soldiers for three days assisted by two local Monpa girls named Sela and Nura (in some versions one or the other girl is mentioned).

Some sources say that he was escorted by one lady of the local village named Bum La during the War. They set up weapons at separated spots and maintained a volume of fire that made the Chinese think they were opposed by a body of troops. Finally the Chinese captured the man who was supplying rations to Jaswant and he revealed to them that they were opposed by only one man.Theyattacked in force,Sela died in a grenade burst, Nura was captured and Jaswant supposedly shot himself with his last cartridge when he realized that he was about to be captured. It is alleged that the Chinese cut off Jaswant Singh's head and took it back to China. It is claimed by some that he killed more than 300 Chinese Soldiers in the war.

However, after the ceasefire, the Chinese commander, impressed by the soldier's bravery, returned the head along with a brass bust of Jaswant Singh. The bust, created in China to honor the brave Indian soldier, is now installed at the site of the battle.

Jaswant Singh's saga of valor and sacrifice continues to serve as an inspiration to all army personnel posted in this sector. He has become a 'Baba', a saint. At the spot where he fought,a small temple has come up with a bust of his and many of his personal effects. A marble plaque commemorates him and 161 other men of his battalion who died in the battle of Nuranang, which was awarded to Garhwal Rifles as a battle honour.This shrine known as Jaswant Garh is between Se La and Jang. All Indian Army personnel passing by this route from General or a jawan, make it a point to pay their respects here.So do civilians. Jaswant is treated as if he is alive, his boots shined and his uniform and accoutrements cared for by Army personnel posted at the shrine. He has received all his promotions in time, and has reached the rank of Honorary Captain.

## BIOGRAPHY OF JASWANT SINGH RAWAT

Rifleman Jaswant Singh Rawat was an Indian soldier who won the Maha Vir Chakra posthumously at the Battle of Nuranang.

Rifleman (RFN) Jaswant Singh, number 4039009, was serving with the 4th Battalion of the Garhwal Rifles. On 17 November the battalion was subjected to repeated Chinese assaults. A Chinese medium machine gun (MMG) located at a vantage point close to the A company lines was proving to be a dangerous menace. Jaswant, Lance Naik Trilok Singh Negi and RFN Gopal Singh Gusain went after the Chinese MMG and after approaching within 12 metres threw grenades at the bunker and charged it, killing a number of Chinese and capturing the MMG.

Jaswant took the MMG and began crawling back towards the Indian lines but he and Trilok were fatally hit by Chinese automatic fire when nearing safety. Gopal Gusain was wounded but managed to drag the MMG into the Indian post. This turned the course of the battle and the Chinese retreated, leaving some 300 dead behind. Jaswant was awarded the Maha Vir Chakra (posthumous) and Trilok and Gopal the Vir Chakra.

A popular and widely-disseminated local story goes as follows : It was the final phase of the Sino-Indian War in November 1962. Even as his company was asked to fall back, Jaswant Singh remained at his post at an altitude of 10,000 feet and held back Chinese soldiers for three days assisted by two local Monpa girls named Sela and Nura (in some versions one or the other girl is mentioned). They set up weapons at separated spots and maintained a volume of fire that made the Chinese think they were opposed by a body of troops. Finally the Chinese captured the man who was supplying rations to Jaswant and he revealed to them that they were opposed by only one man.They attacked in force, Sela died in a grenade burst, Nura was captured and Jaswant supposedly shot himself with his last cartridge when he realized that he was about to be captured. It is alleged that the Chinese cut off Jaswant Singh's head and took it back to China. However, after the ceasefire, the Chinese commander, impressed by the soldier's bravery, returned the head along with a brass bust of Jaswant Singh. The bust, created in China to honor the brave Indian soldier, is now installed at the site of the battle.

Jaswant Singh's saga of valor and sacrifice continues to serve as an inspiration to all army personnel posted in this sector. He has become a 'Baba', a saint. At the spot where he fought,a small temple has come up with a bust of his and many of his personal effects. A marble plaque commemorates him and 161 other men of his battalion who died in the battle of Nuranang, which was awarded to Garhwal Rifles as a battle honour. This shrine known as Jaswant Garh is between Se La and Jang. Indian Army personnel passing by this route traditionally pay their respects here, irrespective of rank. Jaswant is treated as if he is alive, his boots shined and his uniform and accoutrements cared for by Army personnel posted at the shrine. It is also said that if someone misses to respect him while passing the temple misfortune drives him through the way.He has received all his promotions in time, and has reached the rank of Honorary Captain. He is a source of inspiration to people of Arunachal Pradesh.

## Unique love story of Jaswant Singh and Sela in Arunachal

An hour after Sela Pass in Arunachal Pradesh, people come across a unique memorial-cum-mandir of Jaswant Singh Rawat alias Jaswant Baba. The story of Jaswant Singh Rawat is inscribed in a plaque at the memorial. The caretaker of the memorial also takes pride in recounting Jasawant Singh's heroics. Jaswant Singh of the 4th Battalion Garhwal Rifles held off the enemy for 72 hours single-handedly. He ran from bunker to bunker- firing and creating an illusion of many soldiers present. Two local girls helped him to carry the ammunition. The story goes that rather than give in when the Chinese soldiers were at their doorstep, Singh hanged himself. Army convoys on the way to the border make it a point to stop and pay homage at the beautifully maintained memorial. The jawans (soldiers of the Indian army) at the outpost treat everybody passing through with tea.

It was the final phase of the China war in November 1962. Even as his company was asked to fall back, Jaswant Singh remained at his post at an altitude of 10,000 feet and held back the rampaging Chinese for three days single-handedly. He was helped by two local girls — Sela and Nura — during the heroic battle that ended after the Chinese discovered the post was being defended by a solitary soldier. His love story with Sela is still remembered in Arunachal and on her honour the Sela Pass is named!

So enraged were the attackers that they cut off Jaswant Singh's head and took it back to China. However, after the ceasefire, the Chinese commander, impressed by the soldier's bravery, returned the head along with a brass bust of Jaswant Singh. The bust, created in China to honour the brave Indian soldier, is now installed at the site of the battle, a location now known as Jaswantgarh. Jaswant Singh's saga of valour and sacrifice continues to serve as an inspiration to all army personnel posted in this sector.

Army personnel passing by this route, be it a general or a jawan, make it a point to pay their respects here. Jaswant, who was awarded a Mahavir Chakra for his bravery is not the only soldier to be honoured thus. We find several memorials built along the way. One of them in fact is right on the border at Bumla honouring Subedar Joginder Singh who won a posthumous Param Vir Chakra for his bravery.

In a way, the Indian Army is trying to overcome the one big blot it has on its record by officially recognizing the 2420 dead warriors in the 1962 conflict. The Army has constructed a huge war memorial at Tawang. The magnificent Tawang War Memorial, inaugurated by the then Eastern Army Commander Lt. Gen. H R S Kalkat in November 1999, has a 40-feet high Stupa as its centrepiece.

A plaque at the entrance which says, 'A nation that does not honour its dead warriors will perish' indicates the Army's willingness to accept its defeat and learn lesson from it. Old timers say the war memorial is the first real attempt by the Army to honour those who died fighting a vastly superior and well-prepared enemy.

## Forgotten Sino-India War hero Shere Thapa is no less a martyr than Jaswant Singh Rawat

His light machine gun boomed relentlessly, like a roaring tiger. One after another unsuspecting Chinese soldiers were killed and fell into the Ngo River without anyone to count. The day was October 18 half-a-century ago. A brave Shere Thapa of the Indian Army's 2 Jammu and Kashmir Rifles, hiding in a very advantageous position, fired non-stop as his lone soldier-mate continued changing the carbines.

The People's Liberation Army of China had sneaked through the Tama Chung Chung Ridge. Thapa had positioned himself on a vertical slope - invincible high mountain ridge on one side, steep slope down to the Ngo stream, the source of the Subansiri River, on the other side. He had located the most strategic place, either to stop or kill the advancing Chinese soldiers.

Thapa did not notice anymore Chinese after emptying all magazines with the fired brash khokas lying scattered. He confidently came out of his bunker for a recce. Death was waiting for him. He peeped towards the heap of corpses with great satisfaction. A wounded, but alive Chinese soldier, lying on the heap along with his colleagues fired, killing him instantly.

The corpses of the Chinese soldiers were piled up so much that the river failed to carry them. This is the folklore. The great soldier is highly revered in the area for his gallantry act.

Comparatively, brave Thapa was no less a war hero than subedar Jaswant Singh Rawat (No. 4039009 of the 4th Garhwal Rifles Bn), who had fought a lone battle against the invading Chinese in Eastern Sector (Tawang). He was conferred the highest military honour, the Param Vir Chakra, for his bravery. Jaswant Garh, a few km ahead of the pass, stands tall today as a testimony to his heroism.

Locals claim that when the Indian troops retreated from Nurangang, Rawat was the only solider who refused to buzz from his post. With the help of local girls, Sela and Nura, he managed to stave off the enemy advance for 72 hours.

Located at an advantageous position on a hilltop overlooking the two river valleys, Rawat positioned himself in a long trench with guns and enough ammunition. He kept running from one end to another firing at the enemy from one point after the other. The Chinese realized that the Indian Army had retreated after the girls' father betrayed Rawat. The invaders in local outfits surrounded his position and CAPTURED HIM. He was tied to a tree with a telephone wire and beheaded. Sela escaped and jumped off a hilltop. The place later came to be known asSelaPass.Nura was captured and taken away by the invaders. Jagjit Prasad Jain, who died in Dec 2009, after serving the state for 59 years since 1950, had set up P J Canteen at Kimin to supply PDS items to inaccessible areas. Damodar Saram was manager of his canteen at Jang in Tawang district. Despite order to close down the canteen, Sarma stayed back and heed himself behind the huge stock of rice bags. Sela and Nura had informed Samra that the Chinese had tied Rawat to a post and killed him before proceeding towards Bomdila.

Ṡarma, who saw the mortal remains of Rawat, had narrated his experience to Jain (Jain's manager saw Jaswant Singh's mortal remains, Beyond the Horizon, 08-12-2010).

While the Army's official version significantly differs, but legend has it that the Chinese troops after killing Rawat beheaded him and carried his torso as a trophy after he had stood alone against them, firing from a.303 rifle. After the ceasefire, the Chinese commander, impressed by Rawat's bravery, returned the head along with a brass bust of the gallant soldier. The bust is now installed at the site of the battle. He was promoted to the rank of Major General in 2002.

Thapa would have been of the same rank today had his saga of gallantry been recognized. Such discrimination is shameful for the consecutive Arunachal Pradesh and Central governments, particularly the Indian Army.

Political interpreter Chader Mangha along with many villagers, who carried supplies, arms and ammunition for Thapa's Army section, were witness to his bravery. Mangha, who died in 1994,was given a commendation certificate by the GoI in recognition of his service to the nation and promoted to the rank of political assistant. He had also narrated the entire episode to his daughter Yating Byaling a resident of Gosing Taying village under Taksing circle, wife of RD Minister Tanga Byaling. Byaling also vouch of the bravery of Thapa and the village folk.

Even the Chinese had respectfully buried him and left a small note praising his bravery. Why none ever bothered to honour his brave act, even posthumously is intriguing? I have high respect for Rawat as he was a great martyr, but Thapa deserves equal honour.

While correct information on 1962 Indo-China War is still shrouded in mystery, but conclusive evidences are proof of the pitch battle, beyond Tawang and Walong (Tibet-Burma-India tri-junction) sectors.

Villagers inhabiting the Indo-China border claim that the PLA had sent its troops through passes, including Taksing,

Mechuka, Anini, etc where the forces camped waiting for orders. Had the war prolonged,Chinawould have launched a multi-pronged attack but withdrew its forces after cessation of firing, following 29 days (Oct 18 to Nov 16, 1962) of fierce battle, leading to the humiliating defeat of the Indian Army.

Supply line was cut off following retreat order which never reached the duo. Left with no food and insufficient ammunition, they feared any eventuality and decided to fight till death. Thapa sacrificed his life in Middle sector (Upper Subansiridistrict) while protecting Mother India. His mortal remains were brought to Lemiking, last rites performed and a grave built there. The neglected grave and a bridge named after him are evidences of his heroism.

"The first bridge, named after soldier Shere Thapa, with a 600m steep climb...." is the reference about him with picture of his grave found in 'Secrets of Subansiri, Himalayan Club, recoding the 2005 expedition report by a group of trekkers to famous Buddhist pilgrimage Takpa Shiri; Arunachal Expedition - Takpa Shiri; In Search of Old Pilgrimage Route to Takpa Siri 2005 and India 2005 - Alpine Journal.

Indian Army had sizeable presence in Tawang sector connected by road and the saga of Rawat's valour came to limelight as he courageously prevented the PLA's movement expecting reinforcement.

Unprepared Army HQs failed in sending reinforcement as the fleeing Indian forces retreated while brave Rawat stayed back. Jaswantgarh, few km ahead of the battle field, is proof of his patriotism. Any one passing through the Bhalukpong-Tawang road, even a general, without fail salutes the great martyr, believing his soul still guards the frontier.

Thapa knew well that without any road and communication then, expecting any support from the base camp was well neigh impossible. He decided to face the enemies as a brave soldier of Mother India. Shouldn't he be recognized, albeit late, and due honour given by bringing his heroic story before the nation. Septuagenarians in border villages still recall their unforgettable memory when Chinese forces appeared on the horizon of the high hills. They could not understand anything as Indian soldiers used to be occasional visitors, friendly with them and take their help for reconnaissance of the border areas.

The same practice continued today as was told by the war veterans of Kibithoo area. Septuagenarians Menjum Meyor and Thega Meyor of Anjaw district's Kaho, the last Indian village located on Tibet-Burma-India tri-junction, had assisted the Indian Army in digging trenches, carrying arms and ammunition, escorting them for maintaining surveillance when the Battle of Walong was fought at Namti. During an interview recently, they had admitted continuing do so even today, but their services during the war were neither recognized nor remunerated.

Their plain speaking begging with 'Jai Hind' reflected patriotism: "We do not recognize anyone as our forefathers were living inIndiaand we have followed suit. We are son of the soil."

Shockingly, 75-year-old Mayaso Pul had lost his left hand after ammunition carrying on shoulder got accidentally ignited. He regretted while talking to me: "Neither was I paid any remuneration nor any certificate given to me as a freedom fighter, though I have become handicapped for my life and living in penury." Pul along with villagers had treated a solider (Sardarji) with bullet injuries on his neck and facilitated his return to the mainland.

## THE FOURTH BATTLE IN ARUNACHAL PRADESH

The army rather succinctly draws up the military actions that lead to the final stand. Indian troops had withdrawn from Tawang and 4 Garhwal Rifles was deployed to guard Sela, one of the vital installations in the Area.

An attempt by the Chinese to infiltrate, dressed like local monpas, had already been thwarted. The Chinese followed up the attack with two more attacks on the same day – this time supported by artillery, mortars and MMGs. Indian army though continued to hold their ground. According to Indian Army accounts, it's the fourth attack that gave rise to the legend of the immortal Baba Jaswant Singh who guards India's borders in the East.

The fourth attack by the Chinese Army on 4 Garhwal was probably the deadliest. Hell bent on capturing Nauranang, the Chinese managed to move an MMG (Medium Machine Gun) close to where 4 Garhwal was, bringing them under immense fire.

This also prevented the men of 4 Garhwal from using their Light Machine Guns and it's here that Lance Naik Trilok Singh, Rifleman Jaswant Singh and Rifleman Gopal Singh undertook a suicide mission – they crawled through rocks and bushes under heavy enemy fire to take out the Chinese MMG with hand grenades. They succeeded too – lobbing grenades from as close to 15 yards. Jaswant Singh snatched the MMG from the wounded Chinese soldier who still clung on to it and crawled back to his trench.

It would have probably been a very different story if he'd succeeded – but just as he was about to reach the trench – he was shot in the head. But by then the enemy had already been delivered a big blow and Gopal Singh managed to drag the MMG back to Indian trenches.

This 15 minute act of self-sacrificing bravado changed the course of the Battle Of Nauranang, Indian LMGs came alive and beat the Chinese back – Arunachal Pradesh could never come under Chinese control.

What made rifleman Jaswant Singh a legend? But locals have a somewhat different version of Jaswant Singh's actions on November 17th, 1962. While his company had fallen back, Jaswant Singh remained at his post at an altitude of 10,000 ft.

Jaswant Singh along with the help of two local Monpa girls Sela and Nura who worked as porters managed to set up weapons at separate spots and maintained a huge volume of fire on the Chinese. This led the Chinese to believe that they were facing an entire battalion, and not just one man. It's said that Jaswant Singh managed to kill more than 300 enemy soldiers before the Chinese captured the man supplying him rations and told them about the lone rifleman who opposed them. While Sela died in a grenade attack and Nura was captured, Jaswant Singh sensing that he was about to be captured, shot himself with the last bullet.

It is alleged that the Chinese carried Jaswant Singh's severed head back to China till a Chinese Commander who was impressed by his valor returned it. The Chinese Army even had a brass bust of the soldier commissioned which now sits at the site of the battle.

Regardless of what the real story of Jaswant Singh was, for locals, the jawans who are posted for his upkeep and all travellers who pass by – he remains the guardian ghost of India's Eastern Border – the man who saved Arunachal Pradesh from the Chinese. The silver lining in what was otherwise a disappointing battle.

For their work in the field, 4 Garhwal Rifles was awarded the battle honour 'Nauranang' the only one bestowed during the 1962 war. Jaswant Singh's comrades Lance Naik Trilok Singh Negi (posthumously), Rifle Man Gopal Singh were awarded the Vir Chakra.

# 5

# Naib Subedar Bana Singh: The Hero of Siachen

Subedar Major and Honorary Captain Bana Singh, PVC (6 January 1949) is a retired Indian soldier and a recipient of the nation's highest military award, the Param Vir Chakra. He has held the ranks Naib Subedar, Subedar, Subedar Major and Honorary Captain in the Indian Army. As a Naib Subedar, he led the team which conquered the highest peak in the Siachen area as part of Operation Rajiv. The peak was named as "Bana Post" in his honour.

In June 1987 Naib Subedar Bana Singh was volunteering as one of the member of crew men who were especially joined together as the task force, for evicting the enemy intruders from the Siachen Glacier area at an altitude of 21,000 feet. The post situated over there, was actually an indestructible glacier fortress having ice walls that to 1500 feet higher. Clearing the intruders from such a position was immensely a crucial and tough task but fearless Subedar Bana Singh tremendously encouraged his crew men to move on that hazardous route and to accomplish the mission. While seeing the invincible spirit of Bana Singh, his crew men got highly moved and inspirited that they got ready to face any kind of adverse and horrendous condition that comes in their way. The crew men were crawling to get close to the enemy crew. Naib Subedar Bana Singh was a true leader for his crew, he was leading his men with utmost determination and dauntless, no frigid condition was able to stop his indomitable spirit. He was constantly motivating his crew to even face the death, since the route was dangerous and steep and considering the heights of Siachen also, but they had to reach the highest peak; "The Quaid".

Our soldiers were persistently moving towards the target, they were climbing inch by inch at a 90 degree angle. Naik Subedar Bana Singh was unmindful of his personal safety or security, he could not even assert whether it was day or night, since the heavy snowfall had darkened and created illusionary weather. But Subedar Bana Singh was fearless, four of his men were following him closely on that dangerous trek, slowly and gradually they were reaching the heights of the icy walls and now the top of the peak was virtually closer.

Suddenly Bana Singh and his men felt to be little more cautious because they were quite closer to the target point now and from where the enemy could easily detect them. And that is what happened too, enemy threw fire on them that forcibly shoved them in the hostile area and they fell recklessly in the snowy graves.

But sooner Bana Singh somehow tried to muster up his shattered strength and recalled the words of Guru Gobind Singh ji that were conveyed to him in an enlightened experience a night before ; " I want to test you Bana". Now Bana Singh regained his wrecked condition and he again led his crew men. The crew also felt elevated and recharged by seeing the high morale of Subedar Bana Singh.

On the top of the peak at the height of 21,000 feet, the Pakistani were quite carefree they were confident to be safe. They were infused with the nasty and critical remarking for Indian troops. When Naib Subedar and his follower men were reaching the height of the jingoistic banter, suddenly a grenade was dropped over them. And before they could resettle themselves, the grenade exploded and everything became numb for a moment. But Subedar Bana Singh was determined, thus he moved fast. He stood up and unmindful of his security he singlehandedly led the attack on the remaining Pakistanis outside the bunker. Then began a hand to hand fight with the enemies during which some were crushed and some fell down or slipped from the icy walls.

And ultimately on June 26, 1987, Indian Army hosted the flag of its victory by capturing the post with the support of the great soldiers; Rifleman Chunni Lal, Laxman Das, Om Raj and Kashmir Chand under the great leadership of; Fearless Bana Singh. The post earlier used to known as the "Quaid" now got renamed as the "Bana Post". It was because of the invincible leadership and bravery of Naib Subedar Bana Singh that the "Quaid" post could be captured finally otherwise the whole of the Saltoro range would have become an easy target of the Pakistani. Capture of the "Quaid" post was a huge success for the Indian Army and the Nation.

## LIFE AND WORK OF NAIB SUBEDAR BANA SINGH

Naib Subedar Bana Singh, born in Kadyal, Jammu on 6 January 1949, was enrolled in the Indian Army on 6 January 1969 into the Jammu & Kashmir Light Infantry (JAK LI). During June 1987, the 8 JAK LI, was deployed in the Siachen area. It was then found that a large number of Pakistani infiltrators had intruded in the Siachen Glacier. The ejection of these infiltrators was considered difficult but necessary and a special task force was, constituted for the purpose. Naib Subedar Singh volunteered to join this force.

The Pakistani intrusion had taken place at a height of 6500 metres. The enemy post was virtually an impregnable glacier fortress with ice walls, 457 metres high, on either side. Naib Subedar Bana Singh led his men through an extremely difficult and hazardous route. He inspired them by his courage and leadership. He and his men crawled and closed in on the adversary. Lobbing hand-grenades, charging with a bayonet and moving from trench to trench, he cleared the post of all intruders. Naib Subedar Bana Singh was awarded theParam Vir Chakra, the highest wartime gallantry medal, for conspicuous bravery and leadership under most adverse conditions.

## EARLY LIFE

Bana Singh was born into a Sikh family at Kadyal in Jammu and Kashmir, on 6 January 1949. His father was a farmer, and his uncles were soldiers in the Indian Army. He enrolled in the Indian Army on 6 January 1969 into the 8th Battalion of the Jammu and Kashmir Light Infantry (JAK LI). He was trained at the High Altitude Warfare School in Gulmarg, and also at another school at Sonamarg.

## Operation Rajiv

In 1987, the strategically important Siachen area had been infiltrated by the Pakistani forces. The Pakistanis had captured an important position, which they called "Quaidpost" (from Quaid-e-Azam, the title of Muhammad Ali Jinnah). The post was located at a height of 6500 metres on the highest peak in the Siachen Glacier area (the peak was later renamed to "Bana Top" by the Indians, in honour of Bana Singh). From this feature the Pakistanis could snipe at Indian army positions since the height gave a clear view of the entire Saltoro range and Siachen glacier. The enemy post was virtually an impregnable glacier fortress with ice walls, 457 metres high, on either side.

On 18 April 1987, the Pakistanis from Quaid Post fired on the Indian troops at Point Sonam (6,400 m), killing two soldiers. The Indian Army then decided to evict the Pakistanis from the Post. Naib Subedar Bana Singh was posted in Siachen on 20 April 1987, as part of the 8th JAK LI regiment, which was given the task of capturing the Quaid Post. On 29 May, a JAK LI patrol led by Second lieutenant Rajiv Pande made at an unsuccessful attempt at capturing the post, resulting in deaths of 10 Indian soldiers. After a month of preparation, the Indian Army launched a fresh operation to capture the post. This operation, called "Operation Rajiv" in honour of Rajiv Pande, was headed by Major Varinder Singh.

Starting on 23 June 1987, Varinder Singh's task force launched multiple attacks to capture the post. After initial failures, the 5-member team led by Bana Singh successfully captured the Quaid post on 26 June. Bana Singh and his fellow soldiers, including Chuni Lal, climbed the steep 457 m high wall of ice. The team approached the Quaid Post from an unexpected direction, using a longer and more difficult approach than the other teams. There was a blizzard, resulting in poor visibility, which gave cover to the Indian soldiers. After reaching the top, Bana Singh found that there was a single Pakistani bunker. He lobbed a grenade into the bunker and closed the door, killing those inside. The two sides also got involved in a hand-to-hand combat, in which the Indian soldiers bayoneted some of the Pakistani soldiers outside the bunker. A few Pakistani soldiers jumped off the peak. Later, the Indians found six dead bodies of Pakistani soldiers.

On 26 January 1988, Bana Singh was awarded the Param Vir Chakra, the highest wartime gallantry medal in India, for his bravery during Operation Rajiv. The peak which he captured was renamed Bana Top in his honour. At the time of the Kargil War, he was the only PVC awardee who was still serving in the Army.

## Param Vir Chakra Citation

The Param Vir Chakra citation on the Official Indian Army Website reads as follows:

**CITATION**
**NB SUB BANA SINGH**
**8 JAK LI (JC-155825)**

Naib Subedar Bana Singh volunteered to be a member of a task force constituted in June 1987 to clear an intrusion by an adversary in the Siachen Glacier area at an altitude of 21,000 feet. The post was virtually an impregnable glacier fortress with ice walls, 1500 feet high, on both sides. Naib Subedar Bana Singh led his men through an extremely difficult and hazardous route. He inspired them by his indomitable courage and leadership. The brave Naib Subedar and his men crawled and closed in on the adversary. Moving from trench to trench, lobbing hand grenades, and charging with the bayonet, he cleared the post all intruders.

Nb Subedar Bana Singh displayed the most conspicuous gallantry and leadership under the most adverse conditions.

In a country which has only three living winners of the Param Vir Chakra, it is a rare honour to meet one.

"It is an honour to meet you, Sir," we say and Param Vir Chakra winner Honorary Captain Bana Singh replies, "What I did was my duty to the country. I was given a task and I did it."

There is no trace of arrogance that a decorated soldier would perhaps be fully entitled to -- he should after all be an icon of courage in a nation woefully short of heroes -- but Captain Bana Singh makes you feel that what he did was part of a soldier's day at work.

The difference being that when he set out for work that morning 29 years ago he was at the world's highest battlefield on the Siachen Glacier, leading an operation to recapture a Pakistani post at a height of 21,000 feet, scaling vertical walls of ice 1,500 feet high under blinding snowfall.

Pakistani troops sat on top of this brutal climb as Bana Singh and his men launched a brilliant attack, clearing the post of every Pakistani soldier, setting an example in high altitude warfare which would bring him the country's highest ranking gallantry award.

The man sitting in front of us in his modest village home flanked with green fields, dressed in a simple pyjama and light sweater, had not only defeated the enemy but nature itself on the most vicious battle terrain known to man, one that has taken the lives of countless Indian and Pakistani soldiers.

## After retirement

Bana Singh retired on 31 October 2000. The Jammu & Kashmir Government gave him a pension of  166 per month. Bana Singh protested against the low amount, pointing out that the neighbouring states of Punjab and Himachal Pradesh provided a monthly pension above 10,000 to the Param Vir Chakra winners. In October 2006, the Punjab Government led by Captain Amarinder Singh announced a cash award of 1,000,000 for him. The cheque was presented to Bana Singh by Amarinder's successor Parkash Singh Badal in March 2007. The Punjab Government also offered him 2,500,000, a monthly allowance of 15,000 and a 25-acre plot, if he moved to Punjab. However, he refused the offer, saying that he is a resident of J&K. The J&K Government named a stadium in the RS Pura area of Jammu after him, and sanctioned an amount of Rs 5,000,000 for its development in 2010. However, in 2013, *The Tribune* reported that the funds had not been released, and the Bana Singh Memorial Stadium was in a poor shape.

Bana Singh's son Rajinder Singh joined the Indian Army in 2008, at the age of 18.

## HONY CAPT BANA SINGH,

The true, heart warming story of the capture against impossible odds of the Pakistani post, Quaid, the worlds highest battlefield post at 22143 feet (6749 metres) above sea level, from personnel of its elite commando force; the Special Services Group (SSG) by Naib Subedar (later Honorary Captain) Bana Singh, PVC, of 8 JAK LI and his brave hearts

The name Siachen, in Balti, refers to a land abundant with black roses. Siachen glacier is located in the eastern Karakoram Range of the Himalayas, near the Line of Control between India and Pakistan. India controls the whole Siachen glacier complex. The main glacier is sandwiched between the Saltoro Ridge to its west, (occupied by India) and the main Karakoram Range to its east.

## The Terrain

The Siachen glacier is 76 km long, with its width varying from 1000-2500 metres. It falls from an altitude of 18,875 ft (5,753 m) at its head at Indira Col, down to 11,875 ft (3,620 m) at its terminus. The average winter snowfall is 35 feet, with temperatures in the upper reaches ranging from minus 30 degrees to minus 80 degrees centigrade. The crest of the dominating Saltoro Ridge which the Indian Army holds, and where Bana won his PVC, ranges in height from 17,880 to 25,330 feet (5,450 to 7,720 m). The major passes on this ridge are Sia La, Bilafond La and Gyong La. The Indian Army pickets are reachable only after a murderous climb and then a suicidal frontal assault, a near-hopeless task in such rarified, oxygen depleted air.

Bana Singh was born on 6 January 1949 into a Punjabi Sikh family, at Kadyal, a border village located in RS Pura, the famous Basmati rice growing belt outside Jammu. He enrolled in the Indian Army on 6 January 1969 into 8 JAK LI.

He was considered a keen and enterprising, intelligent soldier by his officers, handling diverse responsibilities such as being company clerk and handling quarter master duties as an NCO normally tenable a senior JCO.

He had also been trained in mountain warfare by the High Altitude Warfare School in Gulmarg and Sonamarg and was eminently combat fit; in other words he was, at a young age an all round combat soldier whom his officers and peers respected; the peers and immediate seniors albeit with some form of competitive envy.

On 20 April, 1987, Bana's battalion was deployed, after due acclimatization, in the Siachen area. In a interview with the famous author and Tibetologist, Claude Arpi, Bana stated that Quaid Post was already under occupation of the Pakistanis when the battalion arrived in the glacier.

Named after Mohamed Ali Jinnah, the father of Pakistan, it was the most important and highest post in the area; one of the few occupied by Pakistan during its all out assault in 1987 on Saltoro Ridge under the command of then Brig Pervez Musharraf (later President of Pakistan), before being beaten back.

From Quaid Post, as the Indians would later find out, one could see 80 km around; indeed, almost the entire Saltoro range including Indian posts like Amar and Sonam, which could only be supplied by helicopter. The Pakistanis could therefore prevent the supply of these posts as well as interdict any movement by accurate fire. In fact on 18 April, 1987, firing from Quaid resulted in the death of a JCO and five soldiers at Sonam.

It thus became necessary to capture this post for the safety of our men and supporting helicopters.

The CO of 8 JAK LI, Col DS Rawat, proactively decided to send a patrol to find out the strength and disposition of the Pakistanis. On May 29, a 10 man patrol under 2/ Lt Rajiv Pande departed.

Facing this gutsy young officer was a 90 degree climb on slippery ice walls that were 1500 feet in height which had to be negotiated to reach Quaid Post. On top of that, the weather was abysmal and visibility more so.

Unfortunately, nearing Quaid, they were detected by the SSG commandos and eight, including Lt Pande and his JCO killed. The officer was posthumously awarded a Vir Chakra.

Though the death of 2/Lt Rajiv and his men was tragic, the CO was now even more determined to succeed. With the approval of Brig Nugyal, "Operation Rajiv" was thus launched. A total of 62 people participated to the final operation; two officers, three JCO's and 57 jawans.

The operation was conducted in three phases on 23, 25 and 26 June, 1987. The platoon sent on 23 June under Major Varinder Singh, Bana's company commander, had to unfortunately come back half way, losing two soldiers in the bargain.

Lt Pande had managed to fix ropes, but due to heavy snow fall, the ropes were not traceable. The ropes had therefore to be fixed all over again. The second platoon led by Subedar Sansar Singh with 10 jawans, made an attempt on 25 June.

This time, there was no problem with the ropes, but due to a communication gap with the controlling headquarters; the mission had to be aborted. Col Rawat, determined to succeed at all costs, had conveyed his determination to his command: "I don't care what sacrifices we have to pay, but Quaid will be captured. Naib Subedar Bana Singh, hand picked by his CO for the challenging assignment, led the last attack, along with Riflemen Chunni Lal, Laxman Das, Om Raj and Kashmir Chand. It was exactly at eleven minutes after noon on 26 June 1987, when this final phase of "Operation Rajiv" was launched in heavily snowing conditions and gathering darkness

Another incident he recalled was his much loved company commander, Maj (later Brig) Varinder Singh, who had been shot through the chest in the earlier phase of the operation (he was awarded the Vir Chakra), advising him to capture the Pakistanis alive when Quaid was attacked.

Bana vehemently disagreed, saying in choice Punjabi, "Sir, eh... (edited) meri maasi de putt thori na haege!. Bana recalled that Virender's face broke into a broad smile, in spite of all the prevailing tension.

All the starting signs of the final portion of "Operation Vijay" were of grim portent. It was literally darkness at noon, Bana recalled.

The heavy, persistent snow fall and the poor ambient light conditions made you wonder if it was day or night. On top of that, the Pakistanis knew something was going on because of the artillery shelling that we had started from the gun areas in the base camp to make them put their head down and also to divert their attention.

Quaid, as Bana and his men well knew, was an impregnable glacier fortress with ice walls 1500 feet high on two sides. Naib Subedar Bana Singh led his men through an extremely difficult and hazardous route, climbing in near darkness through a snowstorm. He inspired them by his indomitable courage and leadership.

There was a single, deep bunker on the top, Bana recalled. The Pakistanis must have become complacent because of the foul weather; the heavy snowfall; their success in warding the previous two efforts by the Indians to capture the post, and, not the least that the Pakistani soldiers, particularly the SSG under their boastful Brigade commander had come to believe that they were ten feet tall. He and his five men were therefore able to close up to the bunker.

Bana opened the entrance door, threw his grenades inside and closed the doors... His men set up their Light Machine Gun on single shot. In that extreme climate, the automatic weapon could fire only single shot... After the short but intense close quarter battle that took place, a total of six Pakistanis were killed, with two or three having been bayoneted.

Perhaps there were more SSG personnel who may have fallen to their deaths in their effort to escape the Indians bullets, grenades and bayonets. Too much was happening for anyone to have a clear recall.

What Bana recalled with a personal sense of loss still readable on his face 21 years after the operation was that the Pakistanis, on realizing that the post was lost, started shelling it with their viciously effective air-burst ammunition. One of Bana's brave hearts, Sepoy Om Raj had his hand blown off; surgically amputated.

In spite of Bana's best efforts to save his life, bad weather and visibility as well as the intense shelling colluded. Sepoy Om Raj passed away, being awarded a Vir Chakra posthumously. Bana recalls that, following the protocol and ethos of the Indian Army towards the dead, the bodies of the six SSG personnel were brought back by him and later handed over to Pakistan during a flag meeting at Kargil.

On the morning of 27 June 1987, the Brigade Commander, Brig CS Nugyal who had intimately been involved with the planning and execution of the operation, arrived by helicopter at the battalions launch base. Fiercely hugging Bana and his soldiers, he announced that hereafter, the 22143 feet (6749 metres) above sea level post so brazenly taken away from Pakistan by Naib Subedar Bana Singh and his men, would be called Bana Top in his honour; a decision that a grateful nation and a very proud Army indeed, have accepted for posterity.

Naib Subedar Bana Singh was awarded the Param Vir Chakra, the highest wartime gallantry medal in India, for conspicuous bravery and leadership under most adverse conditions. "Operation Rajiv" overall resulted in award of one MVC (for Subedar Sansar Singh), seven Vir Chakra's and one Sena Medal, besides the PVC. 8 JAK LI had reason to be proud; very proud indeed, for their stupendous skill at arms in the toughest high altitude terrain the world has ever known so far.

**CITATION**

**NB SUB BANA SINGH, 8 JAK LI (JC-155825)**

Naib Subedar Bana Singh volunteered to be a member of a task force constituted in June 1987 to clear an intrusion by an adversary in the Siachen Glacier area at an altitude of 21,000 feet. The post was virtually an impregnable glacier fortress with ice walls, 1500 feet high, on both sides. Naib Subedar Bana Singh led his men through an extremely difficult and hazardous route. He inspired them by his indomitable courage and leadership. The brave Naib Subedar and his men crawled and closed in on the adversary. Moving from trench to trench, lobbing hand grenades, and charging with the bayonet, he cleared the post of all intruders. Naib Subedar Bana Singh displayed the most conspicuous gallantry and leadership under the most adverse conditions.

In March 2008, the son of Honorary Capt Bana Singh, PVC, passed out from the JAK LI Regimental Centre, with his proud father watching.

Srinagar: Two decades after his inspiring heroism in the shuddering heights of Siachen, Subedar Major (Honorary Captain) Bana Singh, Param Vir Chakra (PVC), of the 8th Jammu and Kashmir Light Infantry (JAKLI) has sent his son to defend the frontiers in Kashmir

Subedar Major (Honorary Captain) Bana Singh was awarded the PVC for his heroism in the recapturing of a post from the Pakistan Army on June 23, 1987, in the Siachen Glacier (Jammu and Kashmir). He was a Naib Subedar at the time of the military operation.

The post was named after him as Bana Post and now he is his son's idol as the 18-year old, Rajinder Singh, gets ready to defend India's border.

And Subedar Major (Honorary Captain) Bana Singh, PVC, was present at his son's passing out parade at JAKLI Regimental Centre on the outskirts of Srinagar.

Siachen has taken many a lives of brave soldiers of the Indian Army in this highest battle zone in the world. An inscription on the memorial for the war dead at Siachen Base camp reads:

"Quartered in snow,

Silent to remain,

When the bugle calls,

They shall rise and march again"...

India has enough brave hearts like Honorary Captain Bana Singh, PVC, to make sure that, whenever the Bugle calls, soldiers like him will indeed rise and march again.

# 6

# Subedar Joginder Singh Sahnan

Subedar Joginder Singh Sahnan, PVC (26 September 1921 – 23 October 1962), was an Indian Army soldier who posthumously received India's highest military gallantry award, the Param Vir Chakra. Singh joined the British Indian Army in 1936, and served in the 1st battalion of the Sikh Regiment. During the 1962 Sino-Indian War, he was commanding a platoon at the Bum La Pass in the North-East Frontier Agency. Though heavily outnumbered, he led his troops in the face of the enemy and defended his post until he was wounded and killed.

Subedar Joginder Singh Sahnan, PVC (26 September 1921 – 23 October 1962), aSaini Sikh, born in Moga, Punjab (British India), was a Subedar in the Indian Armywho was awarded the distinguished Param Vir Chakra, the highest war-time gallantry award of the Indian Army.

On 28 September 1936, he was enrolled in the 1 Sikh Regiment. His father, Sher Singh Sahnan, belonged to an agricultural Saini Sikh family which had relocated to village Mahla Kalan near Moga from village Munaka of district Hoshiarpur. His mother's name was Bibi Krishan Kaur Bhela. He married Bibi Gurdyal Kaur Banga, who was from a Saini family of village Kothay Rara Singh near Kot Kapura. He went to primary school in village Nathu Ala and to village Daroli for his middle school.

## Military Action

During the 1962 Sino-Indian War, Subedar Joginder Singh commanded a platoon in the Tawang sector of NEFA (North East Frontier Agency). While holding a defensive position on a ridge in Tongpeng La area on Bum La axis, the platoon noticed heavy Chinese concentration opposite Bum La across the McMohan Line on October 20. This was indeed a preparatory to the Chinese advance on Bum La axis on October 23.

At 0530 hours on October 23, the Chinese launched a heavy attack on the Bum La axis. The intention was to achieve a breakthrough to Tawang. The Chinese attacked the ridge in three waves, each about 200 strong. The attack was supported by artillery and mortar fire, besides other weapons. The fierce resistance of the Sikh platoon, however, compelled the Chinese to fall back with heavy losses. But they regrouped quickly and launched a fresh attack under the cover of an artillery barrage.

Subedar Joginder Singh and his platoon stood firm like a rock before the advancing enemy. In this fierce action, the platoon lost half of its men but not the will to fight. Subedar Joginder Singh, despite a thigh wound, refused evacuation. His platoon also refused to yield any ground to the Chinese.

The last wave of the Chinese attack, which was more determined and more forceful followed next. Now the platoon had very few men left to fight. Subedar Joginder Singh, therefore, manned a light machine gun and killed a large number of enemies, about 52 men. But he could not stem the tide of the Chinese advance single-handedly.

The Chinese Army continued advancing with little concern for the casualties. By now all ammunition with the platoon had been exhausted. When the situation became desperate, Subedar Joginder Singh and his men emerged from their position with fixed bayonets, shouting the Sikh battle cry, "Wahe Guruji ka Khalsa, Wahe Guruji ki Fateh." They fell upon the advancing Chinese and bayoneted many to death. Finally better weapons and numerical superiority of the Chinese prevailed and Subedar Singh was captured after this epic battle. He died from his wounds and frostbite as a PoW in Chinese custody. For his inspiring leadership, steadfast courage and devotion to duty beyond all odds, Subedar Joginder Singh was awarded the highest wartime gallantry medal, the Param Vir Chakra, posthumously.

## BIRTH AT MOGA

Subedar Joginder Singh was born on 28 September, 1921, in Mahla Kalan village at Moga, District Faridkot in Punjab in the house of Sher Singh. He enrolled in the army as a Sepoy on 28 September, 1936, in the First Sikh Regiment. He served in the British Indian army at various places on the Burma Front and won many laurels. After Independence, he served with the Sikh regiment at Srinagar in 1948 when Pakistani tribals attacked Kashmir.

During the Sino-Indian War in 1962, the Indian Army was facing successive setbacks from all theatres of wars, especially in the North East Frontier Agency (NEFA) where Indian troops couldn't provide the required resistance which brought great humiliation to the reputation of an army that had proved instrumental in making the British victorious in World War-II.

Joginder Singh was commanding a platoon of 20 soldiers to form the guards of IB Ridge and Twin Peaks. The Chinese, who were eyeing the capture of Tawang from Indian forces, knew they wouldn't get a hold of Tawang without capturing the Twin Peaks because Indian soldiers stationed here could see every movement of the Chinese from miles away. Therefore, it was certain the Chinese would put all their effort to capture IB Ridge and Twin Peaks. In the early hours of 23 October, 1962, the Chinese launched offensive from three sides and Assam Riffles posted at Bum La couldn't pose much resistance, and soon the war at IB Ridge was guarded by Subedar Joginder Singh with his men.

The ridge was quite steep and it was a daunting task for the Chinese as most of the troops were exposed to Indian guns.

Subedar grabbed this opportunity with both hands and killed many Chinese while repulsing the two waves of aggression.

'Jo Bole So Nihal', the war cry of the platoon was fierce enough to scare the Chinese who perished at the bayonets of Khalsas in thick numbers. While many of his fellow soldiers perished in combat, Sub Joginder Singh was badly wounded, captured and taken as POW.

He succumbed to his wounds in the Tibet region under Chinese custody as a POW. He was awarded the PVC posthumously for showing unparalleled courage despite being at the face of annihilation.

When the Chinese learnt that Joginder Singh was awarded the PVC, the Chinese army, as a mark of respect, repatriated his ashes with full military honours to the battalion on May 17, 1963. His urn was later brought to the Sikh Regimental Centre at Meerut. The urn was honoured at a memorial service held at the Gurdwara Sahib the next day. Later, in a poignant ceremony, the urn was handed over to his widow Gurdial Kaur and young son.

Besides the memorial for his heroics in Moga town, the Indian Army paid tribute to this great martyr by building a monument in his memory at IB ridge.

## MILITARY LIFE AND WAR OF TAWANG SECTOR

It was the Sino-Indian War in 1962 when Subedar Joginder Singh was commanding a platoon of the Sikh Regiment in the Tawang sector of NEFA; North East Frontier Agency. On October 20 1962, the platoon was defending the ridge in Tongpeng La area on Bum La axis when suddenly they sensed and noticed that a huge Chinese troop was heading ahead from opposite Bum La across the McMohan Line. And ultimately on 23rd October with the intention to progress in Tawang this Chinese concentration intensively attacked on the Bum La axis. Chinese began to attack with the heavy artilleries, mortar firing and other weapons. The Platoon of Sikh Regiment tried their level best to defend themselves made the Chinese attackers fearful but sooner the Chinese reformed once again and instantly attacked for the second time.

It is Subedar Joginder Singh Sahnan who was constantly fighting with the Chinese enemy even after losing half of the men of the platoon. He got a bad thigh injury but this injury was very small to make down the morale and courage of Subedar Joginder Singh. The Chinese troops now again attacked for the third time and this attack was more fierce and disastrous that made the Sikh platoon to lose its almost men. Now there were very few of the men being left in the battle field but Subedar Joginder Singh refused evacuation. He then guarded a light machine gun and trashed a large number of enemy men about 52 enemies.

The battle was getting horrendous and Subedar Joginder Singh was not able to handle this situation single-handedly. By now there were many causalities and death in the Sikh Platoon. But that's only the situation when Subedar Joginder Singh acted lionheartedly and confronted the enemy in order to bayonate them to death. He along with his few of the men cried aloud the Sikh battle cry; "Wahe Guru ji kaa Khalsa, Wahe Guru ji ki Fateh".

Subedar Joginder Singh was captured by the Chinese and their custody he died due to his severe injuries and frigid conditions. Subedar Joginder Singh Sahnan was an epitome of bravery and courage, he was truly a devoted solider mantained to fight in all the odds in the battle field. He was awarded the Param Vir Chakra posthumously.

## WHY WE MUST SALUTE THE HEROIC SAGA OF JOGINDER SINGH

On learning that Joginder Singh was a Param Vir Chakra awardee, the People's Liberation Army, in a mark of respect for which the Chinese are not renowned, repatriated his ashes with full military honours.

No tribute can be greater than an avowal of valour by the enemy. M P Anil Kumar pays tribute to one of India's brave heroes. Although undemarcated, the Sino-Indian border had by and large existed unaltered for almost three millennia, sanctified by the geographical principle of watershed, which is generally understood as the crest of high mountains.

The eastern border about Jammu & Kashmir, carved at the Treaty of Tingmosgang signed after a war between Ladakh and Tibet in 1684, had remained so since.

The eastern border (North-East Frontier Agency) received its official imprimatur at the tripartite conference of Tibet, India and China held at Shimla in 1913-14. Initialled by the Chinese representative, the McMahon Line did not create a new border but it simply delineated the traditional, prevailing administrative boundary there.

Since Tibet was an independent entity having freed itself from the Chinese yoke at the time of the Shimla Conference, ratification by Beijing was not necessary, and therefore Beijing was deemed to have initialled the Indo-Tibetan agreement as a valued witness.

Mind you, it was Britain, dreading Russia's 'evil' sway over Tibet, who propagated the myth of Chinese suzerainty over Tibet. Thus, the cartographical exercise at Simla had full legal validity.

The Sino-Indian agreement on Tibet signed on April 29, 1954 was a boon for China, for India had recognised Tibet as a region of China and forsook her rights in Tibet that she had inherited from the British government.

With Tibet deep in his pocket, with the 'Five-anti campaign' having cleansed the country of bourgeoisie, with the Korean crisis behind him, with 'liberated' China on course to blossom into a Communist Shangri-La, Chairman Mao thought the time was ripe to elevate his standing further by putting 'high-flying' Nehru in his place.

No better course than injecting venom into the Hindi-Chini brotherliness, eh? No better way to stir the pot than usurping acres of Indian territory, eh?

Even before the ink on the agreement had dried, expansionist China questioned the alignment of the Sino-Indian border. On July 17, 1954, China protested against the presence of Indian troops in Barahoti (Uttar Pradesh).

Soon, emboldened by the passivity of the Indian government, China laid claim to Aksai Chin and NEFA, and the Chinese army commenced calculated intrusions across the border, to shove the boot in.

In August 1962, in an act of belligerence, the People's Liberation Army occupied the Thag La ridge, swooped down 2.2 km southwest and encircled the Dhola post located south of the river Namkha Chu. The Indian government ordered the army chief to 'throw' the Chinese out of Dhola area on September 22.

The Indian Army's newborn IV Corps mobilised troops to carry out this impossible task, for, the Chinese were ensconced on commanding heights at the western extremity of the McMahon Line where marshalling and massing of troops were not just a logistical nightmare, but a tactical blunder as well.

At daybreak on October 20, the PLA launched simultaneous attacks on the Namkha Chu sector, other frontier divisions of NEFA as well as Ladakh. By the 23rd morning, the PLA had grabbed enough terrain to 'throw' the Indians out of the Dhola-Thag La area.

(Titbit: The CIA-mounted Bay of Pigs invasion ultimately snowballed into the Cuban missile crisis that nudged the world to the brink of Armageddon. Coincidentally, the PLA timed the October 20 incursions with the American naval quarantine of Cuba. Very clever move, for the global spotlight was on Cuba, and the Chinese aggression went largely overlooked by the world.)

## THE HEROIC DEFENCE

China coveted Tawang madly, and the Dragon's primary objective in NEFA was the occupation of Tawang, for which the PLA had swarmed the Bum La area with a division. From the

McMahon Line, the 26-km Bum La-Tawang foot-track was the shortest and the least perilous approach to Tawang.

The Bum La pass, at 4,492 metres, is broad and motorable. Approximately 3 km southwest of Bum La, and west of the foot-track stood the feature called 'Twin Peaks', from which one could espy Chinese activities across the McMahon Line.

The 1st Sikh battalion was charged with making this approach to Tawang impassable. To achieve this end, its Delta Company, commanded by Lieutenant Haripal Kaushik, was tasked to base his outfit at Tongpeng La, a pass situated a km southwest of the 'Twin Peaks'.

Between the 'Twin Peaks' and Bum La, there existed an Inspection Bungalow (IB) on a stretch of flatland. The nearby IB ridge, roughly 2 km south of Bum La, was an ideal redoubt to thwart access to 'Twin Peaks'. The 11th platoon of Delta Company, under Subedar Joginder Singh, deployed at the IB ridge, set up defences to halt the Chinese advance in their tracks.

7 (Bengal) Mountain Battery would provide artillery cover to the Sikhs. Captain Gurcharan Singh Gosal was told to operate as the artillery observation post officer from Tongpeng La.

As dawn began to brighten the morning of October 20, a JCO of the Assam Rifles outpost stationed at Bum La noticed hundreds aggregated across the border and he alerted the 11th platoon. Joginder promptly despatched a section under Havildar Sucha Singh to reinforce the Bum La-post, and then sought 'second line' ammunition from his company HQ.

Hair-trigger ready, everybody held their breath, in anticipation of gunfire. Which dragged on, and on, till 0430 hours on October 23. They first let off volleys of mortar and anti-tank guns (to destroy Indian bunkers), and then about 600 Chinese attacked the Assam Rifles post. Sucha Singh led the vanguard to fell several Chinese and then withdrew his contingent to join his parent platoon at the IB ridge.

Having overrun the Assam Rifles outpost, with the objective of capturing 'Twin Peaks', the enemy launched a concerted assault on the IB ridge, at first light. Joginder Singh, born on September 26, 1921 to a land-owning farmer family in Moga (Punjab), was enrolled in the regiment on September 28, 1936. He carried a reputation of being forthright, honest and a professional soldier.

After studying the topography, using the local resources at the platoon locality astride the IB ridge, he made his men fortify themselves in a fieldwork of tactically-sited bunkers and trenches.

The platoon had a stock of four days' rations. Ill-shod (jungle boots) and unsuitably-clad (no winter clothing), the Himalayan chill made his men shiver, but Joginder motivated and rallied them to focus on their task of giving seasoned PLA servicemen blooded in mountain warfare the shivers.

He knew the IB ridge dominated the Bum La bowl, and the climb from the bed of the nullah to their platoon fieldwork was steep, and therefore the Sikhs would be able to mow down the enemy even with outmoded Lee Enfield 303 rifles.

Since the disposition within the establishment (the government and some among the top brass) was pacifist, the armed forces were deficient on many counts.

As ammo was at a premium, each round had to account for a kill, and he therefore made his men hold fire till the enemy shinnied up and was in the weapon-range.

The gunfight began. The mortars and artillery guns engaged the enemy with telling effect. Mounting casualties and sustained fire compelled the Chinese to take cover behind boulders first and then retreat. Only 17, half the platoon, survived the Chinese offensive.

Having repulsed the first wave, Joginder asked again for more ammo from Tongpeng La. While the account of ammo expenditure was being taken, the Chinese had regrouped to hurl themselves all-guns-blazing at the Indians.

Apparently an echelon had climbed unobserved from the right flank. The shooting that ensued was far more ferocious. Joginder, who was scurrying between two sections, took a machinegun burst on his thigh. Dripping blood, he hopped himself into a bunker and tied the field dressing. He refused evacuation, and continued screaming instructions and adjusting defences.

When the gunner died, he took over the 2-inch mortar and fired some rounds to disrupt and disperse the enemy's raid. His platoon soon accounted for most of the Chinese, but by then the majority of his men had been either killed or seriously wounded.

There was just a breather for the men standing, for, before one could drawl 'Zhou En-lai', the Chinese had briskly mustered about 200 troops and resurrected another foray, to snatch the IB ridge. Sensing the gravity, Lieutenant Kaushik radioed Joginder if he could direct SOS fire on own defences to defuse the Chinese onslaught.

"Yes, Sahib," was the prompt reply. That, alas, would be the last communication with Joginder and his platoon.

Lieutenant Kaushik urged Captain Gosal to promptly engage the IB ridge with Red-over-Red artillery barrage (shelling on to own positions with the likelihood of casualties to own troops, but something that would definitely take a heavy toll of the enemy).

By the time the cannonade ceased, the platoon had run out of ammo, and Joginder had readied the remnant of his platoon for a head-on, last-ditch attack.

With fire raging in their belly, screaming the battle cry '*Bole So Nihal Sat Sri Akal*', the Khalsas killed a score of 'shocked-and-awed' Chinese soldiers in the bayonet charge.

But Chinese troops continued to clamber up and overpowered Joginder in close quarter combat. All but four personnel from the platoon perished in the bloody battle. While a badly wounded Joginder was taken as a prisoner of war, the other three gave the slip, trekked on the bridle-path to the main defences at Se La, and narrated the ringside account of the fierce fighting that raged for four attritional hours.

## A memorial to Subedar Joginder Singh, Param Vir Chakra

Joginder Singh passed on a little later in captivity.

Subedar Joginder Singh was decorated with the Param Vir Chakra, posthumously, for his remarkable leadership under fire and the gallant defence of IB ridge.

## Epilogue

On learning that Joginder was a Param Vir Chakra awardee, the PLA, in a mark of respect for which the Chinese are not renowned, repatriated his ashes with full military honours to the battalion on May 17, 1963. No tribute can be greater than an avowal of valour by the enemy.

The urn was later brought to the Sikh Regimental Centre at Meerut, where Colonel Shamsher Singh, the commandant, received it. The urn was honoured at a memorial service held at the Gurdwara Sahib the next day. Later, in a poignant ceremony, the urn was handed over to his widow Gurdial Kaur and young son.

Besides a memorial in Moga town, the Indian Army has canonised the courage of this brave son by building a monument at the forward slope of IB ridge.

## CITATION

The Param Vir Chakra citation on the Official Indian Army Website reads as follows:

**CITATION**
**SUBEDAR JOGINDER SINGH**
**1 SIKH (JC 1547)**

Subedar Joginder Singh was the commander of a platoon of the Sikh Regiment holding a defensive position at a ridge near Tongpen La in NEFA. At 0530 hours on 23 October 1962, the Chinese opened a very heavy attack on the Bumla axis with the intention of breaking through to Towang.

The leading battalion of the enemy attacked the ridge in three waves, each about 200 strong. Subedar Joginder Singh and his men mowed down the first wave, and the enemy was temporarily halted by the heavy losses it suffered. With in a few minutes, a second wave came over and was dealt with similarly. But the platoon had, by then, lost half its men.

Subedar Joginder Singh was wounded in the thigh but refused to be evacuated. Under his inspiring leadership the platoon stubbornly held its ground and would not withdraw.

Meanwhile the position was attacked for the third time. Subedar Joginder Singh himself manned a light machine-gun and shot down a number of the enemy. The Chinese however continued to advance despite heavy losses. When the situation became untenable Subedar Joginder Singh and the few men that were left in the position fixed bayonets and charged the advancing Chinese, bayoneting a number of them before he and his comrades were overpowered. Throughout this action, Subedar joginder Singh displayed devotion to duty, inspiring leadership and bravery of the highest order.

## Memorial in Moga, Punjab

Subedar Joginder Singh Sahnan (PVC) received highest civilian commemoration in his native town of Moga in 2006 when his statue adorned in battle fatigue was inaugurated near district DC office.

## Other honours

The shipping corporation of India has honoured this great man by naming one of their vessels Subedar Joginder Singh PVC.

# 7

# Param Vir Chakra Lieutenant Colonel Ardeshir Burzorji Tarapore

Lieutenant Colonel Ardeshir Burzorji Tarapore, PVC (19 August 1923 – 16 September 1965), was an officer in the Indian Army and a recipient of the Param Vir Chakra, India's highest award for bravery. After completing his schooling in Pune, Tarapore joined the Hyderabad Army, and was commissioned in January 1942. Initially he joined the infantry, but was later transferred to an armoured regiment, the 1st Hyderabad Imperial Service Lancers. During World War II Tarapore saw action in the Middle East.

After Hyderabad State merged with India in 1948, Tarapore was selected to join the Indian Army. He was commissioned again in April 1951, and was posted to 17 Horse. Later he attended a training course on the Centurion tank in the United Kingdom. During the Indo-Pakistani War of 1965, 17 Horse saw action in the Sialkot sector. Tarapore led the regiment in several tank battles between 11 and 16 September, and was killed in one such battle at Butur-Dograndi on 16 September. Under his leadership the regiment destroyed sixty Pakistani tanks, while the Indians suffered the loss of nine.

Lieutenant Colonel Ardeshir Burzorji Tarapore was born in Mumbai on August 18th 1923. He came from the family of

General Ratanjiba. who led the armies of Chatrapati Shivaji Maharaj, He was awarded 100 villages. Among them Tarapore was the main village. The name Tarapore came from there. Later his grandfather went to Hyderabad and started working under the Nizam of Hyderabad in the excise department. After his death Ardeshir's father took up his job and became very successful with his hard work and dedication. Ardeshir demonstrated his courage at the young tender age when he saved his sister from a family cow that was broken loose. Ardeshir did his schooling from Sardar Dastur Boys' Boarding School in Pune and completed his matriculation in 1940. He applied for army and got selected. He did his training at Golconda and upon completion he was sent to Bangalore. He was commissioned as a second Lieutenant in the 7th Hyderabad Infantry.

Ardeshir was popularly called as "Adi". He was not happy joining the Infantry. He wanted to join an armored regiment. During a battalion inspection by the Commander-in-Chief of the state forces Major General El Edroos. Ardeshir impressed him with his exemplary courage when by accident a grenade fell into the bay area at the grenade throwing range and Ardeshir was quick to jump and throw it. The grenade exploded in the middle a flying shapnel hit his chest and left him injured. Major General Edroos was witness to the entire event. He summoned him to his office and congratulated him for his bravery. Ardeshir took this opportunity to request a transfer to an armored regiment. The General accepted his request and transferred him to the 1st Hyderabad Imperial Service Lancers. He served in West Asia during the WWII.

After the Indian independence hyderabad was merged with India. Which eventually amalgamated the Indian Army. Ardeshir was transferred to The Poona Horse. On 1st April 1951 he was commissioned in Poona Horse. He rose to the position of regiment commandant. In 1965 Indo-Pak war he commanded his own regiment in Poona Horse.

The Poona Horse was raised on the 15th of July 1817. Amongst many of its earlier exploits was that at Koregaun (

near Poona) where 300 of its men along with a small detachment of infantry were surrounded by 28,000 troops of the Peshwa's army under command of the Peshwa himself.

After a day's desperate hand to hand fighting in which the medical officer led the sepoy's in a bayonet charge, the small force so successfully resisted the enemy's attack that the Peshwa withdrew his forces in disgust.

In 1857 the regiment was ordered to Persia. The Shah of Persia had invaded Afghanistan in 1856 and captured Herat. This was contrary to the treaties and he was called upon to retire which he did not, so war was declared). In the battle of Kooshab they charged headlong into the square formed by the Persian 1st Khusgai Regiment of Fars whom they practically annihilated.

In this charge a standard of great antiquity was captured from the Persian Regiment. The captured standard was surmounted by a silver hand, the palm of which is inscribed YAD ULLAL FAUK IDAHEEM which roughly translates THE HAND OF GOD IS ABOVE ALL THINGS. Two VC's were won in this action and a number of other awards. This hand was later to become the central device of the badge of Poona Horse. (note: The Commandants ie Colonel Tarapore's tank was named Kooshab, from this campaign)

In the first great war the regiment again distinguished itself and another VC was won.

In 1921-22 a reorganisation of the Indian Cavalry took place and 34th Prince Albert Victors Own Poona Horse and 33rd Queen Victoria's Own Cavalry were merged to form the 17th Queen Victoria's own Poona Horse, Five years later the title changed to The Poona Horse (17th QVO Cavalry).

At the Battle of Chawinda during 1965 Indo-Pak war the biggest tank battle took place at Phillora in Sialkot.

The Commander of 1st Indian Armoured Division had come to the conclusion that it was necessary to outflank Chawinda before attacking it with infantry and selected Jassoran-Buttar Dograndi area to the west of Chawinda for this purpose 84. The

Indian plan for conduct of operations on 16th September was as following:– (1) Poona Horse with under command one infantry battalion to first capture Jassoran and then advance to Buttur Dograndi, (2) 4 Horse to cross the railway line and secure area Sodreke crossing covering roads Chawinda-Badiana and Badiana-Pasrur (3) The places captured by Poona Horse and 4 Horse were to serve as firm base from where 6 Mountain Division would mount a night attack on Chawinda on night 16/ 17 September85.

The Indian attack commenced at 0600 hours 16th September and Buttur Dograndi was captured by 1030 hours. After this the Indian Army did not make much headway and at 1615 hours abandoned Buttur Dograndi since Indian Army did not have sufficient infantry to hold it. Later an attack was made to recapture Buttur. It was counter attacked by enemy forces with heavy shelling from Wazirwali. Unmindful for his injuries Lt. Col. Tarapore further led his regiment to capture Jassoran and Butur-Dograndi. In this battle his own tank was hit many times but in spite of all the odds he maintained his pivots at both these places, which helped the supporting infantry to attack Chawinda from behind.The soldiers were so Inspired by Lt. Col. Tarapore's leadership and bravery that they fiercely attacked and destroyed many enemy tanks. Limiting their casualties to 9 tanks. However, Lt. Colonel Tarapore was enveloped in flames during this attack and died a hero's death. The valour displayed by him in this action, lasting 6 days, was in keeping with the highest traditions of the Indian Army. Lieutenant Colonel Ardeshir Burzorji Tarapore was awarded with the highest wartime gallantry medal, Param Vir Chakra, posthumously.

The Indian Armies failures in making any worthwhile progress on 15th and 16th September had a more intimate connection with poor higher leadership that pigheadedly insisted on a modern charge of heavy brigade of tanks, against Pakistani artillery, which off course took advantage of the errors of enemy leadership at brigade and divisional level in the employment of armour, which was unnecessarily sacrificed in a suicidal manner, rather than being employed in a dynamic war of movement.

## LIFE AND WORK OF ARDESHIR TARAPORE

Lieutenant Colonel Ardeshir Burzorji Tarapore, PVC was born on August 18, 1923 inMumbai. He belongs to the family of *General Ratanjiba* who led the army of Chatrapati Shivaji Maharaj, who was awarded 100 villages of which Tarapore was main village. The name *Tarapore* comes for the same reason. Later his grandfather relocated toHyderabad and started working under the excise department of Nizam of Hyderabad. After his death Burzonji took up his father's job and was comparatively successful due to his hardwork.

From the young tender age Ardeshir's showed his courage when he saved his sister,*Yadgar*, from a family cow that had broken loose. By the time he was seven years old he was sent to the Sardar Dastur Boys' Boarding School, Pune. He completed his matriculation in the year 1940. After school he applied for the army and was selected. he did his initial training in the *Officers' Training School* at Golconda and on completion was sent to Bangalore. He saw himself commissioned in the 7th Hyderabad Infantry as a Second Lieutenant.

Lieutenant Colonel Ardeshir Burzorji Tarapore was born on 18 August 1923 in Bombay, Maharashtra. He joined the Hyderabad State Force in 1942 and saw active service in West Asia during World War-II. He was commissioned in Poona Horse on 01 April 1951. The biggest tank battle of the 1965 Indo-Pak War took place at Phillora in the Sialkot sector. During the southern thrust of the Indian Army on the Kaloi-Phillora axis the 17 Horse commanded by Lt. Col. Tarapore advanced on the right flank. On 11 September 1965, the regiment was assigned the task of delivering the main armoured thrust for capturing Phillora. It decided upon launching a surprise attack on Phillora from the rear. To achieve the surprise, when the regiment was thrusting forward between Phillora and Chawinda, it was suddenly counter-attacked by the enemy's heavy armour from Wazirwali.

Lt. Col. Tarapore defied the enemy's charge, held his ground and gallantly attacked Phillora with one of his squadrons supported by an Infantry battalion. Though under continuous enemy tank and artillery fire, he remain unperturbed throughout this action. When wounded, he refused to be evacuated. On 14 September 1965, he led his regiment to capture Wazirwali. Unmindful of his injury, he again led his regiment and captured Jassoran and Butur-Dograndi on 16 September 1965. In this battle his own tank was hit several times. But despite the odds, he maintained his pivots at both these places and thereby helped the supporting infantry to attack Chawinda from the rear. Inspired by his leadership, the regiment fiercely attacked the enemy armour and destroyed approximately sixty enemy tanks, suffering only nine tank casualties. However, Lt. Colonel Tarapore was enveloped in flames and died a hero's death. The valour displayed by him in this action, lasting 6 days, was in keeping with the highest traditions of the Indian Army. Lieutenant Colonel Ardeshir Burzorji Tarapore was awarded with the highest war-time gallantry medal, Param Vir Chakra, posthumously.

## Hyderabad State Force

He was popularly known as "Adi". Adi was not very happy joining the infantry, instead he wanted to join an armoured regiment. On one fine day his battalion was inspected byMajor General El Edroos, the Commander-in-Chief of the state forces. At the grenadethrowing range due to an accident a grenade fell into the bay area. Adi was quick to jump and throw it. However the grenade exploded in the middle which left him injured as the flying shrapnel hit his chest. Major General Edroos, was a witness to this event which kept him spellbound. He was impressed by the exemplary courage displayed by Ardeshir. Major General Edroos summoned Ardeshir to his office and congratulated him for his efforts. Ardeshir took this as an opportunity and requested that he be transferred to an armoured regiment. The General accepted this and he was transferred to the 1st Hyderabad Imperial Service Lancers. Interestingly, 1st Hyderabad Lancers fought with The Poona Horse in

Operation Polo. He also saw active service in West Asia during World War-II during this part of his career.

## Indian Army

Later Hyderabad was merged with Union of India. This eventually amalgamated the Indian Army. Ardeshir was shifted to The Poona Horseand was commissioned in Poona Horse on 1 April 1951. He rose to become Commanding Officer (CO) and commanded his very own regiment in the Poona Horse in the 1965 war against Pakistan and while leading his regiment in securing a major objective in Pakistan,Lieutenant Colonel A B Tarapore went down fighting on board his Centurion tank in the highest tradition of the army and recognised as the bravest of the brave to be awarded Param Vir Chakra for his action in the battle.

With the merger of Hyderabad with the Union of India, Indian Army hereafter fused. Lieutenant Ardeshir Burzorji was then shifted to The Poona Horse and was accredited in Poona Horse on 1[SUP]st[/SUP] April 1951. He very efficiently commanded his own regiment in the Poona Horse war in 1965 against the Pakistan. He fought in the highest traditions of the Indian army while boarding his Centurion Tank and got recognized for his bravado in the Indo-Pak War of 1965. This only, made him being awarded with the highest gallantry award the Param Vir Chakra.

## Military action

On 11 September 1965, the 17 Horse regiment launched attack on Phillora in the Sialkot sector at the Battle of Chawinda. The southern thrust of the attack, commanded by Tarapore advanced on the right flank. Between Phillora and Chawinda, the attack met with thePakistani Army's heavy armour charge from Wazirwali. He held his ground and attacked Phillora under continuous enemy tank and artillery fire. When wounded, he refused to be evacuated. He led his regiment to capture Wazirwali on 14 September, and Jassoran and Butur-Dograndi on 16 September 1965.

Though his own tank was hit several times, he maintained his pivots at both these places, supporting the infantry attacking Chawinda. Inspired by his leadership, the regiment attacked the enemy armor and destroyed approximately sixty Pakistani Army tanks, suffering only nine tank casualties. However, Tarapore was killed when his tank was hit and was enveloped in flames.

## Battle of Phillora, Sialkot area, Pakistan

Lieutenant Colonel was commanding the Poona Horse Regiment when on September 11[SUP]th[/SUP] 1965, he delegated the task of transporting the main armored thrust in order to capture Phillora, Sialkot sector in Pakistan.

The attack had to be initiated from the rear, while the regiment was nudging between Phillora and Chawinda it was suddenly got counter attacked by the enemy's heavy armour charge from Wazirali.

But Lieutenant Colonel A B Tarapore was not at all deterred from this constant firing from enemy tanks and artillery. He rather refused to evacuate and decided to hold the ground and with the help of one of his squadrons corporate by an infantry battalion, he fought tremendously well.

On 14[SUP]th[/SUP] September, Lieutenant Colonel AB Tarapore along with the regiment succeeded in capturing Wazirwali and later on th 16[SUP]th[/SUP] September Jassoran and Butur-Dograndi.

Lieutenant showed the great heights of leadership and perseverance even when his own tank was intensely attacked and ruined by the enemy. He did not give up his high spirit to fight and tremendously motivated his regiment. Under the command of such a lionhearted leader the regiment destroyed around sixty Pakistani Army tanks. Lieutenant Colonel Ardeshir Burzorji's tank was hit and encased in the horrendous flames of fire. He died on September 16[SUP]th[/SUP] 1965 as a Hero and a great Leader of the battle. He was awarded the Param Vir Chakra posthumously.

## Param Vir Chakra Citation

The Param Vir Chakra citation on the Official Indian Army Website reads as follows:

**CITATION**
**LIEUTENANT COLONEL A.B TARAPORE**
**POONA HORSE (17 HORSE) (IC-5565)**

On 11 September 1965, the Poona Horse Regiment under the command of Lieutenant Colonel Ardeshir Burzarji Tarapore was assigned the task of delivering the main armoured thrust for capturing Phillora in the Sialkot Sector in Pakistan. As a preliminary to making a surprise attack on Phillora from the rear, the regiment was thrusting between Philloira and Chawinda when it was suddenly counter attacked by the enemy's heavy Armour from Wazirali. Lieutenant Colonel A. B. Tarapore who was then at the head of his regiment, defied the enemy's charge, held his ground and gallantly attacked Philloira with one of his squadrons supported by an infantry battalion. Though under continuous enemy tank and artillery fire, Lieutenant Colonel A B Tarapore remained unperturbed throughout this action and when wounded refused to be evacuated.

On 14 September 1965, though still wounded he again led his regiment to capture Wazirali. Such was his grit and determination that unmindful of his injury, he again gallantly led regiment and captured Jassoran and Butur-Dograndi on 16 September. His own tank was hit several times, but despite the odds he maintained his pivots in both these places and thereby allowed the supporting infantry to attack Chawinda from the rear.

Inspired by his leadership, the regiment fiercely attacked the enemy heavy armour destroying approximately 60 enemy tanks at a cost of only 9 tank casualties, and when lieutenant Colonel A. B Tara pore was mortally wounded the regiment continue to defy the enemy.

The valour displayed by lieutenant Colonel A.B. Tarapore in this heroic action, which lasted six days, was in keeping with the highest traditions of the Indian Army.

# 8

# Second Lieutenant Arun Khetarpal

Second Lieutenant Arun Khetarpal, PVC (14 October 1950 – 16 December 1971) born in Pune, Maharashtra, was an officer of the Indian Army and a posthumous recipient of the Param Vir Chakra, India's highest military decoration for valour in face of the enemy. He died in the Battle of Basantar during the Indo-Pakistan War of 1971 where his actions earned him his honour.

## Early life

Arun Khetarpal was born in Pune, Maharashtra on 14 October 1950. His father Lt Col (later Brigadier) M. L. Khetarpal was a Corps of Engineers officer serving in the Indian Army and his family traced a long history of military service. Attending The Lawrence School, Sanawar, he distinguished himself both as an able student and sportsman and was the school prefect. Khetarpal joined the National Defence Academy in June 1967. He belonged to Foxtrot Squadron where he was the Squadron Cadet Captain of the 38th Course. His NDA No was 7498/F/38. He subsequently went on to join the Indian Military Academy. In June 1971, Khetarpal was commissioned into the 17 Poona Horse. 2nd Lieutenant Arun Khetarpal, son of Brigadier M.L. Khetarpal, was born on 14 October 1950, in Pune, Maharashtra. Arun came from a family with a long tradition of service in the Army. In Sanawar he distinguished himself both in academics and sports. In 1967 he joined the National Defense Academy (NDA) and then went on to Indian Military Academy. He was commissioned in the 17 Poona Horse on 13 June 1971. During the 1971 Indo-Pak War, the 47 Inf. Bde., with the 17 Poona Horse under command, was ordered to establish a bridge-head across the Basantar river in Shakargarh sector. The 47 Inf. Bde. completed the task by 2100 hours on December 15th. It was now for the engineers to breach the enemy mine-fields and make a safe lane for the induction of the 17 Poona Horse in support of the bridge-head. While the engineers were half way through their task, the Indian troops at the bridge-head reported alarming activity of the enemy armour.

They requested immediate tank support. But the mine-field had been cleared only partially by that time. At this critical juncture, the 17 Poona Horse decided to push through the mine-field come what may. By first light on December 16th, the regiment established a link-up between the armour and the infantry at the bridge-head. At 0800 hours, the enemy made a counter-attack with an armour regiment, under the cover of a smoke-screen. The target was the regimental pivot at Jarpal. As the Indians troops were heavily outnumbered, the Commander of 'B' Squadron requested reinforcement. At that time, 2nd Lt. Khetarpal was positioned close to the squadron with his troops in two tanks. He answered the call and moved out to face the enemy attack.

On the way, his troops came under fire from enemy strong points and recoilless gun nests, in the bridge-head zone. 2nd Lt. Khetarpal fiercely attacked these strong-points, over-ran enemy defences and captured many enemy soldiers and recoilless guns at gun point. During one of these attacks, the commander of his second tank was killed on the spot leaving him alone. But he continued attack on the enemy strongholds single-handed, until all the enemy positions were overwhelmed. He then raced to the 'B' Squadron position. By the time he reached there, the enemy tanks were on the retreat. He pursued and destroyed one of these tanks. The 'B' Squadron Commander could persuade him to fall back in line after great difficulty. The enemy soon reformed for a second attack. This time they chose the sector held by 2nd Lt. Arun Khetarpal and two other Officers, for the main attack. The enemy employed a complete armoured squadron against these three tanks in order to achieve a breakthrough.

A fierce tank battle followed. As many as ten enemy tanks were destroyed and of these 2nd Lieutenant Khetarpal alone destroyed four. In the thick of the battle, two of the three Indian tanks became casualties - one was hit and another suffered mechanical failure. The third tank, which was 2nd Lt. Khetarpal's tank, also received a shot and burst into flames. The Commander of the tank troops ordered 2nd Lt. Khetarpal to abandon the burning tank. But realising the useful role of his tank in preventing a breakthrough he communicated the following message to his Commander, "No Sir, I will not abandon my tank. My gun is still working and I will get these bastards." Then he set about destroying the remaining enemy tanks. The last enemy tank which he shot was barely 100 metres from his position. At this stage his tank received a second hit. The brave Officer met his death denying the enemy the intended breakthrough. For his conspicuous gallantry in the face of the enemy, 2nd Lt. Arun Khetarpal was honoured with the highest wartime gallantry medal, the Param Vir Chakra, posthumously.

## 1971 WAR

During the Indo-Pakistan War of 1971, the 17 Poona Horse was assigned to the command of the 47th Infantry Brigade of the Indian Army. Through the duration of the conflict, the 47th Brigade saw action in the Shakargarh sector in the Battle of Basantar.

## Battle of Basantar

Among the tasks set for the 47th Brigade was to establish a bridgehead across the River Basantar. By 2100hr of 15 December, the brigade had captured its objectives. However, the place was extensively mined, which prevented the deployment of the tanks of the Poona horse, and the engineers clearing the mines were halfway through their tasks when Indian troops at the bridge-head reported alarming activity of the enemy armour, asking for immediate armour support. It was at this critical juncture that the 17 Poona Horse decided to push through the mine-field. The regiment was able to establish a link-up between the armour and the infantry at the bridge-head by first light the next day.

## Bridge-head

At 0800hr on 16 December, Pakistani armour launched the first of their counter-attacks under the cover of a smokescreen at the pivot of the 17th Poona Horse at Jarpal. At 0800 hours on 16 December, Pakistani 13th Lancers equipped with the then state-of-the-art US-made 50 ton Patton tanks launched the first of their counter-attacks under the cover of a smokescreen at 'B' Squadron, The Poona Horse, at Jarpal. Its squadron commander urgently called for reinforcements. Arun Khetarpal, who was in 'A' squadron and was stationed close by with hisCenturion tank troop, responded with alacrity, as did the rest of his regiment. The first counterattack was decimated by accurate gunnery, coolness by Indian tank troop and individual tank commanders from the iconic CO, Lt Col Hanut Singh, MVC downwards to its troop leader, Arun Khetarpal. 13th Lancers desperately launched two more squadron level counterattacks, but to no avail and at savage cost in men and material to this otherwise old and well established cavalry regiment.

Khetarpal wheeled to meet the Pakistani armour and launched right into the Pakistani attack. With his troop he was able to run over the enemy advance with his tanks and even captured some of the enemy infantry and weapon crews at gunpoint.

However, the commander of the second tank was killed in this attack. Alone in charge, Khetarpal continued his attack on the enemy strongholds until he had overwhelmed the Pakistani positions. Emboldened by his success so far, he pursued the retreating Pakistani troops and artillery gunning down a Pakistani tank in the process. However Pakistani forces regrouped and counterattacked. In the ensuing tank battle ten enemy tanks were hit and destroyed of which Khetarpal accounted for four.

## Death

The skirmish however took its toll on the Lieutenant as he was hit by enemy fire, but instead of abandoning the tank he fought on destroying one final tank before he was finally overwhelmed. However, his actions had denied a vital breakthrough for Pakistani forces and instead put the Indians in a stronger position in the Shakargarh bulge.

His final words over the radio to a superior officer who had ordered him to abandon his burning tank were, "No Sir, I will not abandon my tank. My gun is still working and I will get these bastards."

Then he set about destroying the remaining enemy tanks. The last enemy tank, which he shot, was barely 100 metres from his position. At this stage his tank received a second hit and he was mortally injured. The officer met his death denying the Pakistani Army the intended breakthrough. Khetarpal's tank "Famagusta" was restored and is on display now.

For his conspicuous gallantry in the face of the enemy, Khetarpal was honoured with the highest wartime gallantry medal, the Param Vir Chakra, posthumously.

Arun Khetarpal was cremated on 17 December near Samba district and his ashes sent to his family who did not learn of his death till 26 December.

Famagusta's crew was Sowar Prayag Singh, the driver, Sowar Nand Singh, the Radio Operator, Sowar Nathu Singh, the Gunner and 2/lt Arun Khetarpal, the commander. Nand Singh was first to die. This was just before the fatal encounter with Major Nasser. Then Arun succumbed to his injuries. Both Prayag Singh and Nathu Singh were badly wounded but survived and retired from the army as Honorary Captains.

## PARAM VIR CHAKRA CITATION

The Param Vir Chakra citation on the Official Indian Army Website reads as follows:

### CITATION
### SECOND LIEUTENANT ARUN KHETARPAL
### POONAHORSE (IC-25067)

On 16 December 1971, the squadron Commander of 'B' Squadron, the Poona Horse asked for reinforcements as the Pakistani armour that was superior in strength, counter attacked at Jarpal, in the Shakargarh Sector. On hearing this transmission, 2nd Lt Khetarpal who was in 'A' Squadron, voluntarily moved along with his troop, to assist the other squadron. Enroute, while crossing the Basantar River, Second Lieutenant Arun Khetarpal and his troops came under fire from enemy strong points and RCL gun nests that were still holding out. Time was at a premium and as a critical situation was developing in the 'B' Squadron sector, Second Lieutenant Arun Khetarpal, threw caution to the winds and started attacking the impending enemy strong points by literally charging them, Overrunning the defence works with his tanks and capturing the enemy infantry and weapon crews at pistol point. In the course of one such daring attack one tank commander of his troop was killed. Second Lieutenant Arun Khetarpal continued to attack relentlessly until all enemy opposition was overcome and he broke through towards the 'B' Squadron position, just in time to see the enemy tanks pulling back after their initial probing attack on this squadron. He was so carried away by the wild enthusiasm of battle and the impetus of his own headlong dash that he started chasing the withdrawing tanks and even managed to shoot and destroy one. Soon thereafter, the enemy reformed with a squadron of armour for a second attack and this time they selected the sector held by Second Lieutenant Arun Khetarpal and two other tanks as the point for their main effort. A fierce tank fight ensued: ten enemy tanks were hit and destroyed of which Second Lieutenant Arun Khetarpal personally destroyed four, just then Second Lieutenant Arun Khetarpal was severely wounded. He was asked to abandon his tank but he realized that the enemy though badly decimated was continuing to advance in his sector of responsibility and if he abandoned his tank the enemy would break through, he gallantly fought on and destroyed another enemy tank. At this stage his tank received a second hit which resulted in the death of this gallant officer.

Second Lieutenant Arun Khetarpal was dead but he had, by his intrepid valour saved the day; the enemy was denied the breakthrough he was so desperately seeking. Not one enemy tank got through.

Second Lieutenant Arun Khetarpal had shown the best qualities of leadership, tenacity of purpose and the will to close in with the enemy. This was an act of courage and self-sacrifice far beyond the call of duty.

## Tribute & Facts

Khetrapal is an iconic figure in the ethos of the Indian Army with prominent constructions being named after him. The parade ground at NDA is named Khetarpal Ground while the auditorium and one of the main gates bear his name an the IMA.

Arun Khetarpal's Centurion was called Famagusta Jx 202. It was restored after the war and is presently preserved in the Armoured Corps Centre And School Ahmednagar.

## LEGACY

"The only occasion when a breakthrough could have occurred was when two squadrons of 13 Lancers attacked together in the afternoon, but a gallant last ditch lone stand by 2/Lt Arun Khetarpal of Poona Horse averted the danger." Maj.(Rtd) A. H. Amin ( Pakistan Armour Corps - Columnist and Historian). The Commander of the Pakistan tank battalion is said to have met the Indian battalion commander after the battle and made enquiries about 2nd Lieutenant Khetarpal's tank since he was very impressed with the gallantry of this particular tank's commander.

In 2001, Brigadier M.L. Khetarpal - now 81 years old - felt a strong desire to visit his birthplace at Sargodha, now in Pakistan. At Lahore airport, Brigadier M.L. Khetarpal was met by Brigadier Khawja Mohammad Naser, who took it upon himself to be Brigadier M.L. Khetarpal host and guide. Brigadier Naser really went out of way to ensure that Brigadier M.L. Khetarpal had a satisfying and nostalgic visit to his old house in Sargodha. Upon his return to Lahore he was once again the guest of Brigadier Naser for three days.

Brigadier M.L. Khetarpal was overwhelmed by the extreme kindness, deference, courtesy and respect bestowed upon him by Brigadier Naser and by all the members of his family and his many servants. However Brigadier Khetarpal felt that something was amiss but could not make out what it was. Was it the long silences that punctuated their animated conversation or was it the look of compassion in the eyes of the women in the family? He could not make out but was sure he was being treated as someone very special.

Finally, on the last night before Brigadier M.L. Khetarpal's departure, Brigadier Naser said 'Sir, there is something that I wanted to tell you for many years but I did not know how to get through to you. Finally, fate has intervened and sent you to me as an honoured guest. The last few days we have become close to one another and that has made my task even more difficult. It is regarding your son who is, of course, a national hero in India. However on that fateful day, your son and I were soldiers, unknown to one another, fighting for the respect and safety of our respective countries. I regret to tell you that your son died in my hands. Arun's courage was exemplary and he moved his tank with fearless courage and daring, totally unconcerned about his safety. Tank casualties were very high till finally there were just two of us left facing one another. We both fired simultaneously. It was destined that I was to live and he was to die.

It was only later that I got to know how young he was and who he was.I had all along thought that I would ask your forgiveness, but in telling the story I realize that there is nothing to forgive. Instead I salute your son for what he did at such a young age and I salute you too, because I know how he grew into such a young man. In the end it is character and values that matter."

Brigadier M.L. Khetarpal was silent as he did not know how to react.To be enjoying the hospitality of the person who had killed his son was a confusing feeling. However being a soldier himself he genuinely admired the chivalry of an officer whose complete squadron was decimated by his son.

Both the Brigadiers retired for the night deep in thought. There are never any victors in war; both sides lose and it is the families that have to pay the price and suffer the most. As someone once said 'Wars are created by politicians, compounded by bureaucrats and fought by soldiers.'

The next day photographs were taken and Brigadier M.L. Khetarpal returned to Delhi. Later the photos reached Delhi along with a note from Brigadier Naser that said:

"With Warmest regards and utmost sincerity, To: Brigadier M.L. Khetarpal, father of Shaheed Second Lieutenant Arun Khetarpal, PVC, who stood like an unsurmountable rock, between the victory and failure, of the counterattack by the 'SPEARHEADS' 13 LANCERS on 16 December 1971 in the battle of "Bara Pind' as we call it and battle of "Basantar" as 17 Poona Horse remembers. —Khawja Mohammad Naser, 13 Lancers, 2 March 2001, Lahore, Pakistan.

## IC-25067 SECOND LIEUTENANT KHETARPAL, ARUN, PVC(POSTHUMOUS) 17 HORSE(POONA HORSE)

He was born in Pune,Maharashtra, was an officer of the Indian Army and a posthumous recipient of the Param Vir Chakra from Delhi. India's highest military decoration for valour in face of the enemy. On 16 December 1971 when our position at Jarpal in the Shakargarh Sector was subjected to an attack by a Pakistani armoured regiment and our troops were heavily outnumbered by enemy forces, the squadron commander asked for reinforcements. 2nd Lt Arun Khetarpal, on hearing this transmission over the radio, answered the call and moved with his troop to meet the enemy attack. On the way, his troop came under fire from enemy strong points and recoillless gun nests that were still holding out in the bridgehead established across the Basantar river by our troops. Realising that a critical situation was developing and prompt action was to be taken, 2nd Lt Khetarpal assaulted the enemy strong points, physically overrunning them and capturing the enemy's infantry and weapon crews at pistol point.

In the course of this action, the commander of one of the tanks in his troops was killed but, 2nd Lt Khetarpal continued to attack relentlessly till all opposition was overcome and he broke through towards the location of our squadron. When enemy tanks started pulling back after their initial probing attacks, he chased them and destroyed one of them. When the enemy launched another attack with an armoured squadron, against the sector held by three of our tanks, one of which was manned by 2nd Lt Khetarpal, a fierce battle ensued and 10 enemy tanks were hit and destroyed of which 2nd Lt Khetarpal personally destroyed four.

In the fight 2nd Lt Khetarpal's tank was hit and it burst into flames and he was severely wounded. 2nd Lt Khetarpal was ordered to abandon his tank but realising that the enemy was still pressing the attack in this sector and that if he abandoned his tank, the enemy would break through, he continued engaging the enemy despite the grievous wounds and his own tank burning. He destroyed one more enemy tank before his tank was hit a second time, killing him. But the enemy had been denied the breakthrough he was seeking so desperately. In this action 2nd Lt Arun Khetarpal displayed the most conspicuous gallantry in the face of the enemy, indomitable fighting spirit and tenacity of purpose.

## MAJ GEN RAJ MEHTA, AVSM, VSM (RETD)

What can one say of a shy, self effacing, embodiment of the Chetwode motto who died? That he was disarmingly handsome and brave; that he was an inspirational leader and the *Fakhr-e-Hind* of his beloved country, India? That he was admired in death by his opposing number of the Pakistani Armoured Corps. That much and so much more can be said and written about this bravest of brave young officers, who willingly and selflessly gave up his tomorrow for the Indian Army's priceless historical legacy of *naam, namak* and *nishan*. Go home therefore, dear reader, and tell them of him and say, with pride and with passion, that 2/Lt Arun Khetarpal, PVC, (Posthumous), by the manner of his military skills, deathless spirit and his death, brought rare honour to his distinguished cavalry regiment, *The Poona Horse* and to soldiering, even as his life blood left his shattered body after he had engaged and destroyed his fourth Pakistani Patton tank. He gave up his today for our tomorrow...

Born on 14 October 1950, in Pune, Arun Khetarpal came from a family with a long military tradition. His great-grandfather had served in the Sikh army and fought against the British at the close run battle of Chillianwala in 1848. His grandfather served in the British army during the First World War and Arun's father, Brigadier ML Khetarpal, was a Sapper officer. Arun studied at the famous Lawrence School, Sanawar. He joined the National Defence Academy in 1967 (38th NDA course, 'Foxtrot' Squadron; he became Squadron Cadet Captain). He was commissioned into *The Poona Horse* on June 13, 1971. The unit was termed *'Fakhr-e-Hind'* by Pakistan after its 1965 battle performance in the Sialkot Sector.

My association with him began in those early days in 1971, when we knew with certainty that we would go to war with Pakistan. I was then a young officer in *16 Light Cavalry*, in 16 Independent Armoured Brigade. Just before we mobilized in late September for moving to the border in J&K, my Regiment played a closely contested basketball match with *The Poona Horse*. Playing for them was Arun. Still to do his Young Officers' Course, he was an average player but a wonderful friend; shy, intense, very driven. Given his movie star looks, his tall, slim frame, his deportment and his pedigreed conduct, he endeared himself to all. That evening, we met at his Officers Mess bar.

Arun surprised all the young officers present by suddenly announcing that, in the coming war; he would die and would be rewarded for gallantry. An awkward silence followed but something in his quiet, convincing demeanour and the intensity with which he made his remark made me believe his premonition.

During the 1971 indo- Pak War, 17 Poona Horse was placed under command 47 Infantry Brigade of 54 Infantry Division in the Shakargarh Bulge opposite Samba, J and K. It was superbly victorious in what we term as the Battle of Basantar and Pakistan terms as the Battle of Barapind. The essence of what happened was that the Brigade was tasked to establish a bridgehead on night December 15, 1971, across the Basantar River, using *The Poona Horse* to provide its Infantry operations and the attacking troops protection and later, spearhead its operations. The enemy's 8 Armoured Brigade sensed the danger and chose to counterattack the bridgehead post-haste, to deny the Indian Army further ingress along this axis that was headed straight for Shakargarh town, the physical and psychological centre of gravity of the Shakargarh Bulge.

At 0800 hours on December 16, Pakistani 13 Lancers equipped with the then state of the art US made 50 ton Patton tanks launched the first of their counter-attacks under the cover of a smokescreen at 'B' Squadron, *The Poona Horse*, at Jarpal. Its squadron commander urgently called for reinforcements. Arun Khetarpal, who was in 'A' squadron and was stationed close by with his Centurion tank troop, responded with alacrity. , as did the rest of his regiment. The first counter attack was decimated by accurate gunnery, coolness by our tank troop and individual tank commanders from the iconic CO,Lt Col (later Lt Gen) Hanut Singh, MVC downwards to its dashing troop leader, Arun Khetarpal. 13 Lancers desperately launched two more squadron level counterattacks, but to no avail and at savage cost in men and material to this otherwise old and well established cavalry regiment.

Arun destroyed three tanks, but was seriously wounded, along with the driver of his tank, *'Famagusta'* when firing at the third tank. When engaging his fourth tank manned by then Major (later Brigadier) Khwaja Mohammad Naser, the opposing squadron commander, his tank was hit for the second time. Deployed across the Basantar River on December 16, 1971, a few kilometres away from his battle, I heard his last radio message. Mortally injured and bleeding, he radioed his squadron commander: "No Sir, I will not abandon my tank. My gun is still working and I will get these ......" He did, dying as he knocked off his fourth Patton tank. He was awarded the Param Vir Chakra posthumously. He was the embodiment of the spirit of*Naam, Namak* and *Nishan* and of the Chetwode Motto.

Many years later, India and Pakistan established 'people to people' contact also known as 'Twin Track Diplomacy'. In 2001, Brigadier Khetarpal felt a strong desire to visit his birthplace at Sargodha, now in Pakistan. Twin Track Diplomacy and contacts thereof ensured that the visit took place. At Lahore airport, Brigadier Khetarpal was met by Brigadier Khwaja Mohammad Naser, who took it upon himself to be his host and guide. Brigadier Naser really went out of way to ensure that Brigadier Khetarpal had a satisfying and nostalgic visit to his old house. The hospitality of Pakistanis is legendary, but Arun's father sensed that behind the exceptional treatment he got from Brigadier Naser and his family, there was some unusual motivation, but could not pinpoint it. Finally the stunning disclosure was made. On the eve of his departure, Brigadier Naser told him that "I regret to tell you that your son died in my hands. Arun's courage was exemplary and he moved his tank with fearless courage and daring, totally unconcerned about his safety. Tank casualties were very high till finally there were just two of us left facing one another. We both fired simultaneously. It was destined that I was to live and he was to die"... The brave father realised that the Pakistani officer had, in confessing, paid a great tribute to Arun and, in so doing, put his own soldier's conscience at causing Arun's death at rest. Later, Brig Khetarpal received a letter from Brigadier Naser that said that Arun had "stood like an insurmountable rock, between the victory and failure of the counter attack by the

'SPEARHEADS' – 13 LANCERS – on December 16, 1971 in the battle of "Bara Pind' as we call it and battle of 'Basantar' as *The 17 Poona Horse* remembers it...

In 1981, I was shocked to receive my posting to the NDA as an Instructor. By an unwritten convention, only ex NDA officers are posted there. I was amongst the privileged few from the OTS who broke this convention as I was an "outsider". I remember standing in front of Arun Khetarpal's portrait in Sudan Block, where the bravest of the brave are eternally sequestered within frames of gold-rimmed portraits; testimony to the Academy's motto of Service Before Self and a source of deathless inspiration. I took an oath then, that I would honour the NDA spirit in all I did in my military career. In subsequent command of my Regiment, a Rashtriya Rifles Sector in Kashmir, an Armoured Brigade, a Division on the Line of Control in Kashmir, I never forgot this pledge.

When I lay seriously wounded on the snow after an encounter with Pakistani terrorists in South Kashmir in January 1998 (I was then a Brigadier in command of a Rashtriya Rifles Sector in South Kashmir), I remembered Arun's gutsy 'spirit and slogged on, refusing pain killing morphine. Hours after I was wounded, we had shot three of the terrorists (we lost two soldiers) and it was only then that I allowed myself to be carried on a stretcher for evacuation by helicopter toSrinagar'sArmyBaseHospital.

West Point, the United States Military Academy after which NDA is modeled, has a poignant unofficial motto: "Much of the history we teach was made by soldier's we taught." One realises how true the motto is for the NDA and, indeed, for soldiers and soldiering worldwide.

Much of modern India's military history has been written by brave hearts like Arun Khetarpal who departed NDA's portals carrying the torch held by Tanaji Malusare, the General who left his son's marriage on Shivaji's command to capture the strategic fortress of Sinhgarh that today overlooks the NDA campus and for whom Shivaji, in February 1670, paid the ultimate eulogy: *'Garh Ala pan Sinh Gela'* (I have got the Fort but have lost my Lion). Indeed, the Sinhgad Fort today oversees the NDA spirit both physically and metaphorically. The 26/29 November terror strike at Mumbai yet again saw the NDA spirit on display in the ultimate sacrifice paid by young Major Sandeep Unnikrishnan, an ex NDA whose heroic death paved the way to the NSG's success in a hugely complex and difficult operation that held the world's attention riveted during its tenancy.

The Indian armed forces and certainly the Indian Mechanised Forces carry the flag once carried by 2/Lt Arun Khetarpal high, very high indeed. Whether NDA, Direct Entry or from the OTA; whether they are men or women officers or simple tank men; Arun's tank *'Famagusta'* now restored, is displayed at the Armoured Corps Centre and School at Ahmednagar. It is here that future Arun Khetarpal's whether tank men or of mechanized infantry learn their profession of arms. Arun's memorial remains a powerful, irresistible beacon encouraging new generations of soldiers and officers across gender to walk the extra mile; to embody the Army's motto of 'Service Before Self' always and every time the need arises.

# 9

# Param Vir Capt Gurbachan Singh Salaria

Captain Gurbachan Singh Salaria, PVC (born 29 November 1935; Gurdaspur, Punjab – 5 December 1961) is a military war hero, who was awarded the Param Vir Chakra, India's highest wartime military award. In the 1988 television serial *Param Vir Chakra* by Chetan Anand, Captain G.S. Salaria was played by actor Brando Bakshi.

Two bullets had pierced his neck. The blood was seeping down and soaking his shirt. Right ahead he could see the gendarmerie running away. Some of his brave and gutsy Gorkhas were still giving chase.

He did not resist when an immense weariness enveloped him. He had lost too much blood. His task had been achieved and he was at peace.

Closing his eyes, Capt Gurbachan Singh Salaria of 3/1 Gorkha Rifles, dropped his rifle and fell, drifting into unconsciousness from which he would never awaken. Many years earlier, when Salaria had joined the Gorkha Rifles, he had been told that his regiment's motto was: It is better to die than to be a coward: Kafar hunu bhanda marnu ramro.

Salaria had lived up to the motto. Salaria fancied himself a palmist. Before the Congo deployment in February 1961, he had visited Chotta Shimla for some work and run into an excise officer, who used to read people's palms.

Reading Salaria's hand, the officer told him that there was a star on his mount of Jupiter, which would bring him great fame. Salaria took the prediction very seriously and would often point it out to fellow officers in lighter moments.

Maj Gen RP Singh recalls Salaria showing him his own right hand. He pointed out the star on his mount of Jupiter. 'Wait and see, this star will take me to great heights,' he said. Singh had leaned over to feel the mount, but only out of politeness. 'I just shrugged it off as I never took his knowledge of palmistry seriously,' the general recounts.

'I did not know that his day of reckoning and attaining fame was just a few days away. Or that he would never know of this fame since it would come when he was in his heavenly abode,' he says quietly.

Gurbachan Singh Salaria was born on 29 November 1935 in a village called Janwal, near Shakargarh, now in Pakistan. The second of five children, he was a favourite of his grandmother, who would tie a black thread around his waist to keep the evil eye away from him.

Gurbachan's father Munshi Ram was in the Armoured Corps of the British Indian Army and would move from one Army cantonment to another, coming home only on annual or casual leave.

When he did come home, it was celebration time. Friends and family would drop in to listen to his awe-inspiring tales of faraway places where soldiers performed great acts of bravery. Little Gurbachan and his siblings would listen to their father in rapt attention. Quite possibly this is how Gurbachan was inspired to be courageous.

Gurbachan would go to school regularly, but was always more occupied with games and outdoor activities rather than studying. He was a good kabaddi player, and continued to be good at sports even after he cleared the entrance to King George's Royal Military College (KGRMC), Bangalore. Though he was initially rejected in the physical exam because his chest was found to be an inch less than the stipulated measurements, he was given a month to try again. He took the challenge head on, drinking one litre of goat's milk every day and exercising passionately.

When he went back for his medical, he had managed to increase his chest by two-and-a-half inches and was immediately admitted. He joined the college in August 1946 as a cadet. In 1947, he was transferred to KGRMC Jullundur, which was closer to his village. When he was in his second year, Gurbachan and a friend were once bullied and insulted by another cadet. Gurbachan's self-respect took a blow but he challenged the bully to a boxing match the next day. He boxed with such fury that the bully was knocked out and had to apologise. The operation in Congo was very reminiscent of this incident; where Gurbachan took on a much bigger and better equipped enemy fighting force just because he wanted to teach them a lesson in war ethics.

Gurbachan went on to the National Defence Academy and then the Indian Military Academy. He joined 2/3 Gorkha Rifles in July 1954 where he was nicknamed Khan Saheb by his commanding officer because of his cropped hair cut and upturned moustache.

In March 1960, he received orders, transferring him to 3/1 Gorkha Rifles. And that was where General R P Singh, who was then the battalion adjutant, met him. General Singh found Salaria to be a simple man, spartan and very careful with money, unlike other young officers, many of whom had extravagant tastes. In fact, Salaria once told him, he recalled, that he was sending money home to FINANCE the education of his younger brother Sukhdev, at college in Jammu. Sukhdev is now 75 and lives in Pathankot. He is bedridden and has lost his sense of balance, but he remembers fondly how, when he and Gurbachan were little boys - Gurbachan was older by two years - they would go swimming in the small stream that ran across their village.

'We had no worries then; we would splash around in the stream. What beautiful days they were. Now Gurbachan is gone and I can't walk, but whenever I think of him that is the first memory that streams into my head,' says the old man, sinking back into silence. He has more memories to recount but his strength fails him.

## EARLY LIFE

He was born in a Rajput family of Punjab State. He started his education at the famousBangalore Military School, Bangalore (erstwhile King George School, Bangalore (more popularly known as King George Royal Indian Military College [KGRIMC], Bangalore) before moving to King George School, Jalandhar (now known as Chail Military School). He joined the 9th batch of National Defence Academy at Khadakwasla. He was in 'Bravo' squadron. His cadet number was 1317.

### Salaria Sainis

Salaria is the largest Saini clan in rural Gurdaspur, Shakargarh, Jammu and the area bordering Sialkot district of Pakistan. Salaria Sainis dominte in over 17 villages in this area which includes village Jangla which Captain Gurbachan Singh Salaria hailed from.

There are a number of Saini clans which are common with Hill Rajputs. Salaria is one such clan. Some other Saini clans , besides Salaria, overlapping with Rajputs on hills are : Dhamrait (Dhamrial) , Mangar (Mangwal/Mangral), Gahunia (Gohaina), Dheri (Dheria), Oghre (Oghial), Gaheer (Gahotra), Aannay (Anotra), Maheru (Mahotra), Khar Khatri, Farad, Basuta (Basotra), Masuta (Masotra), Dhanota (Dhanotra), Biloria, Baunsar, Jagait (Jaggi), Badwal, Chandel, Vaid, etc.

### Attack of Elizabethville, Katanga

It was December 5th 1961 when the Gorkha Rifles were delegated the responsibility of clearing a roadblock created by constabulary at Elizabthville, Katanga. The plan was preconceived that one company along with two Swedish armored cars would attack from the front, whereas Captain Gurbachan Singh Salaria will take two sections of Gorkhas and two Swedish armored personnel carriers with him and would pursue the attack from the airfield. The moment Captain Gurbachan arrived near the roadblock at a distance if 1500 yards he came under a severe attack of small-arms firing from an unseen and predetermined positions of the enemy.

The enemy had armored cars of 90 men that were ready to attack Captain Gurbachan and his small section of men force. While seeing his sections being trapped by the enemy, he decided to terminate every single member of the enemy crew. Gurbachan ran into a subsidiary roadblock in order to hide himself for the moment and planned his strategy to end the enemy. He then took up the charge with khukris, knives and grenades sustained by a rocket launcher. Nothing could stop Captain Gurbachan, then he bayoneted 40 men of the enemy crew and trashed two armored cars.

The enemy was completely astonished to see such bravado of Gurbachan Singh in front of them and this made them so frightened that even being bigger in numbers they rather decided to back out and fled away. Captain Gurbachan Singh Salaria was badly wounded in his neck and had a severe blood loss, but he still continued to fight the battle because he was much more concerned and focused towards his responsibility of succeeding in the operation. His gallantry actions made him achieve his operation, he was successful in rescuing the UN headquarters and motivated the small strength of his men force to fight against a big number of enemies. He subsequently died of his injuries. But his persistent leadership spirit made him a deserving receiver of the Param Vir Chakra.

## MILITARY CAREER

Commissioned in the 1st Gorkha Rifles (the Malaun Regiment) on 9 June 1957, he was posted to the third battalion of the Regiment. In 1961, Salaria was posted abroad with his battalion in Katanga.

After the Belgians quit Congo, a civil war situation developed in that country. When the United Nations decided upon military intervention to retrieve the situation, Indiacontributed a brigade of around 3000 men to the U.N. force. In November 1961, the U.N.Security Council decided to put a stop to the hostile activities of the Katangese troops in Congo. This greatly angered Tshombe, Katanga's secessionist leader, and he intensified his 'hate the UN' campaign. The result was more violence against UN personnel.

On 5 December 1961, a 3/1 GR Company supported by 3-inch mortar attacked a road-block, established by the Katangese troops, between HQ Katanga command and the Elizabethville airfield at a strategic roundabout. The enemy roadblock was destroyed and the Gorkhas established a UN roadblock there. When Captain Salaria, with his platoon, tried to link up with the Gorkha Company to reinforce the roadblock, he met strong opposition in the old airfield area.

The enemy held the area strongly with two armoured cars and 90 men and brought down heavy automatic and small arms fire on his force from a dug-in position on the right flank. Undeterred by the superior enemy strength and firepower, Salaria decided to take the enemy, head-on, to achieve the objective. The Gorkhas then charged the enemy with bayonets, khukris and hand-grenades. A rocket launcher supported them in the attack. In this sharp encounter, Captain Salaria and his men killed 40 of the enemy and knocked out two enemy cars. His bold action completely demoralised the enemy who fled despite numerical superiority and well-fortified positions. In the engagement, Captain Salaria was wounded in the neck by a burst of enemy automatic fire. Ignoring the injury, he continued to fight till he collapsed due to excessive bleeding, dying subsequently of his wounds.

Captain Salaria's actions prevented the Katangese rebels from encircling the UN Headquarters in Elisabethville. His leadership, courage, unflinching devotion to duty and disregard for personal safety were in the best traditions of the Indian Army and for which Captain Gurbachan Singh Salaria was posthumously awarded the highest wartime medal, Param Vir Chakra.

## Citation

The Param Vir Chakra citation on the Official Indian Army Website reads as follows:

**CITATION**

**CAPTAIN GURBACHAN SINGH SALARIA**

**3/1 GORKHA RIFLES (IC-8947)**

On 5 December 1961, 3/1 Gorkha Rifles was ordered to clear a roadblock established by the gendarmerie at a strategic roundabout at Elizabethville , Katanga. The plan was that one company with 2 Swedish armoured cars would attack the position frontally and Captain Gurbachan Singh Salaria with two sections of Gorkhas and two Swedish armoured personnel carriers would advance towards this roadblock from the airfield to act as a cutting-off force.

Captain Salaria with his small force arrived at a distance of 1500 yards from the roadblock at approximately 1312 hours on 5 December 1961 and came under heavy automatic and small-arms fire from an undetected enemy position dug in on his right flank. The enemy also had two armoured cars and about 90 men opposing Captain Salaria's small force.

Captain Salaria appreciating that he had run into a subsidiary roadblock and ambush and that this enemy force might reinforce the strategic roundabout and thus jeopardise the main operation, decided to remove this opposition. He led a charge with bayonets, khukris, and grenades supported by a rocket launcher. In this gallant engagement, Captain Salaria killed 40 of the enemy and knocked out the two armoured cars. This unexpected bold action completely demoralised the enemy who fled despite their numerical superiority and protected positions.

Captain Salaria was wounded in his neck by a burst of automatic fire but continued to fight till he collapsed due to profuse bleeding. Captain Salaria's gallant action prevented any enemy movement of the enemy force towards the main battle scene and thus contributed very largely to the success of the main battalion's action at the roundabout and prevented the encirclement of UN Headquarters in Elizabethville. Captain Salaria subsequently died of his wounds.

## Gallantry Award Citation

*"On 5 December 1961, 3/1 Gorkha Rifles was ordered to clear a roadblock established by the gendarmerie at a strategic roundabout at Elizabethville, Katanga. The plan was that one company with 2 Swedish armoured cars would attack the position frontally and Captain Gurbachan Singh Salaria with two sections of Gorkhas and two Swedish armoured personnel carriers would advance towards this roadblock from the airfield to act as a cutting-off force.*

*Captain Salaria with his small force arrived at a distance of 1500 yards from the roadblock at approximately 1312 hours on 5 December 1961 and came under heavy automatic and small-arms fire from an undetected enemy position dug in on his right flank. The enemy also had two armoured cars and about 90 men opposing Captain Salaria's small force.*

*Captain Salaria appreciating that he had run into a subsidiary roadblock and ambush and that this enemy force might reinforce the strategic roundabout and thus jeopardize the main operation, decided to remove this opposition. He led a charge with bayonets, khukris, and grenades supported by a rocket launcher. In this gallant engagement, Captain Salaria killed 40 of the enemy and knocked out the two armoured cars. This unexpected bold action completely demoralised the enemy who fled despite their numerical superiority and protected positions.*

*Captain Salaria was wounded in his neck by a burst of automatic fire but continued to fight till he collapsed due to profuse bleeding. Captain Salaria's gallant action prevented any enemy movement of the enemy force towards the main battle scene and thus contributed very largely to the success of the main battalion's action at the roundabout and prevented the encirclement of UN Headquarters in Elizabethville. Captain Salaria subsequently died of his wounds.*

*Captain Salaira's personal example, utter disregard for personal safety and dauntless leadership inspired his small but gallant force of sixteen Gorkhas to hold on to their position, dominate the enemy and to inflict heavy casualties despite the enemy's superiority in numbers and tactical position.*

*Captain Gurbachan Singh Salaria's leadership, courage, and unflinching devotion to duty and disregard for personal safety were in the best traditions of our Army."*

# 10

# Captain Vikram Batra

Captain Vikram Batra, another champion of India's 1999 Kargil War, was instrumental in recovering Peak 5140 situated at a height of 17,000 feet from the enemy. Batra knew the vital criticalness of the crest and completed a challenging mission in power to recover the peak. An enemy counterattack cut short his life but not before he had recaptured Peak 5140 with his last words – Jai Mata Di. Here's a bit of trivia: Abhishek Bachchan played Batra's part in the film LOC Kargil.

Vikram Batra is one of the recipients of Param Vir Chakra, the highest military decoration of India.

Captain Vikram Batra PVC (September 9, 1974 – July 7, 1999) was an officer of the Indian Army, posthumously awarded the Param Vir Chakra, India's highest award for valour, for his actions during the 1999Kargil War in Kashmir between India and Pakistan.

Captain Vikram Batra was awarded the Param Vir Chakra, India's highest military honor on 15 August 1999, the 52nd anniversary of India's independence. His father Mr. G.L. Batra received the honor for his deceased son from the President of India, the late K.R. Narayanan.

Captain Vikram Batra, 13 JAK Rifles, and his Delta Company was given the task of recapturing Point 5140. Nicknamed *Sher Shah* ('Lion King' in Hindi) for his unstinting courage, he decided to lead the rear, as an element of surprise would help stupefy the enemy. He and his men ascended the sheer rock-cliff, but as the group neared the top, the enemy pinned them on the face of the bare cliff with machine gun fire. Captain Batra, along with five of his men, climbed up regardless and after reaching the top, hurled two grenades at the machine gun post. He single-handedly killed three enemy soldiers in close combat. He was seriously injured during this, but insisted on regrouping his men to continue with the mission. Inspired by the courage displayed by Captain Batra, the soldiers of 13 JAK Rifles charged the enemy position and captured Point 5140 at 3:30 a.m. on 20 June 1999. His company is credited with killing at least eight Pakistani soldiers and recovering a heavy machine gun.

The capture of Point 5140 set in motion a string of successes, such as Point 5100, Point 4700, Junction Peak and Three Pimples. Along with fellow Captain Anuj Nayyar, Batra led his men to victory with the recapture of Point 4750 and Point 4875. He was killed when he tried to rescue an injured officer during an enemy counterattack against Point 4875 in the early morning hours of 7 July 1999. His last words were, "*Jai Mata Di.*" (which means in Punjabi 'Hail the Divine Mother'). For his sustained display of the most conspicuous personal bravery and leadership of the highest order in the face of the enemy, Captain Vikram Batra was awarded the Param Vir Chakra.

## EARLY LIFE AND CAREER

Vikram Batra was born on 9 September 1974 in Ghuggar village near Palampur,Himachal Pradesh, to G.L. Batra and Jai Kamal Batra. He got his primary education from his mother, who herself is a teacher. He received his education up to Middle Standard at the D.A.V. Public School in Palampur and up to senior secondary stage in Central School, Palampur. After passing his 10+2 in 1992 from Central School Palampur, he got admitted in D.A.V. College, Chandigarh in B.Sc where he was adjudged the best N.C.C. Cadet (Air Wing) in two zones. Later, he was selected to join the Indian Military Academy in Dehradun in 1996 in Jessore company of Manekshaw Battalion, and was commissioned in the Indian Army as a Lieutenant of the 13

Jammu & Kashmir Rifles at Sopore, in Jammu and Kashmir. He rose to the rank of Captain.

## Kargil War

On 1 June 1999, his unit proceeded to the Kargil Sector on the eruption of a war-like situation in Kargil, Drass and Batalik sub-sectors from where he was sent along with his company on the first strategic and daring operation to recapture the first peak of utmost importance - Point 5140, which was at an altitude of 17,000 feet.

Captain Vikram Batra, 13 JAK Rifles, and his Delta Company was given the task of recapturing Point 5140. Nicknamed *Sher Shah* ('Lion King') inHindi for his courage which also doubled as his call sign, he decided to lead the rear, as an element of surprise would help stupefy the enemy.

He and his men ascended the sheer rock-cliff, but as the group neared the top, the enemy pinned them on the face of the bare cliff with machine gun fire. Captain Batra, along with five of his men, climbed up regardless and after reaching the top,hurled two grenades at the machine gun post. He single-handedly killed three enemy soldiers in close combat.

He was seriously injured during this, but insisted on regrouping his men to continue with the mission. Inspired by the courage displayed by Captain Batra, the soldiers of 13 JAK Rifles charged the enemy position and captured Point 5140 at 3:30 a.m. on 20 June 1999. His company is credited with killing at least eight Pakistani soldiers and recovering a heavy machine gun.

The capture of Point 5140 set in motion a string of successes, such as Point 5100, Point 4700, Junction Peak and Three Pimples. Along with fellow Captain Anuj Nayyar, Batra led his men to victory with the recapture of Point 4750 and Point 4875. In the early morning hours of 7 July 1999, he was commanding a mission to rescue an injured officer during an enemy counterattack against Point 4875. During the rescue attempt, he pushed aside his Subedar, saying *"Tu baal-bacchedar hain, hat ja peeche."(You have children, step aside)* and waskilled in action while clearing enemy positions. His last words were, "*Jai Mata Di.*", which is a Punjabi creed referring to Durgadevi, theHindu Goddess of Victory.

## PARAM VIR CHAKRA

The Param Vir Chakra citation on the Official Indian Army Website reads as follows:

**CITATION: CAPTAIN VIKRAM BATRA**
**13 JAMMU AND KASHMIR RIFLES (IC 57556)**

During 'Operation Vijay', on 20 June 1999, Captain Vikram Batra, Commander Delta Company was tasked to attack Point 5140. Captain Batra with his company skirted around the feature from the East and maintaining surprise reached within assaulting distance of the enemy. Captain Batra reorganized his column and motivated his men to physically assault the enemy positions.

Leading from the front, he in a daredevil assault, pounced on the enemy and killed four of them in a hand-to hand fight. On 7 July 1999, in another operation in the area Pt 4875, his company was tasked to clear a narrow feature with sharp cuttings on either side and heavily fortified enemy defences that covered the only approach to it. For speedy operation, Captain Batra assaulted the enemy position along a narrow ridge and engaged the enemy in a fierce hand –to-hand fight and killed five enemy soldiers at point blank range.

Despite sustaining grave injuries, he crawled towards the enemy and hurled grenades clearing the position with utter disregard to his personal safety, leading from the front, he rallied his men and pressed on the attack and achieved a near impossible military task in the face of heavy enemy fire. The officer, however, succumbed to his injuries. Inspired by his daredevil act, his troops fell upon the enemy with vengeance, annihilated them and captured Point 4875.

Captain Vikram Batra, thus, displayed the most conspicuous personal bravery and leadership of the highest order in the face of the enemy and made the supreme sacrifice in the highest traditions of the Indian Army.

## Legacy

Captain Batra is also well known in India for using the slogan, *Yeh Dil Maange More!* as his signal to communicate mission success. He is also known for an interview in which he stated that Pakistani Soldiers were aware of him as "Sher Shah" and addressed him as such in the middle of engagements. He is also honoured with several landmarks being named after him: A hall at Service Selection Center Allahabad is named 'Vikram Batra Block', a residential area in the Jabalpur Cantonment is called 'Captain Vikram Batra Enclave' and the combined cadet's mess at the IMA is named 'Vikram Batra Mess'.

## LEGENDARY TALE OF 'CAPTAIN VIKRAM BATRA': THE 'SHER SHAH' OF INDIAN ARMY

New Delhi: "I'll either come back after raising the Indian flag in victory or return wrapped in it, but I will come for sure," last words of brave Captain Vikram Batra who snatched point 4875 from the enemies and waved the Indian flag there. In his honour, Indian government renamed it as Vikram Batra top. On 19 June 1999, under the leadership of Captain Vikarm Batra, Indian army had snatched point 5140, a strategic peak, from right under the enemy's nose.

After this successful operation of Point 5140, Captain Batra volunteered himself for the next mission to recapture point 4875. Though it was an uphill task considering it the point was 17,000 feet above the sea level, 80 degree steep centigrade along with razor sharp edges from both the sides.

However, recapturing point 4875 was crucial from India's perspective, as heavily armed infiltrators sitting at top could have dominated the road to Leh, accessed Mushkoh Valley and launched hefty attack on Indian troops. The army was marching ahead under the leadership of Lieutenant Naveen (aide of Batra). On July 7, after a 36 hour long battle, Captain Naveen got badly injured after a deadly hand grenade attack from the enemy.

Soon after, Captain Batra rescued Captain Naveen and he himself took the charge saying "tu baal bache wala hai, piche hat".

As he took the charge, enemy started playing the physiological game and demoralized Captain Batra saying, "Sher Shah naam rakhne se koi sher nhi ban jaate"

They even taunted Captain Batra saying, "If India handovers Bollywood actress Madhuri Dixit to them, they will leave the place forever". Captain Batra gave a fitting reply "Madhuri ji to busy hain, me aa jata hun".

Amid deadly firing from the enemy, Captain Batra continually charged ahead holding gun in his hand, as he kept firing at the infiltrators. Until a bullet hit on his chest; with the words 'Jai Mata Di' on his lips, he fell down and as he lay there another bullet hit him in the waist by an artillery splinter.

Before giving away to his grievous injuries, this brave son of India killed another five enemy soldiers. The point 4875 was now under the control of Indian contingent, the national flag was waving there, but alas Captain was no more alive to celebrate the victory.

For his gallant act, unmatched bravery, contribution and excellence, the government of India honored him with highest military honor, The Param Vir Chakra and renamed the Point 4875 as Captain Vikram Batra Top.

Before going to war, Captian Batra had said "I'll either come back after raising the Indian flag in victory or return wrapped in it, but I will come for sure."

This great soldier will always remain alive in the hearts of Indians who are safe in their houses. You can also pay tribute to Vikram Batra.

# 11

# Captain Manoj Kumar Pandey

Born on 25 June 1975 in family of Shri Gopi Chand Pandey, Captain Manoj was a brilliant student & sportsman. He was always top in his academics & won hundreds of certificates and cups during his schooling. He cleared NDA in his first attempt, in his SSB interview his assessor asked why do you want to join army-he replayed, to get PARAM VIR CHAKRA.......& he got it.

Capt. Manoj Kumar Pandey was a man with a laughing face and happy disposition. He did his schooling at "Rani Laxmibai College" , from there he went to "U.P.Sainik school. He always got first rank in his academics, besides, he was a an all round sports man. His hobbies were Hockey, Swimming and athletics.

His mother Smt. Mohini Pandey inspired him towards the morality and spirituality. He did faith in God and had very clear thought about life and death. He firmly believed that everyone has a certain period of life hence one should do something great to inspire the people. he loved children very much. He tried to collect every kind of knowledge so he chose different books to read, even he studied the books of astrology and palmistry.

About his son Captain Manoj Kumar Pandey by his own words by father :

"I am the father of a great son. I know, I can never explain him for he was beyond my understanding and imagination. But

I would like to mention some facts the country must know about him. "We belong to a small village Rudha in Sitapur district, UP. I was not well-off when Manoj was born in the same village on June 25, 1975, as my eldest son. I remember, he was very lovable and affectionate to his grand parents as well as to other family members. He was unique in every manner. At school, his subject or syllabus could never rule him, he always ruled over them. In spite of being seriously ill he got unexpected marks in his 10th examination and was appreciated by everyone.

Manoj always understood my economic condition and whenever any crisis knocked my doorstep, I found him beside me. Observing the family's condition, he started helping me in my business. He was adjudged the best cadet in NCC and was awarded by the Governor of UP. I had to spend no money on his education as he took care of himself through his scholarships.

"After Intermediate, Manoj was selected for NDA. I think this was the happiest day in his life as he had always desired to go to the Army. I cannot forget his answer to a question at SSB that he wanted to join the Force to be awarded Param Vir Chakra. This answer subsequently shocked everyone related to him as he achieved what he had said.In his own words : "One should join the Infantry in Army and in Infantry one must prefer the Gorkha Regiment". I am happy that he got both his desires fulfilled.

On commissioning, he was posted in Kashmir Valley at first. He was then posted to Siachen. On the glacier, he came across varied experiences. After coming back from the glacier, he shared all his experiences with us. He explained about the glacier's problems and Army's efforts for survival there. In his own words : "On glacier, people fight the climate more than they fight the enemy".

"His holidays were the happiest days in our family. I know those days can not come back. Those days are over with the Kargil war. But in my memory those days are still fresh. In Kargil, my dearest son made his family and the nation proud. It was Khalubar where my son displayed extraordinary courage and great leadership. In spite of knowing very well that he was going to face death, he motivated his troops through his patriotic words. He did not care for his life for he thought the nation is above everything else. I respect his feelings. Only with hand-grenades and a khukri he scared his enemy and left none to flee. And for this great deed of courage, he had to sacrifice his life. His martyrdom will continue to be an inspiration for thousands who want to follow him.

"I am proud of you, my son! You are with me every moment in my memory. You are still guiding me. Whenever I am faced with any problem I go in front of his photo, see his face and the solution is always there."

His Victories ::

Captain Manoj Kumar Pandey's regiment was in Siachen from there they got order to move to Batalik sector. His commanding officer Colonel Lalit Rai gave him responsibility to re capture Khalubar post.

Earlier, two petrol party belongs to 16 Grenadiers and 3 Punjab had gone but after 16 days there was no news of them, they all were killed by enemy's mortar and heavy machineguns fire. Here enemy has sat on an advantageous high positions.

Captain. Manoj moved to Kukarthan on where he faced heavy fire, then, he decided to get enemy in night. He halted there and waited till the night. As night falls, by taking advantage of darkness he attacked on enemy, they fought whole night to take on the post. In early morning hours, Capt. Manoj decided to end the night long battle, he, then, went up to the post without caring possible mines. He finally captured the post but lost 9 of his men.

Insatiable Capt. Manoj got yet another and difficult task to recapture Jubar post on 11 June 1999. Jubar task was critical as he was to fought in day lighted vulnerable area. He led his to enemy position through a narrow ridge. Enemy started discriminate fire on Indian Troop, he volunteered himself to locate the position of enemy and hit by a bullet in his sholder. But, determined Capt. charged at the enemy with a full throught battle cry Jai Maha Kali, Aayo Gorkhali!!! in between he was again titted by a bullet in his waist. Indomitable Capt. Manoj continued firing at enemy's bunker.

Then he charged at enemy with his Khukhari, in hand-to-hand battle he kill two more enemy and cleared first bunker area and inspired by him his the troop fell upon the enemy. Unmindful of his grievous wounds, he rushed from bunker to bunker urging his men on. Critically bleeding, he collapsed at the final bunker and finally succumbed to his injuries, but not before the last of the enemy had been annihilated. His last words were, "Na Chodnu" (Don't Leave Them). For his sustained display of the most conspicuous personal bravery and junior leadership of the highest order in the face of the enemy, Lieutenant Manoj Kumar Pandey was awarded the Param Vir Chakra, India's highest medal for gallantry, posthumously.

## BIOGRAPHY

Born on 25$^{th}$ June, 1975, Sitapur Uttar Pradesh, he was the eldest in the family and from a middle class background. He was a keen sportsman since childhood and graduated from NDA in the 90$^{th}$ course, and joined Gorkha Rifles. Destiny had planted a fire for PVC since his teen years, as he had quoted in his SSB interview that he wanted to join the army to win PVC. He had taken an active part in many attacks during the Kargil War. On the night of 2-3$^{rd}$ July, he was leading his platoon with the objective of clearing Jubar Top, which was a very strategic point in the war. On being fired upon by the army, while still on a narrow ledge, he showed exceptional courage. He let out a battle cry and charged on the enemy and inspired his troops to display bravery, too. He killed two enemy soldiers in a hand combat and went on to capture the point. However, due to critical bullet wounds, he went down as a martyr for the country.

### Early life

Captain Manoj Pandey, PVC belonged to Vill - Kamlapur District-Sitapur in Uttar Pradesh. He was the son of Shri Gopi

Chand Pandey, a small time businessman living in lucknow. He was eldest in his family. He was educated at Uttar Pradesh Sainik School, Lucknow, Uttar Pradesh and Rani Laxmi Bai Memorial Senior Secondary School. He had a keen interest in sports with boxing and body building in particular. He passed out from National Defence Academy in 90th course and stayed in MIKE squadron. He wanted to join Gorkha Rifles and got commissioned in the 1/11 Gorkha Rifles of the Indian Army.

Prior to his selection, during his Services Selection Board (SSB) interview, the interviewer asked him, "Why do you want to join the Army?" He immediately replied, "I want to win the Param Vir Chakra." True to his words, Captain Manoj Kumar Pandey did win the country's highest gallantry honour but posthumously.

## Kargil

He forced back the intruders on 11 June 1999 at Batalik Sector in the Kargil War. He led his men to capture the Jubar top which was considered as important due to its strategic location. Quickly sizing up the situation, the young officer led his platoon along a narrow, treacherous ridge that led to the enemy position. While still short of the objective, the enemy fired upon the Indian soldiers effectively stalling the Indian attack. Displaying great courage, he surged ahead of his troops and charged at the enemy with a full-throated battle cry through a hail of bullets.

Although wounded in the shoulder and leg, he pressed on his solitary charge with grim determination, until he closed in on the first bunker. Then in ferocious hand-to-hand combat, he killed two of the enemy and cleared the first bunker. It was the turning point.

Inspired by their leader's spontaneous valour, the troops charged at the enemy and fell upon them. Unmindful of his grievous wounds, he rushed from bunker to bunker urging his men on. Critically injured, he collapsed at the final bunker and finally succumbed to his injuries. But by this time he had already captured the bunker with his men.

## OPERATION VIJAY

Captain Manoj Kumar Pandey took part in a series of boldly led attacks during Operation Vijay; forcing back the intruders with heavy losses in Battlik including the capture of Jubbar Top.

On the night of 3 July 1999 during the advance to Khalubar as his platoon approached its final objective, it came under heavy and intense enemy fire from the surrounding heights. Captain Pandey was tasked to clear the interfering enemy positions to prevent his battalion from getting day lighted, being in a vulnerable position. He quickly moved his platoon to an advantageous position under intense enemy fire, sent one section to clear the enemy positions from the right and himself proceeded to clear the enemy positions from the left.

Captain Manoj Kumar Pandey, PVC (25 June 1975, Sitapur, Uttar Pradesh - 2/3 July 1999, Kashmir), was an officer of the Indian Army of the regiment 1/11 Gorkha Rifles, posthumously awarded the India's highest military honour, Param Vir Chakra for his audacious courage and leadership during adverse times. He died during the attack on Jubar Top, Khalubar Hills in Batalik Sector, Kargil.

Lieutenant Manoj Kumar Pandey, 1/11 Gorkha Rifles, forced back the intruders from the Batalik sector on 11 June 1999. He led his men to recapture the Jubar Top, a feature of great operational importance. But his finest hour was in the capture of Khalubar in the early morning hours of 3 July 1999. On the night of 2/3 July 1999 the battalion's progress on to its final objective, was halted by a determined enemy firmly entrenched on commanding heights. Clearing it was critical as the battalion faced the prospect of being day lighted in a vulnerable area. Lieutenant Pandey stepped forward to take on the mission. Quickly sizing up the situation, the young officer led his platoon along a narrow, treacherous ridge that led to the enemy position. While still short of the objective, the enemy fired upon the Indian soldiers effectively stalling the Indian attack. Displaying great courage, he surged ahead of his troops and charged at the enemy with a full throated battle cry through a hail of bullets.

Although wounded in the shoulder and leg, he pressed on his solitary charge with grim determination, till he closed in on the first bunker. Then in ferocious hand-to-hand combat, he killed two of the enemy and cleared the first bunker. It was the turning point. Inspired by their leader's spontaneous valour, the troops charged at the enemy and fell upon them. Unmindful of his grievous wounds, he rushed from bunker to bunker urging his men on.

Critically bleeding, he collapsed at the final bunker and finally succumbed to his injuries, but not before the last of the enemy had been annihilated. His last words were, *"Na Chodnu" (Don't Leave Them).* For his sustained display of the most conspicuous personal bravery and junior leadership of the highest order in the face of the enemy, Lieutenant Manoj Kumar Pandey was awarded the Param Vir Chakra, India's highest medal for gallantry, posthumously. His father, Mr. Gopichand Pandey, received the award from the President of India, on behalf of his brave son.

## Death

Fearlessly assaulting the first enemy position, he killed two enemy personnel and destroyed the second position by killing two more. He was injured on the shoulder and legs while clearing the third position. Undaunted and without caring for his grievous injuries, he continued to lead the assault on the fourth position urging his men and destroyed the same with a grenade, even as he got a fatal burst on his forehead.

His last words were "Na chhodnu" ("Don't Spare Them" in Nepali language). This singular daredevil act of Captain Pandey provided the critical firm base for the companies, which finally led to capture of Khalubar. The officer, however, succumbed to his injuries. Captain Manoj Kumar Pandey, thus, displayed most conspicuous bravery, indomitable courage, outstanding leadership and devotion to duty and made the supreme sacrifice in the highest traditions of the Indian Army.

## Param Vir Chakra

The citation for the Param Vir Chakra awarded to him reads:

### CITATION
### (LIEUTENANT MANOJ KUMAR PANDEY)

Lieutenant Manoj Kumar Pandey took part in a series of boldly led attacks during 'operation Vijay ', forcing back the intruders with heavy losses in Battlik including the capture of Jaubar Top.

On the night of 2/3 July 1999 during the advance to Khalubar as his platoon approached its final objective, it came under heavy and intense enemy fire from the surrounding heights.

Lieutenant Pandey was tasked to clear the interfering enemy positions to prevent his battalion from getting day lighted, being in a vulnerable position.

He quickly moved his platoon to an advantageous position under intense enemy fire, sent one section to clear the enemy positions from the right and himself proceeded to clear the enemy positions from the left. Fearlessly assaulting the first enemy position, he killed two enemy personnel and destroyed the second position by killing two more.

He was injured on the shoulder and legs while clearing the third position. Undaunted and without caring for his grievous injuries, he continued to lead the assault on the fourth position urging his men and destroyed the same with a grenade, even as he got a fatal burst on his forehead.

This singular daredevil act of Lieutenant Manoj Kumar Pandey provided the critical firm base for the companies, which finally led to capture of Khalubar. The officer, however, succumbed to his injuries.

Lieutenant Manoj Kumar Pandey, thus, displayed most conspicuous bravery, indomitable courage, outstanding leadership and devotion to duty and made the supreme sacrifice in the highest traditions of the Indian Army.

## Legacy

- Manoj Kumar Pandey was awarded the Param Vir Chakra, India's highest medal for gallantry, posthumously.
- His father, Mr. Gopichand Pandey, received the award from the President of India on the 52nd Indian Republic Day.
- Uttar Pradesh Sainik School, Lucknow has its assembly hall named after Capt. Manoj Kumar Pandey.
- Uttar Pradesh Sainik School, Lucknow conducts an inter school football tournament annually as ' Late Captain Manoj Kumar Pandey memorial inter school football tournament' in school itself.
- Uttar Pradesh Sainik School, Lucknow has its main gate named after him.
- The Army Welfare Housing Organization (AWHO) designed and constructed an apartment complex for veterans in Ghaziabad district, Uttar Pradesh, and named it for Pandey as Manoj Vihar.
- The army quarters near the Cardio Thoracic Center(CTC) hospital in Pune is named after Martyr Capt Manoj Pandey as 'Capt. Manoj Pandey Enclave'
- The National Defence Academy named the science block as the 'Manoj Pandey Block'.
- A roundabout is also named after Martyr Capt.Manoj Pandey as "Captain Manoj Pandey Chowk" in his home district Sitapur, Uttar Pradesh and center of Gomti Nagar, Lucknow, Uttar Pradesh, India.
- A hall is made in the name of Capt. Manoj at Service Selection Center Allahabad named as Manoj Pandey Block.
- A gallery in the Kargil War Museum at Drass is named after him.
- In the memory of his greatest efforts to save the nation from the enemy forces, Rani Lakshmi Bai Memorial Senior Secondary School constructed an auditorium in

his name, which was inaugurated by his father and mother.

## His diary

- In his personal diary he wrote "Some goals are so worthy, it's glorious even to fail".
- In the memory of his mother read: "She is the star which shines brightly in the darkness, some one who will always give and bless."
- Just below the poem, are the four lines written in bold letters: "If death strikes before I prove my blood, I promise (swear), I will kill death."

## LIEUTENANT MANOJ KUMAR PANDEY 1/11 GORKHA RIFLES (IC 56959W)

Lieutenant Manoj Kumar Panday took part in a series of boldly led attacks during 'operation Vijay; forcing back the intruders with heavy losses in Batalik including the capture of Jabbar Top.

On the night of 2/3 July 1999 during the advance to Khalubar as his platoon approached its final objective, it came under heavy and intense enemy fire from the surrounding heights. Lieutenant Pandey was tasked to clear the interfering enemy positions to prevent his battalion from getting day lighted, being in a vulnerable position.

He quickly moved his platoon to an advantageous position under intense enemy fire, sent one section to clear the enemy positions from the right and himself proceeded to clear the enemy positions from the left. Fearlessly assaulting the first enemy position, he killed two enemy personnel and destroyed the second position by killing two more.

He was injured on the shoulder and legs while clearing the third position. Undaunted and without caring for his grievous injuries, he continued to lead the assault on the fourth position urging his men and destroyed the same with a grenade, even as he got a fatal burst on his forehead.

This singular daredevil act of Lieutenant Pandey provided the critical firm base for the companies, which finally led to capture of Khalubar. The officer, however, succumbed to his injuries.

Lieutenant Manoj Kumar Pandey, thus, displayed most conspicuous bravery, indomitable courage, outstanding leadership and devotion to duty and made the supreme sacrifice in the highest traditions of the Indian Army.

# 12

# Shaheed Lt. Saurabh Kalia

Captain Saurabh Kalia (1976–1999) was an officer of the Indian Army who died during the Kargil War while being held as a prisoner of war by the Pakistani security forces. He along with five other soldiers of his patrolling team was captured alive and kept in captivity where they were Investigated.

## Early years

Saurabh was born on 29 June 1976 at Amritsar, India to Mrs. Vijay and Dr. N.K. Kalia. His schooling took place in the D.A.V Public School Palampur. Saurabh graduated in (BSc Med.) from H. P. Agricultural University, Palampur, Himachal Pradesh in 1997. He excelled at school, securing first Division and winning scholarships throughout his academic career.

## Military career

He was selected in the Indian Military Academy, Dehradun in August 1997 through Combined Defense Services and was commissioned on 12 December 1998. His first posting was in the 4 JAT Regiment (Infantry) in the Kargil Sector. Saurabh arrived there in mid-January 1999 after reporting at the Jat Regimental Centre, Bareilly on 31 December 1998.

## Kargil war

In the first two weeks of May 1999, several patrols were conducted in the Kaksar Langpa area of Kargil to check whether the snow had retreated enough for the summer positions to be re-occupied. He was the first Indian army officer to observe and reported large-scale intrusion of Pakistani Army and foreign mercenaries in Indian side of the Line of Control (LoC) at Kargil. He assumed guard of "Bajrang Post" at the height 13,000–14,000 feet to check infiltration in the Kaksar area.

On 15 May 1999 Saurabh Kalia along with five soldiers – Sepoys Arjun Ram, Bhanwar Lal Bagaria, Bhika Ram, Moola Ram and Naresh Singh of the 4 Jat Regiment had gone for a routine patrol of the Bajrang Post in the Kaksar sector in the rugged, treeless Ladakh mountains. After a continuous cross fire with Pakistan armed forces from across the LoC, he and his troops ran out of ammunition. They were finally encircled by a platoon of Pakistan rangers and captured alive before any Indian reinforcement could reach for their help. No trace of this entire patrol was left meanwhile Radio Skardu of Pakistan announced that Captain Saurabh Kalia had been captured by the Pakistani troops. It was after this that India discovered hundreds of guerrillas had established fortified positions on the peaks of the hills deep inside the Indian side of the Line of control, with sophisticated equipment and supply lines back to Pakistan-controlled Kashmir.

Captain Kalia and his men were in captivity for over twenty-two (15 May 1999 – 7 June 1999) days and subjected to torture as evident from their bodies handed over by Pakistan Army on 9 June 1999.

The postmortem revealed that the Pakistan army had tortured their prisoners by burning their bodies with cigarettes, piercing ear-drums with hot rods, puncturing eyes before removing them, breaking most of the teeth and bones, fractures of the skull, cutting the lips, chipping of nose, chopping off limbs and private organs of these soldiers besides inflicting all sorts of physical and mental tortures and finally shooting them dead, as evidenced by the bullet wound to the temple. The postmortem report also confirmed that injuries were inflicted ante-mortem (before death)

On 9 June 1999, NK Kalia had received the body of his son, Captain Saurabh Kalia, handed over by the Pakistani army to

Indian army commanders at the Kargil sector, with evidence of torture.

## Reaction

On 15 June 1999 The Deputy high commissioner of the Pakistani Embassy in New Delhi was summoned and a notice for the breach of the Geneva Convention was submitted for the torture and killing of the prisoners of War during the Kargil War. The minister of external affairs Jaswant Singh raised the issue with Sartaj Aziz, the foreign minister of Pakistan for the identification and punishment of the guilty, but Pakistan continues to deny the charges of torture.

On 14 December 2012 Pakistan's Interior Minister Rehman Malik expressed that Captain Kalia may have died because of weather conditions. He said that he came to know about Captain Saurabh Kalia's case very recently, and added that it is not known whether he was killed with the Pakistani bullet or he died because of the weather. He also said he would like to meet Captain Kalia's father to find out what exactly had happened with his son. The same day, the Supreme Court issued notice to the Centre and sought response within ten weeks on a petition filed by Captain Kalia's father N.K. Kalia.

## Efforts by family

Moved by the torture meted out to his son by Pakistan army, N.K. Kalia launched a struggle to declare the act a war crime. Kalia wrote a series of letters to the then Minister for External Affairs Jaswant Singh.

Even after more than a decade since their son's death, the Kalia family has been trying to get justice from the government and to highlight the war crimes that were committed against their son and other Indian soldiers. N.K. Kalia, his father has been following his son's case and wants the act to be declared a war crime by the UN, and the people responsible for the war crimes punished as per the rulings of the Geneva Convention. However, numerous letters to the Centre have failed to move the government to pursue the matter with the world body. Five other soldiers were tortured and killed along with Capt Kalia. "I am ashamed of being an Indian. The country has spineless leaders," said N.K. Kalia. He also started an online signature campaign to highlight the plight of the war victims.

His father approached various national and international organisations to put pressure on Pakistan to identify, book and punish the persons responsible for the inhuman and unpardonable crime of keeping his son in captivity for three weeks and subjecting to unprecedented brutal torture as evident from his body. But in spite of his efforts he is yet to achieve a fruitful result.

He received replies from embassies and high commission of various countries.

Britain: *We are seeking from the Indian Army a full report of the postmortem, unfortunately without any success so far.*

Israel: *Israel does not have diplomatic relations with Pakistan.*

Germany: *They had contacted the ministry of external affairs and had not received a reply.*

Pakistan denied the torture of the six soldiers and rejected India's demand to punish the guilty.

N.K. Kalia said that if such events had happened to an American or Israeli soldier then the culprits would have been hounded around the globe. Despite assurances from the government, the cases is still pending and his family plans to pursue the case till the end.

N.K. Kalia's petition was pursued by Rajeev Chandrasekhar, Member of Parliament who wrote to the External Affairs Minister and raised questions in Parliament on why the Government has not taken up the case of Capt. Saurabh Kalia with the UN Human Rights Council, to declare this act as a war crime, and identify and punish all the perpetrators. In response to a question raised by Chandrasekhar, Defence Minister A. K. Antony wrote to Kalia's parents in October 2013 that India was bound by the Simla Agreement, and any differences with Pakistan will be settled bilaterally.

"In order to declare a war crime, the ministry of defence needs to write to the ministry of external affairs, which then takes up the matter with the UN Human Rights Council. The council then refers the matter to the General Assembly, which can declare war crime. It then goes to the international court of justice (ICJ). It is the ministry of external affairs that did not follow up the case with the UN" said Colonel (retd) SK Aggarwal, former judge advocate general (JAG) officer. An affidavit filed by the External Affairs ministry in November 2013, said that "moving the ICJ is not a legally enforceable right" and that Pakistan may not permit India submitting a proposal to ICJ.

Indian Army Chief General Bikram Singh has also supported the efforts of Mr. N K Kalia. He reportedly wrote to the Ministry of Defence and National Human Rights Commission conveying his concerns in the matter.

N.K. Kalia, along with Rajeev Chandrasekhar, and the Flags of Honour Foundation, an organisation dedicated to building ceaseless engagement between society and the families of our martyrs, filed a petition with the United Nations Human Rights Council (UNHRC) against war crimes and the torture inflicted on Captain Kalia and five jawans by Pakistani forces during the Kargil war in 1999. The petition was filed on 7 December 2012, with Juan E. Mendez, Special Rapporteur on Torture, of the Office of High Commissioner of Human Rights in Geneva. The Indian External Affairs Ministry said it would look at the nature of the petition, as the UNHRC is an inter-state body and usually acts only in terms of initiatives taken by its member states.

## Memorial

Saurabh Kalia's personal belongings such as photographs, uniforms, shoes and mementoes are kept in a separate room, named as 'Saurabh Smriti Kaksha' (a museum), in his house 'Saurabh Niketan' in the hills of Palampur.

In his memory the government of the state of Himachal Pradesh has raised a memorial park named as 'Saurabh Van

Vihar' in an area of 35 acres (14 ha) in Palampur and renamed a street in the town as Capt Saurabh Kalia Marg and the locality as 'Saurabh Nagar'.

A nursing college in the proposed Vivekanand Medical Research Trust Hospital in Palampur has been raised in his memory. In Amritsar, Kaliya's birthplace his statue has been erected in a memorial. A Liquefied petroleum gas agency has been allotted by the Indian Oil Corporationto the parents of Saurabh Kalia.

# 13

# Shaheed Capt. Anuj Nayyar

Anuj Nayyar (August 28, 1975 - July 7, 1999) was an officer of the 17 Jat Regiment of the Indian Army, who was posthumously awarded the Maha Vir Chakra, India's second highest gallantry award, for exemplary valour in combat during operations in the Kargil War in 1999.

## Early years and career

He was born and grew up in Delhi, India in a Hindu family. His father, S.K. Nayyar, worked as a visiting professor in Delhi School of Economics while his mother, Meena Nayyar, worked for the South Campus library of Delhi University.

Capt. Nayyar received his high-school education from Army Public School, Dhaula Kuan, New Delhi (1993 batch). He was a bright student who consistently performed well in academics and sports. He graduated from the National Defence Academy (90th course, Echo Squadron) and later was commissioned into the 17th Battalion Jat Regiment in June 1997 from the Indian Military Academy (100 Reg).

## Kargil conflict

### *Background*

In 1999, the Indian Army detected a massive infiltration by Pakistani military and paramilitary forces in the Kargil region of Jammu and Kashmir. The army quickly mobilized its forces to drive out the Pakistani infiltrators from Indian territory. Capt. Nayyar, a junior commander in the 17 Jat Regiment, was one of the more than 500,000 Indian troops deployed in the region. His first major operation involved securing Pt. 4875, also known as *Pimple II*, a strategic mountain peak on the western side of Tiger Hill which was occupied by Pakistani infiltrators.

Due to its strategic location, securing Pt. 4875 was a top priority for the Indian Army. The peak, which stood at 15,990 feet above sea level, had extremely steep slopes and capturing the peak without aerial support was considered near impossible. In a last-ditch attempt, Nayyar's Charlie Company decided to secure the peak without waiting for any aerial support on July 6, 1999.

## Operation

During the initial phase of assault on Pt. 4875, the Company Commander of the platoon was injured. After the initial setback, the assault team split into two groups, one led by Captain Vikram Batra and other by Capt. Nayyar. The Pakistani infiltrators had constructed several bunkers on Pt. 4875. Nayyar's company, which consisted of 7 personnel, located 4 enemy bunkers. The company began to ascend Pt. 4875 during which it came under heavy artillery and mortar fire from Pakistani infiltrators. However, the team counter-attacked, which also included hand-to-hand combat, forcing the Pakistani soldiers to retreat. During the battle, Nayyar killed 9 Pakistani soldiers and destroyed three medium machine gun bunkers.

Under Captain Nayyar's leadership, the company had successfully cleared three of the four bunkers and began its assault on the last remaining bunker. While clearing the fourth bunker, an enemy rocket propelled grenade fell directly on Nayyar. Despite being grievously injured, Nayyar continued to lead the remaining men in his company. He succumbed to his injuries but not before clearing the last bunker on Pt. 4875.

None of the soldiers from Nayyar's team of the Charlie Company survived the battle. Two days after Pt. 4875 was secured, it was counter-attacked by Pakistani infiltrators during which the second team of the Charlie Company, led by Captain Batra, successfully defended the peak. During the entire battle for the Pimple complex area, 46 regular members of Pakistani Army, an unknown number of Pakistani paramilitary troopers and militants, and 11 Indian Army men, including Captain Nayyar and Captain Batra, were killed.

The securing of the Pimple Complex area paved the way for the recapture of Tiger Hill which finally forced Pakistan to retreat its forces to pre-conflict positions.

## Recognition and legacy

Capt. Nayyar was posthumously awarded the Mahavir Chakra for his bravery and leadership in combat.

## Mahavir Chakra Citation

Gazette Notification: 17 Pres/2000,15.8.99

Operation: Vijay - Kargil

Date of Award: 1999

**Citation:** On 06 July 1999, Charlie Company was tasked to capture an objective, which was a part of the Pimple Complex on the Western Slopes of Point 4875, in the Mushkoh Valley. At the beginning of the attack the Company Commander got injured and the command of the company devolved on Captain Anuj Nayyar. Captain Nayyar continued to command his leading platoon into the attack under heavy enemy artillery and mortar fire. As the platoon advanced, the leading section reported location of 3 to 4 enemy positions. Captain Nayyar moved forward towards the first enemy position and fired rocket launcher and lobbed grenades into it.

Thereafter, the section, along with Captain Nayyar, physically assaulted and cleared the position. The enemy, which was well entrenched, brought heavy volume of automatic fire. Captain Anuj Nayyar, unmindful of his personal safety, motivated his men and cleared two more enemy positions. While clearing the fourth position an enemy rocket propelled grenade hit the officer killing him on the spot. This action led by Captain Anuj Nayyar resulted in killing nine enemy soldiers and destruction of three medium machine gun positions of the enemy. The success ofthis operation after a brief setback was largely due to the outstanding personal bravery and exemplary junior leadership of this daring officer. Captain Anuj Nayyar displayed indomitable resolve, grit and determination and motivated his command by personal example acting beyond the call of duty and made the supreme sacrifice in true traditions of the Indian Army.

S.K. Nayyar, Anuj's father, was allotted a gas station in Delhi by the Government of India in recognition of the services of his son. Tejbir Singh, a fellow soldier of the Jat Regiment, named his son Anuj in honour of Captain Nayyar.

## In Media

Following Capt. Nayyar's death, his heroics during the war were widely covered by Delhi's print media with editorials like Times of India andHindustan Times running full-page description of his Kargil mission. The plight and ill-treatment of his parents by Indian government officials after his death became the subject of several short telefilms and was widely reported in the Indian news media. Several books and Indian films were made to depict Anuj's life and glorify his contribution to the Indian Army.

- In 2003, LOC Kargil, a Hindi film directed by J.P. Dutta which depicted the endeavours of the Indian Army during the Kargil War, was released in which Bollywood superstar Saif Ali Khan played the role of Anuj Nayyar.
- In 2003, Hindi movie named "Dhoop" directed by national award winner, Ashwini Chaudhary, was released which depicted the life of Anuj's parents after his death. Om Puri plays the role of S.K. Nayyar, Anuj's father.

Capt Anuj Nayyar, of 17 JAT, was killed on Pimple 1 in the South West sector of Tiger Hills, on July 5. "All the six persons with him were killed," said a jawan from the same unit who had come to Delhi with the bodies. Paying respects to the 35 martyrs, most of who are from the JAT regiment, was the

Western Army Commander, Lt Gen HBS Kala, who is also the Colonel of the Regiment.

Among the dead who were paid homage today are Capt Anuj Nayyar, Capt Jerry Premraj, L/Nk Balwan Singh, Nk Ram Sarup, Sep Satyavir Singh, Sep Sheesh Ram, Sep Varinder Kumar, Sep Karan Singh, Nk Ganesh Prasad, Sep Pramod Kumar, Sep Anil Kumar, Sep Dharamveer, Sep Jitendra Singh, Sep Rajindra Singh and five personnel from the Grenadiers. This morning, 16 bodies were paid homage. These include those of Grenadiers Riasat Ali, Zuber Ahmed, Hussain Ali Khan, Rizawan, Hassan Mohammad, Mohammad Ishaq Khan, L/Nk Ahmad Ali, Zakir Hussain, Abid Khan, CQMH Annuruddin, Hav Brij Bhushan Tiwari and Sep Pramod Kumar and Maj Sarvanan who was killed on May 29.

# 14

# Shaheed Major Rajesh Singh Adhikari

It was an unlikely place for a husband to read a letter from his wife of 10 months. It was May 14 and the inky blackness of night was falling on the icy expanse of the Himalayas. On a rocky ride at 16,000 ft, Major Rajesh Adhikari had just received a letter from his wife Kiran. With a map in one hand, an AK-47 assault rifle in the other and a mission to lead an assault on a vital position called the Tololing heights, Adhikari stuffed the letter in his pocket. "He said, 'I want to read it in peace tomorrow after the operation is over'," recalls a fellow officer.

Adhikari never got the chance. That night he and a 10-man Grenadiers team began climbing towards their fortified objective with picks and axes.

Sniper fire killed a JCO and when it dropped to six below freezing, the mission was called off. The next day, three teams of 10 men began a new assault. Adhikari led the central charge, three metres ahead of his men. Hit on the chest, he grimly drove forward. The bunker fell, but Adhikari lay dead 20 m short of his objective. His body was finally recovered last week and sent back to his family in Nainital.

In the hills of Garhwal, where they say every third home is a soldier's home, Nainital joined the family in the long wait, his mother hoping if there was no body, maybe her son wasn't dead, maybe he would one day walk in, that eternal smile on his face.

She had seen it all through his school, St Joseph's, Nainital, all through his college years and on his visits home, while recounting his river rafting exploits, while playing old Hindi favourites on his old guitar. In the end she accepted reality — and bade him farewell on his last journey to a pyre beside the Gola river.

The Mechanized Infantry's Major Rajesh Singh Adhikari, the second army officer to die in the operations against infiltrators, had caused heavy casualties to the intruders and forced them to withdraw before succumbing to injuries in Drass sector, the army said today.

It said the officer, who was presently with the Grenadiers, had been given the task of clearing a height which he carried out after making the supreme sacrifice.

Major Rajesh Singh Adhikari (December 25, 1970 – May 30, 1999), Maha Vir Chakrawas an Indian Army officer who died during the Kargil War. He was posthumously awarded the second highest Indian military honour, the Maha Vir Chakra for bravery on the battlefield.

## Early life

Adhikari was brought up in Nainital, a picturesque hill station in northern India. He completed his schooling from St. Joseph's College in 1987, Intermediate from Government Inter College, Nainital and B.Sc. from Kumaon University in the year 1992.

## Career

He attended the Indian Military Academy, a premier military academy in India.Major Rajesh Singh was commissioned on 11 December 1993 from the Indian Military Academy. After graduating from the Academy, he joined the 2 Mech. Infantry of the Indian Army.He was posted in 18th Grenadiers at the time of kargil war.

## During War

When heavy fighting broke out in the Kargil region of the Indian state of Jammu and Kashmir owing to planned infiltration by militantsbacked by the Pakistan army, the Indian Army was ordered to clear the heights of those intruders. Many tough battles took place in the region.The Mechanized Infantry's Major Rajesh Singh Adhikari, the second army officer to die in the operations against infiltrators, had caused heavy casualties to the intruders and forced them to withdraw before succumbing to injuries in Drass sector. It was one of the most significant battles, the Battle of Tololing, where Rajesh made a valiant sacrifice.

On 30 May 1999, as a part of battalion operations to capture the Tololing feature, Major Rajesh Singh Adhikari, 18 Grenadiers (2 Mech. Inf.) was tasked to secure the initial foothold by capturing its forward spur where the enemy held a strongly fortified advance position. The post was located in a treacherous, mountainous terrain at about 15,000 feet and covered with snow. While Major Rajesh Singh Adhikari was leading his team towards the objective, he was fired at from two mutually supporting bunkers with universal machine guns. The officer immediately directed the rocket launcher detachment to engage the bunker and without waiting, rushed into the bunker and killed two intruders in close quarter combat.

Thereafter, the officer, displaying presence of mind under heavy fire, ordered his medium machine gun (MMG) detachment to fix position behind a rocky feature and engage the enemy. The assault party continued to inch their way up. Despite suffering grievous bullet injuries, Major Rajesh Singh Adhikari continued to direct his sub unit. Refusing to be evacuated, the officer charged at the second bunker and killed one more occupant, thus capturing the second bunker at Tololing which later facilitated capture of Point 4590. For conspicuous gallantry and supreme sacrifice, Major Rajesh Singh Adhikari was posthumously awarded the second highest Indian Army decoration Maha Vir Chakra for his actions in the battle.

Maj Adhikari, 29, belonged to Tallital in Nainital district of Uttar Pradesh and was commissioned as an officer in 1993. Married last year to Kiran Negi, he was going to celebrate his first wedding anniversary on June 9.

On 30 May 1999, Major Rajesh Singh Adhikari of 18 Grenadiers (Mech. Inf.) laid down his life in the attempt to capture the Tololing Feature. His task was to secure the initial foothold by capturing its forward spur where the enemy held a strongly fortified advance position. The post was located in a rough, mountainous terrain. While leading his team towards the objective, he was fired at from two mutually supporting bunkers. The Major immediately directed the rocket launcher detachment to engage the bunker, rushed in and killed two intruders in close quarter combat. Despite suffering severe bullet injuries, Major Adhikari continued to direct and guide his team. Refusing to be evacuated, the officer charged at the second bunker and killed one more occupant, thus capturing the second bunker at Tololing, which later facilitated the capture of Point 4590. Major Adhikari, 29, belonged to Tallital in Nainital district of Uttar Pradesh and was commissioned as an officer in 1993. Married in 1998 to Kiran Negi, he died nine days before celebrating his first wedding anniversary. For his gallantry and sacrifice, Major Rajesh Singh Adhikari was honoured with the Maha Vir Chakra, posthumously.

# 15

# Shaheed Acting Major Mariappan Saravanan

The bodies of Acting Major Mariappan Saravanan and a soldier can be seen on the snow where they were killed on May 28 night. But their colleagues have not been able to recover them yet. Heavy firing from the heights — the very heights that the major was trying to free from intruders — makes the task difficult. "We made several attempts to retrieve the bodies of our dead colleagues," says an army officer, "We will have to get their (that of the intruders)heads down a bit before we can try again. We don't want more casualties."

The army's concern about casualties is stronger since Monday. "Heavy casualties" have been reported in the Batalik region in overnight operations on Sunday, which spilled on to the next day and is still continuing.

The official casualty figures are "33 plus five" on Monday — 33 soldiers and five officers. But army sources admit on Tuesday that the figures have "crossed 40, around 50."

"Saravanan was leading a small assault group when he fell," sources say, "We hope to recover the bodies shortly."

Ironically, if it had not been for the war, the 26-year-old major, would have been either readying to travel to Trichy, his hometown, or already there — he was to get engaged in June. From 1 Bihar regiment, he was a short service officer commissioned in March 1995.

Acting Major R S Adhikari, another officer killed belonged to 2 Mechanised Infantry. He had been deputed for a year to the 18 Grenadiers, now fighting a battle in bitter terrain. His deputation was about to end. May be, if the action had started a little later, he would be alive now...

Major Adhikari has much in common with Major Saravanan. He too was 26. He too fell in the same area. And he too considered June a good month — the 9th was his first wedding anniversary.

Army officers say over 30 bodies have been recovered till now. The majority has already been flown out, while the most recent ones are on their way to Srinagar. And the air-strikes are still on, with the Chorbatla area, where fresh intrusions were reported a few days earlier, coming in for attention.

Major Mariappan Saravanan (10 August 1972 – 29 May 1999), was an officer in the prestigious Bihar Regiment of the Indian Army who was killed during the Kargil War. He was killed in hand to hand combat with intruders after killing four intruders in the Batalik area of Kargil Sector on 29 May 1999, along with 33 soldiers and four other officers. Saravanan had just completed four years of service on 10 March 1999.

Major Sarvanan was possibly the first officer killed in the Kargil War. The attack led by him came in the early stages of the conflict when adequate information was not available. The men in 1 Bihar took an oath after Maj. Sarvanan's fall to fight to the finish and recover the heights, to the battle cry of 'Bajrang Bali ki Jai', they launched subsequent offensives that saw it not just take the heights but drive the Pakistanis all the way across the Line of Control. His actions have led to him being referred to as the "Hero of Batalik".

## Biography

### *Childhood*

Born on 10 August 1972 on the island of Rameswaram in the Indian state of Tamil Nadu, Saravanan was commissioned into the famous Bihar Regiment on 11 March 1995 from OTA

Chennai. He began his schooling at Kendriya Vidyalaya in Gaya district and later graduated from St. Joseph's College, Tiruchirapalli in 1992.

Saravanan was also the president of the student union at St. Joseph's College in 1992, an interesting development since the most popular candidate (Thirichelvam) could not stand for election that year and all support went to Saravanan. Saravanan at college had a thin body frame and is a C certificate holder of NCC INFANTRY UNIT.

His father Lt. Colonel Adi Mariappan died in a road accident in Bangalore in 1989 while serving in the Indian Peace Keeping Force duringOperation Pawan in Sri Lanka. Major M Saravanan was survived by Mrs A Mariappan, his mother, and two sisters. The elder one, Chitra, is a doctor whereas the younger one Revathi is a Computer Engineer.

## Military career

The 27-year-old officer Saravanan, as a Major in the Indian Army fell defending the peaks of Batalik in the Kargil war. After completing his schooling in various places—Belgaum, Kannoor, Gurdaspur, Jorhat and Bihar, he joined St Joseph's College in Tiruchi. "After college he tried to get into the National Defence Academy and landed up in the Officers Training Academy," says his closest friend Amalraj. He graduated from the OTA in 1995 and joined the First Bihar regiment as a lieutenant. After joining the Army he had served at places like Tamulpur, Cooch Behar and Bhutan before moving to Kargil. He was made captain the following year and major in 1999.

They were a bunch of three friends—Saravanan, Karthik and Amalraj. A few years ago, they had made a trip to Kanyakumari. On the way, their bus driver fell asleep on the wheel and crashed headlong into an incoming lorry. "Seven people died on the spot and many were injured. We students were in a shock. But not Saravanan, he was cool. He went about checking the dead. Then he helped the injured into passing vehicles and took them to hospital. It was his army background that made him react to an emergency so calmly and resolutely."

Amalraj is an IPS officer now and the Deputy Inspector General of Police in the Trichy Range of Tamil Nadu.

## The Kargil War

The First Bihar Regiment was in Assam when the Kargil War broke out. They were ordered to move to Kargil, Jammu and Kashmir. From the heat of Assam to the cold of Kargil wasn't an easy change. There wasn't enough protective weather gear.

On the night of May 28, 1999, Major Sarvanan was assigned the task of capturing a well-fortified Pakistani position at 14,229 feet (4,337 m) in the Batalik sector. He and his men launched an attack at 04:00. Despite intensive firing from the enemy with artillery and automatic weapons, they charged into a volley of bullets. Saravanan fired a rocket launcher into the enemy position that killed two enemy soldiers. During the combat, he was hit by shrapnel and injured but continued fighting. His commanding officer ordered him to retreat because too many Indian soldiers had been injured. 'Genghis Khan fall back,' came the order. 'Not today sir, we are very close to the objective,' replied Sarvanan who was code named Genghis Khan. He killed two more invaders but this time he was hit by a bullet in the head at 06:30, his body nestled in the snow. A friend in Bangalore called his mother and told her Saravanan had died in Kargil. "We switched on the television and saw it in a news bulletin." Two days later, the official telegram arrived. "He was the first officer to fall".

The Vir Chakra was awarded to Saravanan posthumously and presented to his mother by President K. R. Narayanan. Its citation reads: "For our tomorrow..... he gave his today......".

## MSMT-Major Saravanan Memorial Trust

The family of Saravanan had a long cherished desire to establish a Public Charitable Trust to Immortalize the name of the Great Martyr.

Many of his friends and relatives are desirous of contributing money and kind of this purpose. It has hence become necessary to streamline the inflow of money and ensure proper spending of the same in the name of Late Major Saravanan.Vr.C., In order to have a permanent arrangement, this trust has been made.

The Trust is meant for the welfare of the poor, indigent and needy to serve the society at large without any discrimination as to caste, colour and creed. Also it aims at motivating the youngsters to “Join the Army and serve the nation”.

## War Memorial

Major Saravanan, the legend, has been enshrined in the history of one of the most difficult and brutal wars ever fought by any Army. His name and his saga of extreme bravery has been etched in golden letters in the annals of the Indian Army as the entire nation stands as one to salute him.

Eight years post Kargil war, the memories of the gory battle fought on the inhospitable terrain of Dras and Batalik sectors in Jammu and Kashmir seem to be fading. Through the fading images of our heroes, one figure which looms larger than life is of Major Saravanan, the brave son of Tiruchirapalli city.

At a colourful function organised by 117 (TA) Battalion, Trichy, Major General B. Sivasankar, general officer commanding, headquarters, Andhra, Tamil Nadu, Karnataka and Kerala area, unveiled the War Memorial on the Collector Office road, in the presence of Major General M S Balhara, colonel of the Bihar Regiment and a large number of officials and men of the army, District Collector Ashish Vachchani, senior police officials and a large number of common people.

The first side of the memorial has the portrait of Major Saravanan while the other two sides bear the citation of the brave martyr engraved in marbles, both in Tamil and English. A replica of his assault gun and cap is also mounted atop the memorial.

Mrs. Amirthavalli Mariyappan, the mother of Saravanan and his family were the first to place a wreath on the memorial, followed by army officials with full army honours.

In his address, Major General Sivashankar praised the war hero for his bravery and his mother for giving a son, who made the army and country proud, in a befitting manner. Saravana's sacrifice will continue to inspire the future generation to serve the army and will be remembered fondly by one and all in the Indian army.

This historic memorial constructed and maintained by Major Saravanan Memorial Trust and construction cost Rs.725,000, fully spent by his mother Mrs. Amirthavalli Mariappan.

## Special cover and cancellation

On the occasion of Kargil Vijay Divas on Saturday, 26 July 2008, the Postal Department brought out a special cover and cancellation in memory of Major M. Saravanan, the 'Hero of Batalik'.

The Postmaster General, Central Region, Tiruchi S.P. Rajalingam released the first special cover and handed it over to K.K. Tripathi, Chief Commissioner of Income Tax, Tiruchi at a function organised by Major Saravanan Memorial Trust here.

Praising late Major Saravanan for his bravery during the Kargil War, Mr. Rajalingam said that the Postal Department took pride in bringing out a special cover in memory of the Kargil hero. Mr. Tripathi said that the release of a special cover brought out in memory of Major Saravanan was a befitting tribute to the late Army officer who made the supreme sacrifice while fighting for the country.

"The sacrifices of our defence personnel should always be remembered", he said, adding that "Major Saravanan's sacrifice did not go in vain".

Collector T. Soundiah, Mayor Sarubala R. Tondaiman, Colonel C.P. Medappa, Commanding Officer, 117 Infantry Battalion (Territorial Army) The Guards, Tiruchi, R.K. Jain, General Manager, Ordnance Factory, Tiruchi, Colonel Benz K. Jacob, Group Commander, NCC Group, Tiruchi, Mrs. Amirthavalli Mariappan, the mother of late Major Saravanan, and senior Army officers took part in the function. "I am often referred to as the mother of the HERO OF BATTALIK I am proud that my son kept vigil over the frontiers even after his death, I am proud that my son was the first officer martyr from the Indian Army, and the last to come back home" said Mrs. Amirthavalli Mariappan, the mother of late Major Saravanan. Major Saravanan even after his death his body was staking claim of the land that is rightfully India's.

Nation's third highest wartime gallantry award VIR CHAKRA was awarded to Major Mariappan Sarvanan on 15th August 1999.

# 16

# Soldiers As Heroes

Another noteworthy feature was the honour accorded spontaneously to the soldiers who died in battle. Day after day the press carried reports of how thousands of people would turn up to pay their homage to soldiers killed in Kargil battle when their bodies were brought for funerals to their villages and towns. The bereaved families of all the soldiers were made to feel they were not alone in their sorrow, that others not only shared their grief but were also eager to honour those who lost their lives reclaiming or defending Indian territory.

For example, at the cremation of Major Manoj Talwar in Meerut "...all roads leading to the cremation ground were jampacked and vehicular traffic came to a halt at different places, when an army motorcade carrying the body of the dead Major wrapped in the tricolour flag, passed through the city for its cremation with full military honours. Earlier with the arrival of the body more than 50,000 people belonging to Meerut, Baghpat and their nearby districts began to pour in his residence to pay homage to Major Talwar." (*The Times of India*, July 17, 1999)

Similar scenes were repeated in virtually every part of the country: cities, towns and even villages including in the insurgency ridden Northeast. In Assam, people even braved the ULFA's (United Liberation Front of Assam) directives against honouring the army heroes of Kargil and mustered courage to stand up against ULFA's murderous and extortionist politics for the first time since this terrorist outfit came into prominence.

A *Times of India* report on 29th July tells us that the Army Headquarters had uptil then received more than six lakh letters during the two month long battle in Kargil. Out of this school children sent 5,10,725 letters. These letters included cheques sent for the Army Central Welfare Fund which has already collected more than 37 crores from such donations. This is not counting the much greater amount being collected by the Prime Minister's Fund for Kargil heroes or by several other organisations which took the lead in such an effort.

Numerous citizens, young and old organised fund raising campaigns on their own initiative for the welfare of the families of the dead and injured soldiers. Reports of school children donating their pocket money and scholarship money came in from all corners of the country. The *dhobi* (washerman's) Union in Delhi donated Rs51,000. Sex workers, lawyers, doctors and housewives and even beggars joined together for collecting donations for the Kargil soldiers. In Delhi Tihar jail inmates alone gave a donation of Rs3.31 lakhs in cash from their meagre earnings and a larger number of them also donated blood. (*The Indian Express*, June 8, 1999) Such efforts cut across class, caste, gender and regional barriers.

In addition, blood donation camps organised in different parts of the country elicited such an enthusiastic response that for the first time our blood banks were flowing with surplus blood. People wouldn't stop giving blood even when they were informed that there was no way that the collected blood could be transported to Kargil. This, when there has always been a perennial shortage of blood donations in India.

The letters to the army headquarters included offers of service from doctors, students, engineers and even retired personnel who expressed a desire to do anything that the army requires from them including a wish to recruit in the army with the readiness to die in battle.

Besides such requests, the army was surprised to find a manifold increase in the applicants coming to join the army during the period of Kargil conflict. The response was so overwhelming that in many places, the army recruitment camps were mobbed with tens of thousands of young men, all desperate to go to Kargil right away. (*The Times of India*, July 10, 1999). Thousands of educated young men in border villages volunteered to be porters for the army. One would expect, people would be more afraid to join the army during wartime. But the Kargil crisis seems to have had the opposite effect.

All this is noteworthy considering that in recent years the army seemed to have lost some of its glamour and allure for educated young men who till recently seemed to prefer even ordinary clerical jobs to joining the army. For years army establishments had been complaining that a large percentage of their officer grade vacancies were not being filled due to lack of enthusiasm for an army career.

## Army Ill-Equipped

It was alarming to read stories of how ill-equipped our army is to fight at such high altitudes on one of the world's most difficult terrains. The soldiers had neither adequate clothes nor some of the most basic equipment like snow goggles so essential to survive and fight effectively. By contrast, the Pakistani soldiers especially the officers seemed far better equipped in every way, as shown in their weaponry, food, clothing, accessories and even facilities like TVs and telephones recovered from their bunkers.

How much of what we were told about the Pakistani officers' accommodations after they were captured was propaganda by the Indian army which has always clamoured for larger allocations in successive budgets, and how much of it speaks of real neglect of the legitimate needs of the Indian soldiers, is hard to tell. But given the track record of our bureaucracy in every field, given their propensity for making a tragic mess of anything they touch with their corrupt and inefficient hands, it is not far-fetched to believe that our soldiers were not nearly as well-equipped as they should and could have been. There could well have been a revolt in the army. Instead, our soldiers fought valiantly, many died heroically, with young officers leading their jawans rather than using them as cannon fodder, as seemed to be the case in many Pakistani military units. The incredibly high proportion of Indian officers who were killed while leading their men is in sharp contrast to the casualty figures of the Pakistani army officers in this conflict.

The extraordinary courage and unity displayed by our military units is especially moving considering that many of the colonial traditions are still preserved in the Indian army. The gap between the ordinary soldier and the officer cadre remains too large to be healthy. The ordinary soldiers largely come from rural poor families. Many are poorly educated and are treated like drudges by the officers. It is a common sight to see up to half a dozen soldiers attached as flunkies to each army officer (depending on his rank) as his personal servants. Often they cook, wash, clean and do many of the menial chores in the homes of their *sahibs* and *memsahibs*. This is certainly not the best way to organise a modern army with a democratic spirit. And yet, our soldiers demonstrated exceptional courage, commitment and a spirit of teamwork during this battle.

## Thwarted Idealism

There is a lot to be learnt from our soldiers' performance and the following public response. The desire to see India do well in living up to its responsibilities is indeed intense among our people, as is a sense of idealism an aspiration to live for goals in addition to and higher than personal enrichment and well-being. But this idealism is not finding expression in a country weighed down by a decaying and exploitative political and economic structure and poor quality leaders. There is a whole sea of enthusiasm and idealism waiting to find creative expression in peacetime. It is being thwarted by the corruption and sheer mismanagement of our gargantuan, inefficient *babudom* and its venal rulers. They have often gone out of their way to divide people on caste, religions, regional and linguistic lines. Yet, they have had only brief and limited successes. People tend to rise above those divides because of a deeply rooted sense that they are repositories of a great common heritage rather than being a mere nation. The Kargil war confirms that in India a sense of belonging to a common civilisation and patriotic feelings for this land survive and even thrive despite all the doings and misdoings of our ruling establishment.

This conflict also showed the changing character of the Indian army and the shift in its recruiting base. During British times when this army was created, even junior officers were recruited mostly from wealthy, aristocratic families. In the early post-independence years the anglicised upper classes provided the recruiting ground for the officer class. As the Kargil casualties showed, that is no longer the case. Most of the officers seem to come from modest middle, lower middle and even working class backgrounds, many even from rural areas. As with the fundraising drives for the army, the middle and lower middle classes seem far more responsive to the call of patriotism than the rich and powerful overall.

## Desperation for Recruitment

For many among the poor, service as a low ranking jawan in the army is the route to upward mobility. Most other avenues for advancement are badly choked due to the mismanagement of our economy. This was demonstrated tragically in the way in which over 30,000 young men from poor families gathered at the Darbhanga Air Force Base, in response to army advertisements announcing a recruitment drive in Bihar's Darbhanga and Chhapra districts for a few hundred jawans. Most of these young men did not possess even the pitifully few minimum qualifications demanded of those seeking to enlist as jawans. They were undersized, malnourished, maleducated young men who had not even cleared their class VIII examination. Yet, given the low literacy and high unemployment rates in these regions, they were desperate to be recruited. An announcement by authorities that only men from Darbhanga were eligible for selection was enough to trigger off eruptions of violence. The police acting in their characteristic crude, ham-handed style, opened fire on these young desperate men, killing dozens in the process. The army closed the main gates. In the prevailing panic, aspirants ran into the murky flood waters that had engulfed the district those days. The full death toll is not yet ascertained because many bodies were washed away, though official sources mentioned 23 dead. (*Outlook*, August 2, 1999)

## Brutalising Our Own

The outrage over the torture and brutal treatment meted out to our captured soldiers by the Pakistani army also reminded one of some unfortunate truths about our own society. Pakistani mutilations of Indian soldiers were attributed to "to some cannibalistic streak" (*Hindustan Times*, June 12, 1999) and evidence of the "steady brutalisation of the Pakistani armed forces." (*The Times of India*, June 12, 1999)

We in India, especially the elites, have hardly ever expressed a similar outrage over similar acts of torture and mangling which are routinely occurring in our police stations. The poor in India have been at the receiving end of such brutalities from the Indian police and even the army. Thousands die in police custody every year. Many are arrested on mere suspicion of having committed some petty theft. I know of any number of people among the elite in India who actively justify such acts. I also know many more who want the police to use third degree methods of punishment on their own servants if there is a theft in their house. All this in a bid to recover their stolen property expeditiously even when they have no real evidence that the theft is actually the servant's doing. Likewise, in the name of curbing insurgency, many innocents have been brutalised and murdered by our army in areas like Nagaland and Kashmir. Whole villages have been burnt down and thousands of women raped and killed by our soldiers in the Northeast. Thousands of people have simply "disappeared" after being taken into custody over the last few decades. Yet, such brutalities on our own people by our own police and our own army have rarely evoked similar outrage or condemnation.

If significant sections of our society had demonstrated similar outrage and condemnation at the violence inflicted by our police and security forces on many vulnerable sections of our own citizens, perhaps we would not be facing long and drawn out insurgencies in certain regions. Prolonged army rule, with all the excesses that go with it, turned many people against the Indian state. If the general population in Kashmir had not felt so disenchanted with the Indian state for treating them with such mistrust and disdain, Pakistan would never have succeeded as much as it has in creating trouble for us in Kashmir.

## Army on Charity?

However, despite the generosity of the public response, there remains something troubling about the fund raising drives among the people for the welfare of the soldiers. It indicates that our citizens do not believe that the government is looking after our soldiers adequately. The government as well as the army establishment seemed to confirm this by inviting donations for the armed forces welfare fund. In few other countries in the world are voluntary donations deemed so central to welfare of the soldiers.

What is the message we are giving the world by making it appear that the welfare of the soldiers and their families is contingent upon contributions from the pocket money of little children? Alongside the tales of the heroism of our soldiers, there was a parallel flow of news reports about many of the heroes of our previous conflicts who were living in penury and how the widows and other dependents of many of our decorated soldiers had spent decades trying to get the benefits due to them from the army all in vain.

What do we learn from the enthusiasm and support expressed spontaneously for the Indian soldiers, considering there was very little sign of war hysteria in the way people responded? No film star, no cricketer or politician has in recent decades received the kind of deep felt upsurge of public honour as did the humblest of army jawans during the Kargil conflict.

All these are unmistakable signs that in this day and age when anti-heroes have come to dominate our public life, people have finally found symbols of inspiration in ordinary soldiers who demonstrated extra ordinary courage and determination in fighting one of the most hazardous battle in literally the most inhospitable terrain in the world.

## Our Rulers Disappoint

In post-Independence India, most politicians and other power wielders in our country have transformed themselves into plain thugs and looters of this country's resources. Their conduct would have turned even angels into hard-boiled cynics. Time and again, our people were given the hope that they had found leaders capable of challenging the corruption and mismanagement which has become the hallmark of our public life.

People thronged enthusiastically to lend support to whoever projected himself/herself as a real crusader J.P. in the 1970s, V.P. Singh in the 1980s, and in more recent times many regional figures like NTR in Andhra Pradesh and Jayalalitha in Tamil Nadu. Most of these men and women betrayed the trust reposed in them. In the past few decades, the quality of public leaders declined so sharply that young people turned to other national icons like cricketers to sustain their patriotic fervour.

However, even at their best, cricketers can provide only momentary relief to a people who feel rudderless on account of the mess our rulers have made of our country. The battle of Kargil showed the Indian soldiers at their best in their commitment to risk their lives to safeguard India's vital interests. Given how badly our

soldiers had been let down by the ruling establishment, who failed to perform even basic intelligence tasks and provide essential amenities to soldiers stationed in freezing temperatures and hazardous living conditions, their fighting spirit was indeed commendable. Even when due to lack of proper intelligence information about enemy positions on the strength of the Pakistani army on those unnerving peaks and knowing well that they were sent on virtual suicide missions the soldiers kept their morale surprisingly high.

## Misuse of the Army

And if the army's actions had been subjected to fair, thorough and appropriate scrutiny all these years, we would have a more efficient army, with fewer intelligence failures. It ought to be a matter of great concern that hundreds of thousands of army men have been for years deployed to quell internal rebellions rather than guard our borders their actual mandate.

Those soldiers risk demoralisation and loss of purpose. They feel frustrated engaged in warring on their own people.

It is much more demoralising for an army to face the hostility of their own citizens as has been happening in Kashmir and the Northeast than to face an external enemy. We have debilitated our army considerably by misusing it for the wrong purposes. Ultimately, all this is the result of the short-sighted, venal politics being pursued by our national and regional leaders.

## Plight of Border Villages

Another sad revelation of the Kargil war which ought not to come as a surprise, is the sad state of our border villages. Rural areas in all of India are worse off than our miserably impoverished towns and cities. However, the condition of border villages is far more pitiable because of the constant insecurity. Forces on both sides exchange intermittent fire which hits innocent civilians living in villages across the Line of Control more often than it does the opposing armies.

One consequence of this insecure atmosphere is that no one is willing to invest in any business or industry around those areas. Even government officials treat these villages with great disdain. Consequently, life for the people in such areas is truly harsh. It was only after the national and international press descended on these god-forsaken villages to report on the ongoing war that we were able to comprehend how woeful are the living conditions in these areas.

The reporters also had a tough time in these terribly deprived circumstances where any evidence of basic infrastructure is virtually non-existent. They had to make herculean efforts to send their reports to their papers because of the paucity and lack of functioning of telephone lines, the absence of electricity and running water and other such essential services. This forced the press to notice how callously the government reacted to the plight of these border villages even during this crisis. Here are a few samples of news snippets that appeared in the press recently:

A report from Malayan village in Kargil district tells us that when the inhabitants had to flee their village following heavy artillery fire, they were not even provided bare shelter by the government. They left their homes in panic. Consequently, they could not carry with them even essentials like warm clothes and utensils. They expected the government to help them till conditions became safe for them to return home. But nothing came by way of assistance. To quote 50 year old Noori, "We have become beggars in our own country... we would have starved were it not for the kindness of the local villagers. They have fed us and allowed us to live in their own homes." The report goes on to add that most of the villagers who have migrated from Malayan are suffering from malnutrition, gastroenteritis and scabies. (*The Indian Express*, June 25)

In most places free food camps (*langars*) were organised by local people. It was voluntary organisations who have come to the rescue of the thousands of starving border migrants camping at various schools on the outskirts of Jammu region. Though government officials and politicians made the mandatory rounds of these camps, assuring the migrants of immediate relief, those promises were not honoured. Government did announce a relief package for the uprooted people consisting of 5 kg grain per person and 5 litres of kerosene per month. But in many places even this inadequate amount failed to appear on time. The business community of the Jammu region pooled money to organise *langars* for thc people putting up at various makeshift camps.

Through this period, we have watched the state government pass on the buck to the Central government, arguing that their failure to provide adequate relief was due to paucity of funds and that they were awaiting more central assistance. The Central government, on its part, is too busy making political capital out of this war to bother much about the plight of its already vulnerable citizens in border areas.

Even during quiet times their lives in this area are difficult. In winter, the temperature drops to minus 50 degrees celsius. They live in mud houses that are completely sealed off for seven months. They live with their cattle on the same floor to get some warmth generated through the animals' body heat. They stock up food like *sattu*(roasted barley flour) and survive on salt tea with yak milk. Health facilities in the area are negligible even in normal times. During war times even the little that is available breaks down. News reports talk of premature deliveries and higher maternal mortality rates since virtually no post-natal care is available to them. The already skeletal health delivery system is being deserted by doctors who have moved away to safer areas.

Even those border villages of Punjab which are situated in normal terrain don't fare any better. For example, a report from village Simbal-Scole off the Gurdaspur border told us that fear and tension run through the lives of the villagers as the battle rages on the border and monsoon threatens to flood the rivers. While gunshots from Pakistan threaten them on one side, flooding rivers do so on the other. Just 50 meters separate the village from Pakistan and three small rivers cut them off from India. The Ujh, the Uni and the Tarnah are already widening their course before meeting the Ravi. In a few weeks, they will overflow as they normally do every year. And if the fighting spills over, the villagers have no escape routes. Their only boat lies broken and abandoned, their sole telephone has never worked since its installation three years ago. The village elder says, "*Je baad aaye, pehle sada* number, *je ladai shuru hoyegi, pher bhi pehle sada* number, (If the floods come, we will be the first to die. If the war starts, we'll be the first to die.)"

The battle at the border has derailed their lives. Those who migrated and returned have belatedly started planting their paddy. Shopkeepers have stopped giving the customary credit for the purchase of fertilisers. Traders are not ready to take any risk.

Many women have been forced to pawn their jewellery to buy agricultural essentials like manure. To reach the village, it is necessary to take a detour from Pathankot to Kathua in J&K, as there is no connecting bridge across the river Ravi. They have to cross the rivers to reach the nearest hospital and school. Every monsoon they are marooned, and subsist on a diet of potatoes, pickles and roti. (*The Indian Express*, July 7, 1999)

Another report from Devi Garh tells us that Swarno, whose husband is bed-ridden since 1971 after he sustained injuries while fleeing his village before the war, has had no help coming to her from the government. Even during this crisis, she herself had to carry him in a bullock cart to a camp. "I do not even have enough money for a *kafan* (shroud) if he dies," she says.

Most villagers are at the brink of destitutions because they have not been able to cultivate their land because of persistent firing. The uncertainty of sowing and harvesting has forced many to take up menial jobs in and around their villages. Some of them feel even a war would be preferrable to this continuous insecurity. At least during war, the government has to pay some attention to their plight because of increased media attention.

A large number of people who left their villages during this period had to live with relatives and friends but some have no where to go and took shelter in government buildings. At many places up to 10 families were sharing a single room. In most places there is no electricity, no bathroom, no water. Many reported that they were given slips stating their entitlement for ration but those slips brought forth no food supplies.

"The focus of the entire nation is on Kargil, and deservedly so, but the nation should not forget that we too are suffering for the nation's cause and deserve some attention,' says Janak

Raj, of Devi Garh whose only source of livelihood - two buffalos - were killed in the firing from across the border." (*The Indian Express*, July 2, 1999)

Reading reports of this kind one cannot help but ask, is this war being fought only for territory? When will people living in that area begin to matter to the "defenders of the nation?" How does one deal with the callousness of the government which is unable to even provide adequate food and shelter to citizens who have been rendered homeless on account of this war?

Most importantly, what does it mean to be an Indian citizen? What does it actually entitle people to, at a very minimum? What advantages, guarantees, securities and entitlements come with being an Indian citizen? If people are expected to fend for themselves even during those times when a war is imposed on their area by the governments of the two countries, shattering their fragile economy and jeopardising their very lives, why then should it make any difference to them whether Pakistani state rules their territory or India?

Strong nations are built when people can see that the state provides them real security of life and property, provides them certain facilities as their minimum due, and that they can count on the state to come to their rescue in time of crisis and calamities_be it war or floods. If none of this can be counted on as a citizen's inalienable right, why have a government at all?

## THE TRAVAILS OF PREVIOUS WAR HEROES

"Octogenarian P.R. Gambhir, a proud father of Second Lieutenant Kamal Gambhir who died fighting for the country at the young age of 20 in the 1971 war feels extremely bitter about the country his son died for. All he has received till now is a solarium of Rs 10,000 and a paltry sum of Rs 200 per month as pension, which has increased now to Rs 2,500. The increase in pension is due to inflation and the government has not done them any favour he rues. They were all busy celebrating their victory over Pakistan... people like us were forgotten. We had the means and the will to continue, but what about those who don't have either? The root of all the trouble was the "permanent residential status" of the Gambhirs. They had migrated from Pakistan in 1947. Kamal was born in Udaipur, Rajasthan, but the family moved to Rourkela soon after. Kamal had given Rourkela as his permanent address, `But the Orissa government said we were not permanent residents of Rourkela and were, therefore, not entitled to any war-related scheme there. In Delhi it was the same story,' Mr Gambhir says. He claims a sub-divisional magistrate in Orissa had offered him a plot but demanded a share as a bribe. `I was made to feel a beggar. I wrote to many people, including the then Prime Minister Indira Gandhi, but did not get any response,' he says, pointing to a thick file." (*The Times of India*, July 13, 1999)

In another case 55 years old Sepoy Sahadeo Prasad had to have both his legs amputated at the young age of 27 because of severe frostbite during the 1971 war against Pakistan. With a paltry pension of Rs 1,275 per month he is supporting a family of eight children in dire poverty.

The fate of many jawans who fought gallantly, gave their life or limb can be glimpsed from the experience of Sepoy Nripen Chandra Saha Roy, 62 who lost both his legs during the 1962 war. He was one of the 11 survivors of the 2nd Rajput regiment. With no help from the state, Roy brought up his four sons and just about makes ends meet. "He says, `Even if they [meaning the government of West Bengal] give us land, it'll be barren. Prime land and plots have gone to party cadres and anti-social elements, who cares for us?' " (*Outlook*, July 12, 1999)

Then there is the sad story of Sepoy S. Thomas who fought during a fortnight of intense fighting that saw the creation of Bangladesh. Thomas lost his left eye and in 1975 was made to retire as an army medical team declared him physically unfit. With no salary or pension he and his wife had to move to their village in Thiruvanamalai in Tamil Nadu where they worked as paid labourers. He says"'I earned Rs 1.50 for a day's labour while my wife made Re 1.' Whenever he could save Rs 10, he would visit the office of the Madras Engineering Regiment in Banglore to enquire about his compensation and pension. 'The stock answer: the files were missing and they were trying their best,' he says. With lot of running around he got a monthly pension of Rs 75 and an annual maintenance of Rs 500. Later through local ex-servicemen's association he got a postman's job. 'I had to strain to read addresses and ride along busy roads,' he says." (*Outlook*, July 12, 1999)

At times even officers had to suffer at the hands of non-caring bureaucrats. Take Major General Dayal for instance. A serving major he was christened "the saviour of Haji Pir." Gen. Dayal was promised land by the Himachal government after his daring feat in 1965, but he is yet to get it after 34 years. (*The Times of India*, June 22, 1999)

Not only the wounded warriors but the widows of soldiers especially of the 1965 and 1971 too have faced a horde of problems. It is in fact shocking that some of them like Manidevi, 51, who lost her husband in the 1971 war when he was blown up in a minefield near Abohar in Punjab receive a meagre Rs 15 as monthly pension. (*Outlook*, July 12, 1999)

This points to a rather sad picture of corruption, inefficiency and mismanagement of funds meant for the welfare of our soldiers by the bureaucratic establishment in our country.

## INDIAN HEROES OF KARGIL WAR

They'd promised their families they'd come back soon. They more than kept their word. Went as mere men. Came back as heroes. In coffins.

"THEY GAVE THEIR TODAY FOR OUR TOMORROW"

Over a 400 of them at last count. Median age 19 to 35. The grim-faced army officers receiving the coffins, draped in the tricolour, the carriage to the army parade ground, the set-jawed shok shastra farewell salute by steely soldiers.

The silent sorrow of upraised guns, slowly brought, barrel downward, to the ground, left arm tautly extended to the right before retracking, the holding of palm to chest, the sudden dropping of head, the 30-second hushed silence, then the regulation rajnigandha and marigold wreaths from the army and air chiefs, the general officer commanding, fellow officers, the battalion, before the body escorted by a comrade begins its last journey home.

Wreathed in white, the colour of the pure; kesariya, the colour and insignia of the brave. Now across mountains, now across rivers, plains.

The Kargil War was an armed conflict between India and Pakistan that took place between May and July in 1999 in and around the area of Kargil in Kashmir, India. The reason of the war was the infiltration of Pakistani soldiers into the Indian side of the Line of Control (LOC) into the area of Kargil. The Pakistani paramilitary forces were led by General Ashraf Rashid. The Indian Army, later on supported by the Indian Air Force, attacked the Pakistani positions and, with international diplomatic support, eventually forced withdrawal of the Pakistani forces across the LOC.

The Kargil war is one of the most recent examples of high altitude warfare in mountainous terrain. This was only the second direct ground war between any two countries after they had developed nuclear weapons, after the Sino-Soviet border conflict of 1969.

The town of Kargil is located 205 km from Srinagar, facing the Northern Areas across the LOC with Pakistan. The National highway (NH 1) connecting Srinagar to Leh cuts through Kargil. The area that witnessed the infiltration and fighting is a 160 km long stretch of ridges overlooking this highway.

The military outposts on the ridges above the highway were generally around 5,000 metres (16,000 ft) high, with a few as high as 5,485 metres (18,000 ft). According to India's then army chief Ved Prakash Malik, and many other scholars, much of the background planning, including construction of logistical supply routes, had been undertaken much earlier. On several occasions during the 1980s and 1990s, the army had given Pakistani leaders (namely Zia ul Haq and Benazir Bhutto) similar proposals for infiltration into the Kargil region, but the plans had been shelved for fear of drawing the nations into all-out war. Some analysts believe that the blueprint of attack was reactivated soon after Pervez Musharraf was appointed chief of army staff in October 1998.

There were three major phases to the Kargil War.

- Pakistan infiltrated forces into the Indian-controlled section of Kashmir and occupied strategic locations enabling it to control NH1.
- The next stage consisted of India discovering the infiltration and mobilizing forces to respond to it.
- The final stage involved major battles by Indian and Pakistani forces resulting in India capturing positions held by Pakistani forces and the withdrawal of Pakistani forces back across the Line of Control.

The incursions into Kargil were not detected for a number of reasons: Indian patrols were not sent into some of the areas infiltrated by the Pakistani forces and heavy artillery fire by Pakistan in some areas provided cover for the infiltrators. Once the intcursions were detected the Government of India responded with Operation Vijay, a mobilisation of 200,000 Indian troops.

However, because of the nature of the terrain, division and corps operations could not be mounted; subsequent fighting was conducted mostly at the regimental or battalion level. In effect, two divisions of the Indian Army, numbering 20,000, plus several thousand from the Paramilitary forces of India and the air force were deployed in the conflict zone. The total number of Indian soldiers that were involved in the military operation on the Kargil-Drass sector was thus close to 30,000.

The number of infiltrators, including those providing logistical backup, has been put at approximately 5,000 at the height of the conflict. This figure includes troops from Pakistan-administered Kashmir who provided additional artillery support. The Indian Air Force launched Operation Safed Sagar in support of the mobilization of Indian land forces, but its effectiveness during the war was limited by the high altitude and weather conditions, which in turn limited bomb loads and the number of airstrips that could be used.

The terrain of Kashmir is mountainous and at high altitudes; even the best roads, such as National Highway No. 1 (NH 1) from Leh to Srinagar, are only two lanes. The rough terrain and narrow roads slowed traffic, and the high altitude, which affected the ability of aircraft to carry loads, made control of NH 1A (the actual stretch of the highway which was under Pakistani fire) a priority for India. From their observation posts, the Pakistani forces had a clear line-of-sight to lay down indirect artillery fire on NH 1A, inflicting heavy casualties on the Indians.

This was a serious problem for the Indian Army as the highway was its main logistical and supply route. The Pakistani shelling of the arterial road posed the threat of Leh being cut off, though an alternative (and longer) road to Leh existed via Himachal Pradesh.

The infiltrators, apart from being equipped with small arms and grenade launchers, were also armed with mortars, artillery and anti-aircraft guns. Many posts were also heavily mined, with India later stating to having recovered more than 8,000 anti-personnel mines according to an ICBL report. Pakistan's reconnaissance was done through unmanned aerial vehicles and AN/TPQ-36 Firefinder radars supplied by the US. The initial Indian attacks were aimed at controlling the hills overlooking NH 1A, with high priority being given to the stretches of the highway near the town of Kargil. The majority of posts along the Line of Control were adjacent to the highway, and therefore the recapture of nearly every infiltrated post increased both the territorial gains and the security of the highway. The protection of this route and the recapture of the forward posts were thus ongoing objectives throughout the war.

The Indian Army's first priority was to recapture peaks that were in the immediate vicinity of NH1a. This resulted in Indian troops first targeting the Tiger Hill and Tololing complex in Dras, which dominated the Srinagar-Leh route. This was soon followed by the Batalik-Turtok sub-sector which provided access to Siachen Glacier.

Some of the peaks that was of vital strategic importance to the Pakistani defensive troops were Point 4590 and Point 5353. While 4590 was the nearest point that had a view of NH1a, point 5353 was the highest feature in the Dras sector, allowing the Pakistani troops to observe NH1A.

The recapture of Point 4590 by Indian troops on June 14 was significant, notwithstanding the fact that Point 4590 resulting in the Indian Army suffering the most casualties in a single battle during the conflict.

Though most of the posts in the vicinity of the highway were cleared by mid-June, some parts of the highway near Drass witnessed sporadic shelling until the end of the war. The tail of an Indian air force MiG-21 fighter shot down by a Pakistani missile.

The pilot Squadron Leader Ajay Ahuja was killed. The IAF lost a MiG-27 strike aircraft which it attributed to an engine failure as well as a MiG-21 fighter which was shot down by Pakistan; Initially Pakistan said it shot down both jets after they crossed into its territory and one Mi-8 helicopter to Stinger SAMs. On May 27 1999, Flt. Lt. Nachiketa developed engine trouble in the Batalik sector and bailed out of his craft. Sqn Ldr Ajay Ahuja went out of his way to locate his comrade but was shot down using a shoulder-fired Stinger missile.

According to reports, he had bailed out of his stricken plane safely but was apparently killed by his captors as his body was returned riddled with bullet wounds.

Some of the brave Indian Soldiers and heroes who died protecting the Indian nation in the Kargil War:

- Officers (Indian Army)
- Lt. Col. Vishwanathan
- Lt. Col. Vijayaragahvan
- Lt. Col. Sachin Kumar

- Major Ajay Singh Jasrotia
- Major Kamlesh Pathak
- Major Padhmaphani Acharya
- Major Marriapan Sarvanan
- Major Rajesh Singh Adhikari
- Major Harmider Pal Singh
- Major Manoj Talwar
- Major Vivek Gupta
- Major Sonam Wangchuk
- Major Ajay Kumar
- Captain Amol Kalia
- Captain Kieshing Clifford Nongrum
- Captain Sumeet Roy
- Captain Amit Verma
- Captain Pannikot Visvanath Vikram
- Captain Anuj Nayyar
- Captain Vikram Batra
- Dy. Commandent Joy Lal(BSF)
- Captain Jintu Gogoi
- Lt. Vijayant Thaper
- Lt. N. Kenguruse
- Lt. Hanif-u-din
- Lt. Suarav Kalia
- Lt. Amit Bhardwaj
- Lt. Balwan Singh
- Lt. Manoj Kumar Pandey
- Officers (Indian Air Force)
- Squadren Leader Ajay Ahuja
- Squadren Leader Rajiv Pundir
- Flt. Lt. S Muhilan
- Flt. Lt. Nachiketa Rao
- Seargent Pvnr Prasad

- Sergeant Raj Kishore Sahu
- Junior Commissioned Officers (Indian Army)
- Naik Chaman Singh
- Naik R Kamraj
- Naik Kudeep Singh
- Naik Birendra Singh Lamba
- Naik Jasvir Singh
- Naik Surendra Pal
- Naik Rajkumar Punia
- Naik S N Malik
- Naik Surjeet Singh
- Naik Jugal Kishore
- Naik Suchha Singh
- Naik Sumer Singh Rathod
- Naik Surendra Singh
- Naik Kishen Lal
- Naik Rampal Singh
- Naik Ganesh Yadav
- Havaldar Major Yashvir Singh
- Lance Naik Ahmed Ali
- Lance Naik Gulam Mohammed Khan
- Lance Naik M R Sahu
- Lance Naik Satpal Singh
- Lance Naik Shatrugan singh
- Lance Naik Shyam Singh
- Lance Naik Vijay Singh
- Naik Degender Kumar
- Havaldar Baldev Raj
- Havaldar Jai Prakash Singh
- Havaldar Mahavir Singh
- Havaldar Mani Ram
- Havaldar Rajbir Singh

- Havaldar Satbir Singh
- Havaldar Abdul Karim
- Havaldar Daler Singh Bahu
- Subedar Bhanwar Singh Rathod
- Rifleman Linkon Pradhan
- Rifleman Bachhan Singh
- Rifleman Satbir Singh
- Rifleman Jagmal Singh
- Rifleman Rattan Chand
- Rifleman Mohamad Farid
- Rifleman Mohamad Aslam
- Rifleman Yogendra Singh
- Rifleman Sanjay Kumar

*Sepoys (Indian Army)*

- Grenadier Manohar Singh
- Gunner Uddabh Das
- Sepoy Amardeep Singh
- Sepoy Vijay Pal Singh
- Sepoy Virendra Kumar
- Sepoy Yashwant Singh
- Sepoy Santokh Singh
- Sepoy Dinesh Bhai
- Sepoy Harendragiri Goswami
- Sepoy Amrish Pal Bangi
- Constable Suraj Bhan (BSF)
- Sepoy Lakhbir Singh
- Sepoy Bajindra Singh
- Sepoy Deep Chand
- Sepoy Dondibha Desai
- Sepoy Keolanand Dwivedi
- Sepoy Harjindra Singh

- Sepoy Jaswant Singh
- Sepoy Jaswinder Singh
- Sepoy Lal Singh
- Sepoy Rakesh Kumar(RAJ)
- Sepoy Rakesh Kumar (Dogra)
- Sepoy Raswinder Singh
- Sepoy Bir Singh
- Sepoy Ashok Kumar Tomar
- Sepoy R. Selvakumar

So after 10 years of Kargil, we take a moment to remember the brave soldiers and Heroes who fought the Kargil War and died for the nation.

# 17

# Glorious History of Indian Military

The dates back several millennia. The first reference to armies is found in the Vedas and the epics Ramayana and Mahabaratha.

From the ancient period through to the 19th century, a succession of powerful dynasties rose and fell in India as smaller rulers also struggled for power through war. The British colonised India during the 19th century.

The predecessors to the modern Army of India were the sepoy regiments, native cavalry, irregular horse and Indian sapper and miner companies raised by the three British presidencies. The Army of India was raised under the British Raj in the 19th century by taking the erstwhile presidency armies, merging them, and bringing them under the Crown. The British Indian Army fought in both World Wars.

The armed forces succeeded the military of British India following India's independence in 1947. After World War II, many of the wartime troops were discharged and units disbanded. The reduced armed forces were partitioned between India and Pakistan.

The Indian armed forces fought in all three wars against Pakistan and a war with the People's Republic of China. India also fought in the Kargil War with Pakistan in 1999, the highest altitudemountain warfare in history. The Indian Armed Forces have participated in several United Nations peacekeeping operations and are presently the second largest contributor of troops to the peacekeeping force.

## THE VEDIC PERIOD

The Rigvedic tribes of Indo-Aryans were led by their tribal chieftains (*raja*) and engaged in wars with each other and other tribes. They used bronze weapons and horse-drawn spoke-wheeled chariots described prominently in the Rigveda. The main share from the booty obtained during cattle raids and battles went to the chief of the tribe. The warriors belonged to the Kshatriya varna.

The Vedas and other associated texts dating to the post-Rigvedic (Iron Age) Vedic period (ca. 1100–500 BC) contain the earliest written references to armies in India. The earliest known application of war elephants dates to this period; the animals are mentioned in several Vedic Sanskrit hymns.

The two great epics of India, the Ramayana and the Mahabharata, centre on conflicts between the emerging Mahajanapadas and refer to military formations, theories of warfare and esoteric weaponry. They discuss standing armies and the use of chariots, war elephants and even flying machines in wars. The Ramayana describes the fortifications of Ayodhyain great detail. The Mahabharata describes various military techniques like Chakravyuha used in the Kurukshetra War.

## THE MAGADHA DYNASTIES

### Shishunaga Dynasty

The expansionist King Bimbisara conquered Anga in what is now West Bengal and strengthened the military of Magadh's capital, Rajagriha. Ajatashatru built a new fort at Pataliputra, Magadh's new capital, to launch an attack on Licchavis across the Ganges River. Jain texts tell that he used two new weapons, a catapult and a covered chariot with swinging mace that has been compared to modern tanks.

## Nanda Dynasty

Mahapadma Nanda defeated Ikshvakus, Panchalas, Kasis, Harhayas, Kalingas, Asmakas, Kurus, Maithilas, Surasenas, and Vitihotras and assumed the title "the destroyer of the kshathriyas". At the time of Dhana Nanda, the Nandas had an army consisting of 80,000 cavalry, 200,000 infantry, 8,000 armed chariots, and 6,000 war elephants.

## Maurya Dynasty

According to Megasthenes, who served as an ambassador from the Seleucid Empire, Chandragupta Maurya built an army consisting of 30,000 cavalry, 9,000 war elephants, and 600,000 infantry. Chandragupta conquered all of northern India, establishing an empire from the Arabian Sea to the Bay of Bengal. He then defeated the Macedonians and Seleucus I Nicator to conquer the regions to the east of the Indus River. He then turned south, taking over much of what is now Central India. His military was administered by six chairs, one for each of the four arms of the army (infantry, cavalry, elephants, and chariots), one chair for the navy, and one for logistics and supply. Infantry at this time was most commonly armed with a longbow made of bamboo and a single- or double-handed broadsword probably similar to the khanda. Other foot soldiers could be armed with a large animal hide tower shield and a spear or javelins. Cavalry carried spears. Elephants were mounted, usually bareback (rarely with a howdah at this time, as it is a Greek invention), by archers or javelin throwers, with a mahout around the animal's neck. Chariots by this time were in definite decline, but remained in the army due to their prestige. In 185 BC, the last Mauryan ruler was assassinated by Pushyamitra Sunga, the Commander-in-Chief of the Mauryan armed forces.

# THE GOLDEN AGE

Classical Indian texts on archery in particular and martial arts in general are known as Dhanurveda. Several classics of the genre date from this period.

## Satavahana Dynasty

According to some interpretations of the Puranas, the Satavahana family belonged to the Andhra-jati ("tribe") and was the first Deccanese dynasty to build an empire in daksinapatha (southern region). The Satavahanas (also called Andhra and Shalivahan) rose to power in modern Maharashtra around 200 B.C. and remained in power for about 400 years. Almost the whole of present day Maharashtra, Madhya Pradesh, Chhattisgarh, Odisha, Goa, Karnataka, and Andhra Pradesh came under Satavahana rule. Their capital was Paithan, then called Pratishthan.

Simuka, the dynasty's founder, conquered Maharashtra, Malwa and part of Madhya Pradesh. His successor and brother Kanha (or Krishna) further extended his kingdom to the west and the south. He was succeeded by Satakarni I, who defeated the Sunga dynasty of North India. His successor, Gautamiputra Satakarni, defeated the invading Sakas (Scythians), Yavanas (Greeks) and Pahlavas (Parthians), as well as the Western Kshatrapas ruler Nahapana. His empire extended up to Banavasi in the south, and included Maharashtra, Konkan, Saurashtra, Malwa, west Rajasthan and Vidharbha. Later, Satavahana rulers lost some of these territories. Satavahana power revived briefly under Yajna Sri Satakarni but declined after his death.

## Kushan Empire

Vima Takto, using the name "Soter Megas" (Great Saviour), conquered Gandhara and northern India in 68 AD. The Kushan warriors were assimilated into Indian society as Kshatriyas. Following Yuezhi's style, most Kushan nobles fought on horseback supported by cataphracts, which were the backbone of the Kushan army and whose use increased with time. Coins depicting Kujula, Vima Takto, Vima Kadphises and Kanishka show the king unarmoured or armoured more lightly than later Kushan kings. On many coins Kanishka appears to have a bow, but this interpretation is debatable. Some Buddhist texts indicate the use of Indian influences like elephants leading the attacks and the use of chariots. Elephants first appeared on the coins of Vima Kadphises and probably went on to become the mount of the kings. The elephants are depicted with towers and a covering; it is unclear whether these were armour or just padding. Buddhist texts mention that the infantry were used to support these elephants. The historian Nikonorov suggests that the elephants used were provided by the Satraps. Greeks, various mountain tribes, Sacas from northern India and Iranian mercenaries also fought in the Kushan army.

## Gupta Dynasty

*Siva-Dhanur-veda* discusses the military of the Gupta Empire. The Guptas relied heavily on armoured war elephants; horses were used little if at all. The use of chariots had declined heavily by the time of the Guptas, as they had not proved very useful against the Macedonians, Scythians, and other invaders. Guptas utilised heavy cavalry clad in mail armour and equipped with maces and lances, who would have used shock action to break the enemy line. They also employed on infantryarchers. Their longbow was composed of bamboo or metal and fired a long bamboo cane arrow with a metal head; iron shafts were used against armoured elephants. They also sometimes used fire arrows. Archers were frequently protected by infantry equipped with shields, javelins, and longswords. The Guptas also maintained a navy, allowing them to control regional waters. Samudragupta seized the kingdoms of Shichchhatra and Padmavati early in his reign. Later, he took the Kota kingdom and attacked the tribes in Malvas, the Yaudheyas, the Arjunayanas, the Madurasand the Abhiras. By his death in 380, he had conquered over twenty kingdoms. Chandragupta IIdefeated his rival, Rudrasimha III, by 395 and defeated the Saka Western Kshatrapas of Malwa, Gujarat and Saurashtra in a campaign lasting until 409. Chandragupta II also crushed the Bengal (Vanga) chiefdoms. Skandagupta defeated Pushyamitra and repelled the attack of Hephthalites or "White Huns" around 455, but the expense of the wars drained the empire's resources and contributed to its decline.

## THE CLASSICAL AGE

### Harsha's Empire

Emperor Harshavardhana (606–648) ruled northern India for over forty years. His father, a king of Thanesar, had gained prominence by successful wars against the Huns. Harsha had plans to conquer the whole of India, and carried on wars for thirty years with considerable success. By 612 he had built up a vast army with which he conquered nearly all North India up to the Narmada river. In 620 he invaded the Deccan Plateau but was repelled by Pulakesi II.

### The Chalukyas and Pallavas

In South India, the Chalukyas and the Pallavas gained prominence. The Chalukya ruler Pulakesi II's expansionism started with minor campaigns against the Alupas, Gangas and others. He defeated the Pallava king Mahendravarman and conquered the Cheras and the Pandyas. His greatest military success, the defeat of Harshavardhana, depleted his treasury, forcing him to end his expansionist campaigns.

The Pallava king Narasimhavarman vowed to avenge Mahendravarman's defeat by Pulakesi II. He invaded Vatapi with an army headed by his general Paranjothi. He defeated the Chalukyas, killing Pulakesi II in 642. Clashes between the Chalukyas and the Pallavas continued for a century, until the Chalukya king Vikramaditya II won a decisive victory against the Pallavas in 740. The Rashtrakutas overthrew the Chalukya empire in 750. During the 970s, Tailapa II overthrew the Rashtrakutas and recovered most of the Chalukya Empire, except for Gujarat. The Chalukyas of this period are known as the Kalyani Chalukyas, as Kalyaniwas their capital. They clashed intermittently with the Cholas.

### The Chola Empire

The Cholas were the first rulers of the Indian subcontinent to maintain a navy and use it to expand their dominion overseas. Vijayalaya Chola defeated the Pallavas and captured Thanjavur.

In the early 10th century the Chola king Parantaka I defeated the Pandyan king Maravarman Rajasimha II and invaded Sri Lanka. The Rashtrakuta ruler Krishna III defeated and killed Parantaka I's son Rajaditya in about 949.

Uttama Chola reigned 970-85. Inscriptions tell that at least from his time, Chola warriors wore waist coats of armour. Hence, one regiment was called *Niyayam-Uttama-Chola-tterinda-andalakattalar*. Paluvettaraiyar Maravan Kandanar served as a general under Uttama and his predecessor, Sundara. Rajaraja Chola began his military career with the conquest of the Cheras in the Kandalur War. He captured the Pandya ruler Amara Bhujanga, the town of Vilinam, and a part of Sri Lanka. In the 14th year of his reign (998–999) he conquered the Gangas of Mysore, the Nolambas of Bellary and Eastern Mysore, Tadigaipadi, Vengi, Coorg, the Pandyas and the Chalukyas of the Deccan. During the next three years, he subdued Quilon and the northern kingdom of Kalinga with the help of his son Rajendra Chola I. Rajendra later completed the conquest of Sri Lanka, crossed the Ganges, and marched across Kalinga to Bengal. He sent out a great naval expedition that occupied parts of Java, Malaya, and Sumatra. The Cholas were brought down by the Hoysalas from the west and Pandyas from the south.

## The Gurjar-Pratiharas, Palas and Rashtrakutas

In middle of 9th century, the Palas under Devapala attacked the Gurjara-Pratiharas. Led by Mihir Bhoja, the Pratiharas and their allies defeated Narayan Pala.

There were many battles between the Gurjar Pratiharas under Bhoj and the Rashtrakutas under Krishna II with mixed results. When the Rashtrakuta king Indra III attacked Kanauj, Mahipala, Mihir Bhoj's successor, fled; he later returned.

Al-Masudi wrote that in 915, during Mahipala's rule, the Pratiharas were at war with the Muslims in the west and the Rashtrakutas in the south, and that the Gurjar Pratiharas had four armies of about 800,000 men each.

## Arab Conquest of Sindh

In 712, an Arab general, named Muhammad bin Qasim Al-Thaqafi (c. 31 December 695–18 July 715), attacked and conquered Sindh kingdom which is mainly situated in Indus valley area (After partition, now in modern day Pakistan), by the time Sindh was ruled by Raja Dahir of Rai Dynasty, this dynasty was at war with Arabs. Though they defeated several Arab invasion before 712 A.D, but this time being deprived of local Buddhist people's support, Sindhu was captured and the first step of Islamic foundation in India was created. Chach Nama ,written by Kàzí Ismáíl briefly discusses the events.

## THE MEDIEVAL ERA

## Delhi Sultanate

The Delhi Sultanate, under the Khilji dynasty, repelled several invasions by the Mongol Empire. Zafar Khan, a general serving Alauddin Khilji, defeated the Mongols near Jalandhar in 1297. In 1299, Zafar Khan fought back a Mongol army of 200,000 soldiers but was killed in the process. Its last sultan, Ibrahim Lodi, died fighting the forces of Babur in the first battle of Panipat in 1526, ending the sultanate and paving the way for the foundation of the Mughal Empire.

## The Rajputs

After Babur's victory over Ibrahim Lodi, the Mewar ruler Rana Sanga led a combined Rajput army of 20,000 intending to defeat Babur and capture Delhi. The Mughals had superiorartillery, which prevailed against the Rajput cavalry. A Tomargeneral betrayed Rana Sanga, resulting in his defeat by Babur at the Battle of Khanua (16 March 1527). During the reign Rana Sanga's son Rana Udai Singh II, Babur's grandson Akbar conquered Chittor, the capital of Mewar.

In the Battle of Haldighati (21 June 1576) between Akbar and Rana Pratap Singh, the Mughal army of 80,000 was headed by a Rajput, Raja Man Singh, and Akbar's son Salim. The Rajput army's strength was 20,000. After a four-hour battle in which most of his soldiers were either killed or captured, Rana Pratap escaped with the help of his estranged brother Sakti Singh. His legendary horse Chetak was killed in the battle. Later, Rana Pratap organized a small army of Bhiltribals funded by a businessman called Bhamashah and started a guerrilla war against Akbar. He retook large parts of Mewar but could not retake Chittor.

## Muzaffarid Dynasty

Sultan Muzaffar Shah I, the Governor of Gujarat, established the Muzaffarid dynasty in 1391. It expanded rapidly and peaked under Sultan Mahmud I, who lost the Battle of Diu to the Portuguese in 1509.

## Calicut

Ruled by the Zamorin, the small Hindu Nair kingdom of Calicut (Malabar) welcomed the Portuguesein 1498 as traders but then fought several naval wars with Portugal in the 1500s. The office of Muslim naval chief in Calicut was known as the Kunhali Marakkar.

## Vijayanagara Empire

In 1509, the Bahamani Sultan declared war against the Vijayanagara Empire. His large coalition army was defeated by Krishnadevaraya in a battle in which the Sultan was wounded. In 1510, Krishnadevaraya launched a counteroffensive against the Sultan at Kovelaconda; Yusuf Adil Shahi of Bijapur died in the battle.

In 1512, Krishnadevaraya captured Raichur and Gulbarga after defeating Barid-i-Mamalik, the titular head of the Bahmani Sultanate, who escaped to Bidar. Later, Bidar also fell to Krishnadevaraya, who restored the Bahmani Sultan to his throne under the terms of their peace treaty.

Between 1512 and 1514, Krishnadevaraya subjugated the Palaigar of Ummattur, who had rebelled against his brother. During this campaign, the Gajapati of Odisha attacked Vijayanagara and occupied two northeast provinces: Udayagiri and Kondavidu. Krishnadevaraya recaptured these lands between 1513 and 1518.

On 26 January 1565, the neighboring kingdoms of Ahmednagar, Berar, Bidar, Bijapur and Golcondacame together to defeat the Vijayanagar decisively in the Battle of Talikota. The surviving Vijaynagar forces fled with a large treasury to re-establish their headquarters at Vellore Fort in Tamil Nadu and Chandragiri (Andhra Pradesh) near Tirupathi. It would be here that the British would seek a land grant to establish the English East India Company Fort St. George in Madras.

Later, the Vijayanagara's southern Telugu governors, in present day Tamil Nadu, became independent. They became the Gingee Nayaks in Gingee Fort, the Tanjore Nayaks, and the Nayaks of Madurai.

## Mughal Empire

The Mughal Empire began in 1526 with the overthrow of Ibrahim Lodi and encompassed most of South Asia by the late 17th and early 18th centuries. Allied with the Maharaja, it extended from Bengal in the east to Balochistan in the west, Kashmir in the north to the Kaveri basin in the south, a territory of over 4 million $km^2$ at its height. Its population at that time has been estimated at between 110 and 130 million. In the year 1540, then Mughal Emperor Humayunwas defeated by Sher Shah Suri, and forced to retreat to Kabul. Suris and their adviser, the Hindu Emperor Hem Chandra Vikramaditya, also called Hemu, ruled North India from 1540 to 1556. Hemu established a 'Hindu' Empire briefly from Delhi in 1556.

The "classic period" of the Empire started in 1556 with the accession of Akbar the Great and ended with the death of Emperor Aurangzeb in 1707, although the dynasty continued for another 150 years. During this period, the Empire was marked by centralized administration and active culture. Following 1725 the empire declined rapidly, weakened by wars of succession; famine and local revolts fueled by it; the growth of religious intolerance; the rise of the Maratha Empire; and finally British colonialism. The last Mughal emperor, Bahadur

Shah II, whose rule was restricted to the city of Delhi, was imprisoned and exiled by the British after the Indian Rebellion of 1857.

## The Marathas

In 1674, Shivaji Bhosale carved an independent Maratha zone around Pune, Maharshtra, from the Bijapur Sultanate and, with that began the emergence of the Marathas as the most important power in India that filled the vacuum created by the decline of the Mughal Empire. Shivaji established an effective civil and military administration. After a lifetime of conquest and guerrilla warfare with the Mughal emperor Aurangzeb, Shivaji died in 1680, leaving behind a kingdom of great but ill-defined extent. This was followed by a period of instability ending with Aurangzeb's death. Shivaji was the second king in Indian history to maintain an active navy. Kanhoji Angre, the first Maratha naval chief under Shivaji's grandson Shahuji, controlled illegal entries into Maratha territory by Dutch, English and Portuguese commercial ships on the Western coast of India in the early 18th century. He remained undefeated until his death in 1729.

Although the descendants of Shivaji continued to rule, the office of the Peshwa, or the Prime Minister, became the focus of Maratha power and patronage. The Peshwas were the effective rulers of the Maratha state and oversaw the period of greatest Maratha expansion, brought to an end by the Maratha's defeat by an Afghanarmy at the Third Battle of Panipat in 1761. The Marathas recovered their position as the dominant power in India by 1772 until the last Peshwa, Baji Rao II, was defeated by the British in the Third Anglo-Maratha War.

## Travancore Kingdom

King Marthanda Varma inherited the small feudal state of Venad in 1723 and built it into Travancore, one of the most powerful kingdoms in southern India, with the help of the British East India Company. Marthanda Varma led the Travancore forces during the Travancore-Dutch War of 1739–46, which culminated in the Battle of Colachel. Marthanda

Varma went on to conquer most of the petty principalities of the native rulers who had allied with the Dutch against him.

During Dharma Raja's reign, Tipu Sultan invaded Travancore, but commander-in-chief Raja Kesavadas led Travancore to victory despite being outnumbered. This attack led to Travancore joining the British against Tipu in the Third Battle of Carnatic.

Pazhsi Raja, Velu Thampi Dalava and Paliath Achan, later leaders of Travancore, fought the British East India Company but lost. Travancore became a British ally in 1805 following a treaty between Colonel Charles Macaulay and Diwan Velu Tampi. It remained so until 1947 when it became part of the newly independent Union of India.

## Mysore Kingdom

Hyder Ali, the *de facto* ruler of Mysore, was one of the first Indian rulers to resist the British, allying instead with France. He was one of the first Indian rulers to use rockets, employing them to defeat a top British unit.

Hyder Ali's son Tipu Sultan was instructed by French military officers. Tipu fought in the First Anglo-Maratha War of 1775–1779. He defeated the Brathwaite on the banks of the Coleroon in February 1782 in the Second Mysore War. After his father's death in 1782, he sought alliances with the Marathas and the Mughals but was rebuffed.

He turned to France instead. In 1789, he ignited the Third Mysore War by invading Travancore, a British protectorate, but was defeated when France failed to come to his aid due to the outbreak of the French Revolution. Later, Horatio Nelson ended Napoleon's ambitions for India at the Battle of the Nile. During the Fourth Mysore Warof 1799, three armies—one from Bombay and two British, one of which was commanded by the future Duke of Wellington—marched into Mysore and besieged the capital, Srirangapatnam. On 4 May 1799, the armies broke through the defending walls. Tipu Sultan died of a gunshot wound near the gates of his fortress.

## Sikh Empire

Maharaja Ranjit Singh was a Sikh ruler of the sovereign country of Punjab and the Sikh Empire. His father Maha Singh led Sukerchakia, a misl within the Sikh Confederacy. Born in 1780 in Gujranwala, Ranjit Singh succeeded his father at the age of 12. He united the Sikh factions into the Sikh Empireand took the title "Maharaja" on 13 April 1801, to coincide with Baisakhi. Lahore was his capital from 1799. In 1802 he conquered Amritsar, a holy city of the Sikh religion. In 1822 Ranjit Singh hired European mercenaries for the first time to train a part of his troops. He modernized his army, creating a military force whose power delayed the eventual British colonization of Punjab. The result was a powerful and heavily armed state. The Battle of Jamrud in 1837 was a major setback for Ranjit Singh: his general Hari Singh Nalwa was killed, the Khyber Pass was established as the western limit of the Sikh Empire's influence.

Ranjit Singh died in 1839, and his empire crumbled under internal strife and poor governance by his heirs. On the east of his realm Gulab Singh extended Sikh authority in the Himalayas until stopped by the Qing Empire in the Sino-Sikh war (1841–1842). After the First Anglo-Sikh War (1845–46), Punjab effectively ceased to be an independent state. The British Empire annexed the Sikh Empire following the Second Anglo-Sikh War (1848–49).

# COLONIAL ERA

## Company Rule

The British Indian Army was raised to guard the factories of the British East India Company. Following the fall of French Pondichéry in 1793, this was divided into Presidency armies of Bengal, Madras and Bombay in 1795. The Dutch trained the Nair Brigade, the military of Travancore.

During the Sepoy Mutiny of 1857–58, some units of the Bengal Native Infantry and Cavalry revolted against the British East India Company. The rebels received less support than they had expected from members of the Bombay and Madras Armies. A number of atrocities took place, among them the Siege of Cawnpore. The mutiny ultimately failed because of lack of resources and coordination among the rebels. Reprisals by the victorious British Army, assisted by Sikh and Afghan regulars and irregulars, were ruthless.

## The British Raj

Following the Sepoy Mutiny, British rule in India was reorganised under the British Raj, made up of areas directly administered by the United Kingdom and princely states under theparamountcy of the British Crown. Under terms of treaties with the Crown, these princely states were allowed some local autonomy in exchange for protection and representation in international affairs by the United Kingdom. The Raj included present-day India, Pakistan, and Bangladesh.

After 1857, the Presidency Armies were abolished in favour of a reconstituted British Indian Army under the control of the British Crown and the Viceroy. Many units were disbanded or reorganised, and new units of Sikhs, Gurkhas, and irregular horsemen were introduced. The majority of the Madras Native Infantry and Cavalry had their class compositions changed to North Indian tribes, considered more "martial" than the darker, shorter "thambis" who made up the majority of the Madras Presidency Army. Indian sepoys were banned from serving as officers or in the artillery corps. Recruiting focused more on Sikhs and Gurkhas, whom the British viewed as loyal. New caste-based and religion-based regiments were formed.

The British Indian Army consisted of members of all the major religious groups in India: Hindus, Sikhs, Christians, and Muslims. The number of Sikhs in the army grew steadily with time as British commanders came to believe they were more loyal and martial, an impression reinforced by their conduct during the Sepoy Mutiny. The Sikhs, for their part, aligned with the British to prevent a resurgence of Muslim rule; Sikhs had been persecuted under the Mughal Empire.

The Indian Air Force was established in 1932.

## British India (1857 to 1947)

The Royal Indian Navy was first established by the British while much of India was under the control of the East India Company. The first Indian to be granted a commission was Sub Lieutenant D. N. Mukherji, who joined the Royal Indian Marine as an engineer officer in 1928. Indian sailors started a rebellion known as the Royal Indian Navy mutiny in 1946, on board ships and in shore establishments which spread all over India. A total of 78 ships, 20 shore establishments and 20,000 sailors were involved in the rebellion.

The Indian Army during World War I contributed a number of divisions and independent brigades to the European, Mediterranean and the Middle East theaters of war. One million Indian troops would serve overseas, of whom 62,000 died and another 67,000 were wounded. In total 74,187 Indian soldiers died during the war. In World War I, the Indian Army fought against the German Empire in German East Africa and on the Western Front. Indian divisions were also sent to Egypt, Gallipoli and nearly 700,000 served in Mesopotamia against the Ottoman Empire.

## Organisation

The Indian Army has its origins in the years after the Indian Rebellion of 1857, often called the Indian Mutiny in British histories, when in 1858 the Crown took over direct rule of British India from the East India Company. Before 1858, the precursor units of the Indian Army were units controlled by the Company and were paid for by their profits. These operated alongside units of the British Army, funded by the British government in London.

The armies of the East India Company were recruited primarily from Muslims in the Bengal Presidency, which consisted of Bengal, Bihar and Uttar Pradesh, and high caste Hindus recruited primarily from the rural plains of Oudh. Many of these troops took part in the Indian Mutiny, with the aim of reinstating the Mughal Emperor Bahadur Shah II at Delhi, partly as a result of insensitive treatment by their British officers. The meaning of the term "Indian Army" has changed over time:

1858–1894: The Indian Army was an informal collective term for the armies of the three presidencies; the Bengal Army, Madras Army and Bombay Army.

1895–1902: The Indian Army had a formal existence and was the "army of the government of India", including British and Indian (sepoy) units.

1903–1947: Lord Kitchener was Commander-in-Chief, India, between 1902 and 1909. He instituted large-scale reforms, the greatest of which was the merger of the three armies of the Presidencies into a unified force. He formed higher level formations, eight army divisions, and brigaded Indian and British units. Following Kitchener's reforms:

- The Indian Army was "the force recruited locally and permanently based in India, together with its expatriate British officers."
- The British Army in India consisted of British Army units posted to India for a tour of duty, and which would then be posted to other parts of the Empire or back to the UK.
- The Army of India consisted of both the Indian Army and the British Army in India.

## Personnel

Commissioned officers, British and Indian, held identical ranks to commissioned officers of the British Army. King's Commissioned Indian Officers (KCIOs), created from the 1920s, held equal powers to British officers. Viceroy's Commissioned Officers were Indians holding officer ranks.

They were treated in almost all respects as commissioned officers, but had authority over Indian troops only, and were subordinate to all British King's (and Queen's) Commissioned Officers and KCIOs. They included Subedar Major or Risaldar-Major (Cavalry), equivalents to a British Major; Subedar or Risaldar (Cavalry) equivalents to Captain; and Jemadars equivalent, to Lieutenant.

Recruitment was entirely voluntary; about 1.3 million men served in the First World War, many on the Western Front and 2.5 million in the Second. Non-Commissioned Officers included Company Havildar Majors equivalents to a Company Sergeant Major; Company Quartermaster Havildars, equivalents to a Company Quartermaster Sergeant; Havildars or Daffadars (Cavalry) equivalents to a Sergeant; Naik orLance-Daffadar (Cavalry) equivalents to a British Corporal; and Lance-Naik or Acting Lance-Daffadar (Cavalry) equivalents to a Lance-Corporal.

Soldier ranks included Sepoys or Sowars (Cavalry), equivalent to a British private. British Army ranks such as gunner and sapper were used by other corps.

## Command

The officer commanding the Army of India was the Commander-in-Chief in India who reported to the civilian Governor-General of India. The title was used before the creation of a unified British Indian Army; the first holder was Major General Stringer Lawrence in 1748. By the early 1900s the Commander-in-Chief and his staff were based at GHQ India. Indian Army postings were less prestigious than British Army positions, but the pay was significantly greater so that officers could live on their salaries instead of having to have a private income. Accordingly vacancies in the Indian Army were much sought after and generally reserved for the higher placed officer-cadets graduating from the Royal Military Academy Sandhurst. British officers in the Indian Army were expected to learn to speak the Indian languages of their men, who tended to be recruited from primarily Hindi speaking areas. Prominent British Indian Army officers included Frederick Roberts, 1st Earl Roberts, William Birdwood, 1st Baron Birdwood, Claude Auchinleck and William Slim, 1st Viscount Slim.

## History

In the aftermath of the Indian Rebellion, the three armies of the former Presidencies of the East India Company passed to the British crown. After the mutiny, recruitment switched to what the British called the "martial races," particularly Sikhs, Awans, Gakhars, and other Punjabi *Mussulmans*, Pashtuns, Marathas, Bunts, Nairs, Rajputs, Yadavs, Kumaonis, Gurkhas, Garhwalis, Mohyals, Dogras, Jats and Sainis.

The three Presidency armies remained separate forces, each with its own Commander-in-Chief. Overall operational control was exercised by the Commander-in-Chief of the Bengal Army, who was formally the Commander-in-Chief of the East Indies. From 1861, most of the officer manpower was pooled in the three Presidential Staff Corps. After the Second Afghan War a Commission of Enquiry recommended the abolition of the presidency armies. The Ordnance, Supply and Transport, and Pay branches were by then unified.

The Punjab Frontier Force was under the direct control of the Lieutenant-Governor of the Punjab during peacetime until 1886, when it came under the C-in-C, India. The Hyderabad Contingent and other local corps remained under direct governmental control. Standing higher formations – divisions and brigades – were abandoned in 1889. No divisional staffs were maintained in peacetime, and troops were dispersed throughout the sub-continent, with internal security as their main function. In 1891 the three staff corps were merged into one Indian Staff Corps.

Two years later the Madras and Bombay Armies lost their posts of Commander-in-Chief. In 1895, the Presidency Armies were abolished and the Indian Army created thereby was re-grouped into four commands: Bengal, Madras (including Burma), Bombay (including Sind, Quetta, and Aden), and the Punjab (including the North-West Frontier and the Punjab Frontier Force). Each was under the command of alieutenant general, who answered directly to the C-in-C, India.

The Presidency armies were abolished with effect from 1 April 1895 by a notification of the Government of India through Army Department Order Number 981 dated 26 October 1894, unifying the three Presidency armies into a single Indian Army. The armies were amalgamated into four commands, Northern,

Southern, Eastern, and Western. The Indian Army, like the Presidency armies, continued to provide armed support to the civil authorities, both in combating banditry and in case of riots and rebellion. One of the first external operations the new unified army faced was the Boxer Rebellion in China from 1899 to 1901.

## Renumbering and Renaming the Regiments

To emphasize that there was now only one Indian Army, and that all units were to be trained and deployed without regard for their regional origins, the regiments were renumbered into single sequences of cavalry, artillery, infantry of the line, and Gúrkha Rifles. Regimental designations were altered to remove all references to the former Presidential Armies. Where appropriate subsidiary titles recalling other identifying details were adopted. Thus the 2nd Bengal Lancers became the 2nd Lancers (Gardner's Horse).

The new order began with the Bengal regiments, followed by the Punjab Frontier Force, then the regiments of Madras, the Hyderabad Contingent, and Bombay. Wherever possible a significant digit was retained in the new number. Thus the 1st Sikh Infantry became the 51st Sikhs, the 1st Madras Pioneers became the 61st Pioneers, and the 1st Bombay Grenadiers became the 101st Grenadiers.

The Gúrkha Regiments had developed into their own Line of rifle regiments since 1861. They were five of these until they were joined by the former 42nd, 43rd, & 44th Gúrkha Regiments of the Bengal Army, who became the 6th, 7th, & 8th Gúrkha Rifles. The numbers 42, 43, & 44 were allocated respectively to the Deoli and Erinpura Irregular Forces and the Mhairwara Battalion from Rajputana. The mountain batteries had already lost their numbers two years earlier. Under the 1903 reforms they were renumbered with twenty added to their original numbers. The army had very little artillery (only 12 batteries of mountain artillery), and Royal Artillery (Royal Indian Artillery) batteries were attached to the divisions. The Indian Army Corps of Engineers was formed by the Group of Madras,

Bengal and Bombay Sappers in their respective presidencies.

The Queen's Own Corps of Guides, Punjab Frontier Force, composed of cavalry squadrons and infantry companies, was renamed the Queen's Own Corps of Guides (Lumsden's) but stayed numberless. The new regimental numbering and namings were notified in *India Army Order 181*, dated 2 October 1903.

In 1903 the title of the Indian Staff Corps was abolished, and thereafter officers were simply appointed to 'the Indian Army.' A General Staff was then created to deal with overall military policy, supervision of training in peacetime, conduct of operations in war, distribution of forces for internal security or external deployment, plans for future operations and collecting intelligence. Functions were divided along British lines into two branches; the Adjutant-General, dealing with training, discipline, and personnel, and the Quartermaster-General, dealing with supplies, accommodation, and communications.

In 1906 a General Branch was established to deal with military policy, organisation and deployment, mobilisation and war plans, and intelligence and the conduct of operations. The Chiefs of the staff branches answered to the Chief of the General Staff, whose post was held by a lieutenant-general. To provide training for staff officers, the Indian Staff College was established in 1905, and permanently based at Quetta from 1907.

With no intermediate chain of command, army headquarters was weighed down with minor administrative details. Divisional commanders were responsible not only for their active formations, but also for internal security and volunteer troops within their respective areas. On mobilisation, divisional staffs took the field, leaving no-one to maintain the local administration. Supporting services were insufficient, and many troops intended for the field force were not moved from their old stations into the areas of their new divisional command. These defects became clear during the First World War, and lead to further reorganisation.

The Indian Army Act 1911 legislated the replacement of the Indian Articles of War 1869. It was passed by the Governor General. It was under aspects of this law that the Army charged defendants during the Indian National Army Trials in 1945. It was replaced by the *"Indian Army Act, 1950"* after partition and independence.

## Kitchener Reforms

The Kitchener reforms began in 1903 when Lord Kitchener of Khartoum, newly appointed Commander-in-Chief, India, completed the unification of the three former Presidency armies, and also the Punjab Frontier Force, the Hyderabad Contingent and other local forces, into one Indian Army.

The principles underlying the reforms were that:

- defence of the North-West Frontier against foreign aggression was the army's primary role
- all units were to have training and experience in that role on that frontier
- the army's organisation should be the same in peace as in war
- maintaining internal security was for the army a secondary role, in support of the police.

Lord Kitchener found the army scattered across the country in stations at brigade or regimental strength, and in effect, providing garrisons for most of the major cities. The reformed Indian Army was to be stationed in operational formations and concentrated in the north of the sub-continent. The Commander-in-Chief's plan called for nine fighting divisions grouped in two corps commands on the main axes through the North-West Frontier. Five divisions were to be grouped on the Lucknow – Peshawar – Khyber axis, and four divisions on the Bombay – Mhow – Quetta axis. However, the cost of abandoning some thirty-four stations and building new ones in the proposed corps areas was considered prohibitive, and that aspect of the plan had to be modified.

Under the compromise adopted in 1905, the four existing commands were reduced to three, and together with Army

Headquarters, arranged in ten standing divisions and four independent brigades:

- Northern Command comprised the 1st (Peshawar) Division, the 2nd (Rawalpindi) Division, the 3rd (Lahore) Division, the Kohat Brigade, the Bannu Brigade, and the Derajat Brigade.
- Western Command comprised the 4th (Quetta) Division, the 5th (Mhow) Division, the 6th (Poona) Division, and the Aden Brigade, located in Aden in the Arabian Peninsula.
- Eastern Command comprised the 7th (Meerut) Division and the 8th (Lucknow) Division.

Army Headquarters retained the 9th (Secunderabad) Division and the Burma Division under its direct control. The numbered divisions were organised so that on mobilisation they could deploy a complete infantry division, a cavalry brigade, and a number of troops for internal security or local frontier defence. Permanent divisional commands were formed with an establishment of staff officers under a Major-General.

After the reforms ended in 1909, the Indian Army was organised along British lines, although it was always behind in terms of equipment. An Indian Army division consisted of three brigades each of four battalions. Three of these battalions were of the Indian Army, and one British. The Indian battalions were often segregated, with companies of different tribes, castes or religions. One and a half million volunteers came forward from the estimated population of 315 million in the Indian subcontinent.

Regimental battalions were not permanently allocated to particular divisions or brigades, but instead spent some years in one formation, and were then posted to another elsewhere. This rotating arrangement was intended both to provide all units with experience of active service on the Frontier, and to prevent them becoming 'localised' in static regimental stations. In contrast, the divisional locations remained constant, as indicated by their respective titles.

## First World War

Prior to the outbreak of the First World War, the strength of the British Indian Army was 155,000. Either in 1914 or before, a ninth division had been formed, the 9th (Secunderabad) Division. By November 1918, the Indian Army rose in size to 573,000 men.

Before the war, the Indian government had decided that India could afford to provide two infantry divisions and a cavalry brigade in the event of a European war. 140,000 soldiers saw active service on the Western Front in France and Belgium – 90,000 in the front-line Indian Corps, and some 50,000 in auxiliary battalions. They felt that any more would jeopardise national security. More than four divisions were eventually sent as Indian Expeditionary Force A formed the Indian Corps and the Indian Cavalry Corps that arrived on the Western Front in 1914. The high number of officer casualties the corps suffered early on had an effect on its later performance. British officers that understood the language, customs, and psychology of their men could not be quickly replaced, and the alien environment of the Western Front had some effect on the soldiers. However, the feared unrest in India never happened, and while the Indian Corps was transferred to the Middle East in 1915 India provided many more divisions for active service during the course of the war. Indians' first engagement was on the Western Front within a month of the start of the war, at the First Battle of Ypres.

Here, Garwhal Rifles were involved in the war's first trench raid on 9–10 November 1914 and Khudadad Khan became the first Indian to win a Victoria Cross. After a year of front-line duty, sickness and casualties had reduced the Indian Corps to the point where it had to be withdrawn.

Nearly 700,000 then served in the Middle East, fighting against the Turks in the Mesopotamian campaign. There they were short of transportation for resupply and operated in extremely hot and dusty conditions. Led by Major General Sir Charles Townshend, they pushed on to capture Baghdad but they were repulsed by Turkish Forces.

In the First World War the Indian Army saw extensive service including:

- Western Front: Battle of Neuve Chapelle
- Battle of Gallipoli
- Sinai and Palestine Campaign
- Mesopotamian Campaign, Siege of Kut
- East Africa, including the Battle of Tanga.

Participants from the Indian subcontinent won 13,000 medals, including 12 Victoria Crosses. By the end of the war a total of 47,746 Indians had been reported dead or missing; 65,126 were wounded.

Also serving in the First World War were so-called "Imperial Service Troops", provided by the semi-autonomous Princely States. About 21,000 were raised in the First World War, mainly consisting of Sikhs of Punjab and Rajputs from Rajputana (such as the Bikaner Camel Corps and the Hyderabad, Mysore and Jodhpur Lancers of the Imperial Service Cavalry Brigade). These forces played a prominent role in the Sinai and Palestine Campaign.

## Interbellum (1918–1939)

Elements of the Army operated around Mary, Turkmenistan in 1918–19. Malleson mission and Entente intervention in the Russian Civil War. The army then took part in the Third Anglo-Afghan War of 1919. In the aftermath of the First World War, the Indian Territorial Forceand Auxiliary Force (India) were created in the 1920s. The Indian Territorial Force was a part-time, paid, all-volunteer organisation within the army. Its units were primarily made up of European officers and Indian other ranks. The ITF was created by the Indian Territorial Force Act 1920 to replace the Indian section of the Indian Defence Force. It was an all-volunteer force modelled after the British Territorial Army. The European parallel to the ITF was the Auxiliary Force (India).

After World War I the British started the process of Indianisation by which Indians were promoted into higher officer ranks. Indian cadets were sent to study at the Royal Military Academy Sandhurst in England and were given full commissions as King's Commissioned Indian Officers. The KCIOs were equivalent in every way to British commissioned officers and had full authority over British troops (unlike VCOs). Some KCIOs were attached to British Army units for a part of their careers.

In 1922, after experience had shown that the large groups of single battalion regiments were unwieldy, a number of large regiments were created, and numerous cavalry regiments amalgamated. The List of regiments of the Indian Army (1922) shows the reduced number of larger regiments. Until 1932 most British Indian Army officers, both British and Indian, were trained at Royal Military Academy Sandhurst, after that date the Indian officers increasingly received their training at the Indian Military Academy in Dehradun which was established that year.

## Second World War

At the outbreak of the Second World War, the Indian Army numbered 205,000 men. Later on during the Second World War the Indian Army would become the largest all-volunteer force in history, rising to over 2.5 million men in size. In doing so the Indian III Corps, Indian IV Corps, Indian XV Corps, Indian XXXIII Corps, Indian XXXIV Corps, 4th, 5th, 6th, 7th, 8th, 9th, 10th, 11th, 12th, 14th, 17th, 19th, 20th, 21st, and 23rd Indian Divisions were formed, as well as other forces. Additionally two armoured divisions and an airborne division were created. In matters of administration, weapons, training, and equipment, the Indian Army had considerable independence; for example, prior to the war the Indian Army adopted the Vickers-Berthier (VB) light machine gun instead of the Bren gun of the British Army, while continuing to manufacture and issue the older SMLE No. 1 Mk III rifle during the Second World War, instead of the Lee-Enfield No.4 Mk I issued to the British Army from the middle of the war.

Particularly notable contributions of the Indian Army during that conflict were the:

- Mediterranean, Middle East and African theatres of World War II
- East African campaign
- North African campaign
- Operation Compass
- Operation Battleaxe
- Operation Crusader
- First Battle of El Alamein
- Second Battle of El Alamein
- Anglo-Iraqi War
- Syria-Lebanon campaign
- Anglo-Soviet invasion of Iran
- Italian campaign
- Battle of Monte Cassino
- Battle of Hong Kong
- Battle of Malaya
- Battle of Singapore
- Burma Campaign
- Battle of Kohima
- Battle of Imphal.

About 87,000 Indian soldiers lost their lives during this conflict. Indian soldiers won 30 Victoria Crossesduring the Second World War.

The Germans and Japanese were relatively successful in recruiting combat forces from Indian prisoners of war. These forces were known as the Tiger Legion and the Indian National Army (INA). Indian nationalist leader Subhas Chandra Bose led the 40,000-strong INA. From a total of about 55,000 Indians taken prisoner in Malaya and Singapore in February 1942, about 30,000 joined the INA, which fought Allied forces in the Burma Campaign. Others became guards at Japanese POW camps. The recruitment was the brainchild of Major Fujiwara Iwaichi who mentions in his memoirs that Captain Mohan Singh Deb, who surrendered after the fall of Jitra became the founder of the INA.

Some Indian Army personnel resisted recruitment and remained POWs. An unknown number captured in Malaya and Singapore were taken to Japanese-occupied areas of New Guinea as forced labour. Many of these men suffered severe hardships and brutality, similar to that experienced by other prisoners of Japan during the Second World War. About 6,000 of them survived until they were liberated by Australian or U.S. forces, in 1943–45.

During World War II, after the fall of Singapore and the ending of ABDACOM in early 1942, until the formation of South East Asia Command (SEAC) in August 1943 some American and Chinese units were placed under British military command.

## World War I

During World War I, over 800,000 volunteered for the army, and more than 400,000 volunteered for non-combat roles, compared with the pre-war annual recruitment of about 15,000 men. The Army saw action on the Western Front within a month of the start of the war, at the First Battle of Ypres where Khudadad Khan became the first Indian to be awarded a Victoria Cross. After a year of front-line duty, sickness and casualties had reduced the Indian Corps to the point where it had to be withdrawn. Nearly 700,000 Indians fought the Turks in the Mesopotamian campaign. Indian formations were also sent to East Africa, Egypt, and Gallipoli.

Indian Army and Imperial Service Troops fought during the Sinai and Palestine Campaign's defence of the Suez Canal in 1915, at Romani in 1916 and to Jerusalem in 1917. India units occupied the Jordan Valley and after the Spring Offensive they became the major force in the Egyptian Expeditionary Force during the Battle of Megiddoand in the Desert Mounted Corps' advance to Damascus and on to Aleppo. Other divisions remained in India guarding the North-West Frontier and fulfilling internal security obligations.

One million Indian troops served abroad during the war. In total, 74,187 died, and another 67,000 were wounded. The roughly 90,000 soldiers who lost their lives fighting in World War I and the Afghan Wars are commemorated by the India Gate.

## World War II

In 1939, the British Indian Army's strength was about 189,000, with about 3,000 British officers and 1,115 Indian officers. The army was expanded greatly to fight in World War II: by 1945, the strength of the Army had risen to about 2.5 million, with about 34,500 British officers and 15,740 Indian officers. The Army took part in campaigns in France, East Africa, North Africa, Syria, Tunisia, Malaya, Burma, Greece, Sicily and Italy.

Particularly significant contributions came in the campaigns in Abyssinia and North Africa, against the Italians; at El Alamain and in Italy, against the Germans; and in the Burma Campaign against Japan. The army ultimately suffered 179,935 casualties: 24,338 killed, 64,354 wounded, 11,762 missing, and 79,481 taken prisoner.

During the war, Indian nationalist expatriates in Southeast Asia and the Japanese Army formed the Indian National Army (INA) to fight for Indian independence from Britain. For manpower, it relied on the approximately 45,000 Indian troops of the Indian Army whom the Japanese captured when Singapore fell in February 1942. Subhas Chandra Bose was parachuted in to lead the INA in 1943, and he greatly expanded the INA to include the mainly Tamil civilian Indian community in Malaya.

He also negotiated a combat role for the INA from the reluctant Japanese, who were more inclined to use it intelligence and propaganda work. In 1944, INA units participated in the Japanese Army‘s offensives against British positions in the Arakan and the Imphal Plain. Not being a military man Bose - or "Netaji" (respected leader" as he had grandly christened himself - naively believed that Indian soldiers of the Indian Army who deployed against the INA would flock to its standard. But these Indian troops stood form, and actually defeated the

INA. Despite this, Bose insisted that the INA be given an independent sector on the Irrawaddy in February 1945. Despite the desperate efforts of some INA troops, their sector was overrun, and desertions became common.lace. Militarily, the INA was finished. After the war, however, it made a political impact, due to the British decision to publicly court-martial three INA commanders. This was a miscalculation, because Indian nationalist politicians, who had previously come out against the INA, now whipped up popular sentiment for the release of the INA accused. Realizing their error, the British acquiesced. In this way, the INA was another Sign that the Raj's days were numbered.

## INDIAN AIR FORCE

The Indian Air Force is the fourth largest air force in the world. In its history, it has generally relied on Soviet technology to support its growth. However, in recent times, India has begun building its own original aircraft, including the HAL Tejas, which is a 4.5 generation fighter. Also India and Russia are currently building a 5th generation stealth aircraft jointly. India has also developed UAV called Nishant and HAL Dhruv, an advanced light helicopter. Recently it has completed a test of long range BVR air to air missile named Astra and also conducted a successful test of Anti ballistic missile defense system and hence became the 4th country after US,Russia and Israel to do so.

## STRUCTURE OF THE INDIAN AIR-FORCE

### Recruitment and Training

Recruitment is through three military related academies. These include the National Defence Academy, Indian Military Academy and Officers Training Academy. For entrance, one must display that they are both physically and mentally fit to be in the military by sitting examinations and undergoing medical checkups. The complete list of institutions training Indian army were listed in Military academies in India section.

## Indian Army

***Strength:*** During a conflict, the air-arm of the Indian army plays a crucial role in providing essential supplies and air cover to the ground forces. Shown here is the Indian Army's HAL Dhruv.

## Indian Army Statistics

| | |
|---|---|
| Active Troops | 1,325,000 (2nd) |
| Artillery | 7100 |
| Battle Tanks | 5010 |
| Aircraft | 52 squadrons of helicopters |
| Surface-to-air missiles | 90,000+ |

The Indian Army is the world's second largest army in terms of military personnel (after China). It is a completely voluntary service, the military draft having never been imposed in India. The army has rich combat experience in diverse terrains, due to India's diverse geography, and also has a distinguished history of serving in United Nations peacekeeping operations.

The force is headed by the Chief of Army Staff, currently General Deepak Kapoor. The highest rank in the Indian Army is Field Marshal, but it is a largely ceremonial rank and appointments are made by the President of India, on the advice of the Union Cabinet of Ministers, only in exceptional circumstances. General S.H.F.J. Manekshaw and the late General K.M. Cariappa are the only two officers who have attained this rank. The Indian Army has seen military action in the Indo-Pakistani War of 1947, the Indo-Pakistani War of 1965,the Indo-Pakistani War of 1971, and others such as Operation Polo in 1948, the Sino-Indian War in 1962 over the McMahon Line, and the Kargil War against Kashmiri insurgents and the Pakistan military personnel. Currently, the Indian army has dedicated one brigade of troops to the UN's standby arrangements.

Through its large, sustained troop commitments India has come in for much praise for taking part in difficult operations for prolonged periods. The Indian Army has participated in several UN peace-keeping operations, including the ones in Cyprus, Lebanon, Congo, Angola, Cambodia, Vietnam, Namibia, El Salvador, Liberia, Mozambique and Somalia. The army also provided a paramedical unit to facilitate the withdrawal of the sick and wounded in Korea.

## INDIAN NAVY

The Indian Navy is the naval branch of the armed forces of India. With 55,000 men and women, including 5,000 naval aviation personnel and 2,000 Marine Commandos (MARCOS), it is the world's fifth largest navy. The Indian Navy currently operates more than 155 vessels, including the aircraft carrier INS Viraat. The navy is considered to have blue-water capabilities. It is fairly advanced in terms of technology and is in control of one of two Asian aircraft carriers. Two more aircraft carriers are on order and will be joining the Indian Navy. The ships of the Indian Navy are of Indian and foreign origin.

In its maritime doctrine, the Indian Navy establishes its role in providing support to maritime neighbours during natural disasters. This was demonstrated during the Asian tsunami crisis during which the Indian Navy sent 35 ships to support relief efforts in neighbouring countries. The Indian navy has taken part in UN missions in the coast of Somalia and has provided security to an African Union summit held in Mozambique. India uses its navy to enhance its international relations through joint exercises, port visits, and humanitarian missions, including disaster relief. The Indian Navy is increasing its capabilities as a true blue-water navy; the Indian Navy's doctrine states that this is for the collective good of nations.

## ARMED FORCES (SPECIAL POWERS) ACT, 1958

The Armed Forces (Special Powers) Act (AFSPA), is an Act of the Parliament of India which was passed on 11 September 1958.

It is a law with just six sections granting special powers to the armed forces in what the act terms as "disturbed areas". Although the usefulness of the act has been universally acknowledged in particular for stabilizing the Kashmir valley and maintaining peace, the Act has received criticism from several sections for alleged concerns about human rights violations in the regions of its enforcement, where arbitrary killings, torture, cruel, inhuman and degrading treatment and enforced disappearances have alleged to have happened.

## History

The Armed Forces Special Powers Ordinance of 1942 was promulgated by the British on 15 August 1942 to suppress the Quit India Movement.

Modeled on these lines, four ordinances—the Bengal Disturbed Areas (Special Powers of Armed Forces) Ordinance; the Assam Disturbed Areas (Special Powers of Armed Forces)Ordinance; the East Bengal Disturbed Areas (Special Powers of Armed Forces) Ordinance; the United provinces Disturbed Areas (Special Powers of Armed Forces) Ordinance were invoked by the central government to deal with the internal security situation in the country in 1947 which arouse out of Partition of India.

## Armed Forces Special Powers (Assam and Manipur) Act, 1958

In 1951, the Naga National Council (NNC) reported that it conducted a 'free and fair plebiscite' in which about 99 per cent Nagas voted for a 'Free Sovereign Naga Nation'. There was a boycott of first general election of 1952 which later, extended to boycott of government schools and officials. In order to deal with the situation, the Assam government imposed the Assam Maintenance of Public Order (Autonomous District) Act in the Naga Hills in 1953 and intensified police action against the rebels. When the situation worsened, Assam deployed the Assam Rifles in the Naga Hills and enacted the Assam Disturbed Areas Act of 1955, providing a legal framework for the paramilitary forces and the armed state police to combat insurgency in the region. But the Assam Rifles and the state armed police could not contain the Naga rebellion and the rebel Naga Nationalist Council (NNC) formed a parallel government "The Federal Government of Nagaland" on 22 March 1956. The Armed Forces (Assam and Manipur) Special Powers Ordinance 1958 was promulgated by the President Dr. Rajendra Prasad on 22 May 1958. It was replaced by Armed Forces (Assam and Manipur) special Powers Act, 1958 on 11 September 1958.

## Armed Forces (Assam and Manipur) Special Powers (Amendment) Act, 1972

The Armed Forces (Assam and Manipur) Special Powers Act,1958 empowered only the Governors of the States and the Administrators of the Union Territories to declare areas in the concerned State or the Union Territory as 'disturbed'. The reason for conferring such a power as per "Objects and Reasons"' appended to the Bill was that, "Keeping in view the duty of the Union under Article 355 of the Constitution, inter alia, to protect every State against internal disturbance, it is considered desirable that the Central government should also have power to declare areas as 'disturbed', to enable its armed forces to exercise the special powers". The territorial scope of Act also expanded to the five states of the North-East, - Assam, Manipur, Meghalaya, Nagaland, Tripura and to the Union Territories Arunachal Pradesh andMizoram. In addition, the words, "The Armed Forces (Assam and Manipur) Special Powers Act, 1958" were substituted by "Armed Forces (Special Powers) Act, 1958", getting the acronym of AFSPA, 1958.

## The Armed Forces (Punjab and Chandigarh) Special Powers Act, 1983

The central government enacted the Armed Forces (Punjab and Chandigarh) Special Powers Act on 6 October 1983, repealing The Armed Forces (Punjab and Chandigarh) Special Powers Ordinance, 1983, to enable the central armed forces to operate in the state of Punjab and the union territory of Chandigarh. The Act was enforced in the whole of Punjab and

Chandigarh on 15 October 1983. The terms of the Act broadly remained the same as that of the Armed Forces Special Powers Act (Assam and Manipur) of 1972 except for two sections, which provided additional powers to the armed forces.

1. Sub-section (e) was added to Section 4 stipulating that any vehicle can be stopped, searched and seized forcibly if it is suspected of carrying proclaimed offenders or ammunition.
2. Section 5 was added to the Act specifying that a soldier has the power to break open any locks "if the key there of is withheld".

The Act was withdrawn in 1997, roughly 14 years after it came to force.

## The Act

The Articles in the Constitution of India empower state governments to declare a state of emergency due to one or more of the following reasons:

- Failure of the administration and the local police to tackle local issues.
- Return of (central) security forces leads to return of miscreants/erosion of the "peace dividend".
- The scale of unrest or instability in the state is too large for local forces to handle.

In such cases, it is the prerogative of the state government to call for central help. In most cases, for example during elections, when the local police may be stretched too thin to simultaneously handle day-to-day tasks, the central government obliges by sending in the BSF and the CRPF. Such cases do not come under the purview of AFSPA. AFSPA is confined to be enacted only when a state, or part of it, is declared a 'disturbed area'. Continued unrest, like in the cases of militancy and insurgency, and especially when borders are threatened, are situations where AFSPA is resorted to.

By Act 7 of 1972, the power to declare areas as being disturbed was extended to the central government.

In a civilian setting, soldiers have no legal tender, and are still bound to the same command chain as they would be in a war theatre. Neither the soldiers nor their superiors have any training in civilian law or policing procedures. This is where and why the AFSPA comes to bear - to legitimize the presence and acts of armed forces in emergency situations which have been deemed war-like.

## Armed Forces (Special Powers) Act

According to the Armed Forces Special Powers Act (AFSPA), in an area that is proclaimed as "disturbed", an officer of the armed forces has powers to:

- After giving such due warning, Fire upon or use other kinds of force even if it causes death, against the person who is acting against law or order in the disturbed area for the maintenance of public order,
- Destroy any arms dump, hide-outs, prepared or fortified position or shelter or training camp from which armed attacks are made by the armed volunteers or armed gangs or absconders wanted for any offence.
- To arrest without a warrant anyone who has committed cognizable offences or is reasonably suspected of having done so and may use force if needed for the arrest.
- To enter and search any premise in order to make such arrests, or to recover any person wrongfully restrained or any arms, ammunition or explosive substances and seize it.
- Stop and search any vehicle or vessel reasonably suspected to be carrying such person or weapons.
- Any person arrested and taken into custody under this Act shall be made over to the officer in charge of the nearest police station with the least possible delay, together with a report of the circumstances occasioning the arrest.
- Army officers have legal immunity for their actions. There can be no prosecution, suit or any other legal proceeding against anyone acting under that law. Nor

is the government's judgment on why an area is found to be disturbed subject to judicial review.

- Protection of persons acting in good faith under this Act from prosecution, suit or other legal proceedings, except with the sanction of the Central Government, in exercise of the powers conferred by this Act.

## Non-state Views and Commentary

### United Nations view

When India presented its second periodic report to the United Nations Human Rights Committee in 1991, members of the UNHRC asked numerous questions about the validity of the AFSPA. They questioned the constitutionality of the AFSPA under Indian law and asked how it could be justified in light of Article 4 of the International Covenant on Civil and Political Rights, ICCPR. On 23 March 2009, UN Commissioner for Human Rights Navanethem Pillay asked India to repeal the AFSPA. She termed the law as "dated and colonial-era law that breach contemporary international human rights standards."

On 31 March 2012, the UN asked India to revoke AFSPA saying it had the no place in Indian democracy. Christof Heyns, UN's Special Rapporteur on extrajudicial, summary or arbitrary executions said "During my visit to Kashmir, AFSPA was described to me as 'hated' and 'draconian'. It clearly violates International Law. A number of UN treaty bodies have pronounced it to be in violation of International Law as well."

### Non-governmental organizations' analysis

The act has been criticized by Human Rights Watch as a "tool of state abuse, oppression and discrimination".

The South Asian Human Rights Documentation Centre argues that the governments' call for increased force is part of the problem.

"This reasoning exemplifies the vicious cycle which has been instituted in the North East due to the AFSPA. The use of the AFSPA pushes the demand for more autonomy, giving the people of the North East more reason to want to secede from a state which enacts such powers and the agitation which ensues continues to justify the use of the AFSPA from the point of view of the Indian Government." - The South Asian Human Rights Documentation Centre

A report by the Institute for Defense Studies and Analysis points to multiple occurrences of violence by security forces against civilians in Manipur since the passage of the Act. The report states that residents believe that the provision for immunity of security forces urge them to act more brutally. The article, however, goes on to say that repeal or withering away of the act will encourage insurgency.

In addition to this, there have been claims of disappearances by the police or the army in Kashmir by several human rights organizations.

Many human rights organizations such as Amnesty International and the Human Rights Watch (HRW) have condemned human rights abuses in Kashmir by police such as "extra-judicial executions", "disappearances", and torture; the "Armed Forces Special Powers Act", which "provides impunity for human rights abuses and fuels cycles of violence. The Armed Forces Special Powers Act (AFSPA) grants the military wide powers of arrest, the right to shoot to kill, and to occupy or destroy property in counterinsurgency operations. Indian officials claim that troops need such powers because the army is only deployed when national security is at serious risk from armed combatants. Such circumstances, they say, call for extraordinary measures." Human rights organizations have also asked Indian government to repeal the Public Safety Act, since "a detainee may be held in administrative detention for a maximum of two years without a court order.".

Activists who are working in J&K for peace and human rights include names of Madhu Kishwar, Ashima Kaul, Ram Jethmalani, Faisal Khan, Ravi Nitesh, Swami Agnivesh, Dr. Sandeep Pandey and many others. They all accept that people to people communication and development of new avenues are the only way for peace, however laws like AFSPA are continuously violating human rights issues there." What [the Indian State] has failed to see is that such small, ethnic groups are resisting the Indian state for 55 years" says legal activist and scholar, Babloo Loitongbom.

## United States leaked diplomatic cables

The Wikileaks diplomatic cables have recently disclosed that Indian government employees agree to acts of human rights violations on part of the Indian armed forces and various paramilitary forces deployed in the north east parts of India especially Manipur. The violations have been carried out under the cover of this very act. Governor S.S. Sidhu admitted to the American Consul General in Kolkata, Henry Jardine, that the Assam Rifles in particular are perpetrators of violations in Manipur which the very same cables described as a state that appeared more of a colony and less of an Indian state.

Earlier leaks had also stated that International Committee of the Red Cross (ICRC) had reported to the United States diplomats in Delhiabout the grave human rights situation in Kashmir which included the use of electrocution, beatings and sexual humiliation against hundreds of detainees. This act is in force in Kashmir since 1990.

## Santosh Hegde commission on Manipur encounter deaths

A high-power commission headed by the retired Supreme Court judge, Santosh Hegde was constituted in January 2013 to probe six encounter deaths in Manipur. The committee, comprising former Supreme Court judge Santosh Hegde, ex-CEC J M Lyngdoh and a senior police officer, has said in its report that the probe showed that none of the victims had any criminal records. The judicial commission set up by the Supreme Court is trying to make the controversial Armed Forces Special Powers Act (AFSPA) more humane, and the security forces more accountable.

The committee has suggested fixing a time frame of three months for the central government to decide whether to prosecute security personnel engaged in extrajudicial killings or unruly behaviour in insurgency-hit regions. The Commission noted that AFSPA was an impediment to achieving peace in regions such as Jammu and Kashmir and the northeast. The commission also said the law needs to be reviewed every six months to see whether its implementation is actually necessary in states where it is being enforced. About Section 6 of the act, which guarantees protection against prosecution to the armed forces, the report said: "It is not that no action can be taken at all. Action can be taken but with prior sanction of the central government.

## MILITARY MODERNIZATION

The military modernization begun in the late 1970s had three major focuses. First, under the political leadership of Deng Xiaoping, the military became disengaged from civilian politics and, for the most part, resumed the political quiescence that characterized its pre-Cultural Revolution role. Deng reestablished civilian control over the military by appointing his supporters to key military leadership positions, by reducing the scope of the PLA's domestic nonmilitary role, and by revitalizing the party political structure and ideological control system within the PLA.

Second, modernization required the reform of military organization, doctrine, education and training, and personnel policies to improve combat effectiveness in combined-arms warfare. Among the organizational reforms that were undertaken were the creation of the state Central Military Commission, the streamlining and reduction of superfluous PLA forces, civilianization of many PLA units, reorganization of military regions, formation of group armies, and enactment of the new Military Service Law in 1984. Doctrine, strategy, and tactics were revised under the rubric of "people's war under modern conditions," which envisaged a forward defence at selected locations near China's borders, to prevent attack on Chinese cities and industrial sites, and emphasized operations using combined-arms tactics. Reforms in education and training emphasized improving the military skills and raising the education levels of officers and troops and conducting combinedarms operations. New personnel policies required upgrading the quality of PLA recruits and officer candidates, improving conditions of service, changing promotion practices to stress professional competence, and providing new uniforms and insignia.

The third focus of military modernization was the transformation of the defence establishment into a system capable of independently maintaining a modern military force. As military expenditures remained relatively constant, reforms concentrated on reorganizing the defence research-and-development and industrial base to integrate civilian and military science and industry more closely. Foreign technology was used selectively to upgrade weapons. Defence industry reforms also resulted in China's entry into the international arms market and the increased production of civilian goods by defence industries. The scope of PLA economic activities was reduced, but the military continued to participate in infrastructure development projects and initiated a program to provide demobilized soldiers with skills useful in the civilian economy.

## Civil-Military Relations

Lines between civilian and military leadership and institutions in China are indistinct. All high-ranking military leaders have high-level party positions, and many high-ranking party officials have some military experience. When military leaders participate in national policy making, therefore, it is not clear whether their positions reflect PLA corporate interests or the interests of groups that cut across institutional lines. In general, in times where there was national leadership consensus on national policy, such as in the 1950s, the PLA was politically quiescent. Once the PLA was drawn into civilian politics during the Cultural Revolution, the military became divided along the lines of civilian factions. As long as the national leadership remained divided on a number of policy issues, the PLA, fearing factional struggles and political instability, was reluctant to leave the political scene. When Deng Xiaoping was rehabilitated in 1977, however, the stage was set for the withdrawal of the military from politics and a partial return to the PLA's previous political passivity.

## Political Role of the People's Liberation Army

Deng Xiaoping's efforts in the 1980s to reduce the political role of the military stemmed from his desire to reassert civilian control over the military and to promote military modernization. To accomplish his objectives, Deng revitalized the civilian party apparatus and leadership and built a consensus on the direction of national policy. He also established personal control over the military through personnel changes, and he reduced the scope of the PLA's domestic political, economic, and social roles. Finally, he strengthened party control over the military through institutional reforms and political and ideological education. The revitalization of the party and the establishment of a consensus on national policy assured top military leaders of political stability and a vigorous party capable of handling national and regional affairs without extensive military participation.

Deng's personal political control was established over the military through his assumption of the position of chairman of the party Central Military Commission in June 1981 and through his appointment of his supporters to key positions in the party Central Military Commission, Ministry of National Defence, and the PLA's General Staff Department, General Political Department, and General Logistics Department. Occasional replacement of military region and military district commanders also strengthened Deng's hand. Military leaders who objected to Deng's policies were replaced with more amenable personnel.

The creation of the state Central Military Commission in 1982 aimed to further strengthen civilian control over the military by stressing the PLA's role as defender of the state and by establishing another layer of supervision parallel to party supervision. The civilianization of several PLA corps and internal security units reduced the size of the PLA and the scope of its involvement in civilian affairs. The placement of defence industries under civilian control and the transfer or opening up of military facilities, such as airports and ports, to civilian authorities also limited the PLA's influence in economic and political matters. Propaganda using the PLA as a model for society also diminished, and emphasis was placed on the PLA's military rather than political role.

## Party Control

In addition to making personnel changes, Deng revitalized party control over the PLA and diffused the military's political power by designating provincial-level, municipal, district, and county party committee secretaries to serve concurrently as the first political commissars of their equivalent-level units in the regional PLA.

The percentage of PLA personnel permitted to join the party was limited by restricting party membership to military academy graduates. Political and ideological training stressed the military rather than the social, ideological, or economic role of the PLA. Special effort was made to discredit the PLA's role in the Cultural Revolution; the PLA's support for the left was described as incorrect because it caused factionalism within the military.

While emphasizing the necessity and appropriateness of reforms to modernize the military, political education also sought to guarantee military support for Deng's reform agenda. Beginning in 1983 a rectification campaign (part of the party-wide rectification campaign aimed primarily at leftists) reinforced this kind of political and ideological training.

Beginning in the late 1970s, Deng Xiaoping succeeded in decreasing military participation in national-level political bodies. Military representation on the Political Bureau fell from 52 percent in 1978 to 30 percent in 1982, and military membership in the party Central Committee declined from 30 percent in 1978 to 22 percent in 1982. Most professional military officers shared common views with the Deng leadership over military modernization and the fundamental direction of national policy, and they willingly limited their concerns to military matters.

Nonetheless, some elements in the PLA continued to voice their opinions on nondefense matters and criticized the Deng reform program. Dissent centered on prestigious military leaders, notably Ye Jianying, who feared that ideological de-Modification, cultural liberalization, and certain agricultural and industrial reforms deviated from Marxist values and ideals. The Deng leadership contained these criticisms with the help of the personnel changes, political education, and the rectification campaign just mentioned. In this way it was able to keep military dissent within bounds that did not adversely affect civil-military relations.

## Popular Attitudes Toward the People's Liberation Army

Starting in the late 1970s, popular attitudes toward the PLA also underwent considerable changes. In the 1950s and 1960s, the military's prestige was very high because of its wartime exploits, because it was held up as a role model for society, and because of its participation in civilian construction projects.

But the power gained by the PLA during the Cultural Revolution reawakened civilian resentment of military privileges and abuses of power. By the early 1980s, with the circumscription of the PLA's domestic role and the implementation of agricultural reforms offering greater opportunities for rural youth, the PLA's reputation as a prestigious, elite, Marxist-model organization and a promising channel for social mobility was severely tarnished.

Society's perception of the military appeared to be returning to the traditional viewpoint that "one doesn't make nails out of good iron; one doesn't make soldiers out of good men." To restore this damaged image in the late 1980s, the media extolled the PLA's martial virtues and the great strides made in military modernization in recent years.

## MILITARY ORGANIZATION

By 1987 changes in military organization indicated the importance Chinese leaders attached to structural reform in building military forces capable of waging modern, combined-arms warfare. These reforms included the creation of the state Central Military Commission parallel to the party Central Military Commission, reduction in force, reorganization of military regions, formation of group armies, enactment of the new Military Service Law, and reorganization of defence industries.

### State and Party Central Military Commissions

At the apex of Chinese military organization stood two bodies—the state and party Central Military Commissions. The 1982 state Constitution created the state Central Military Commission as the state organ subordinate to the National People's Congress responsible for "directing the country's armed forces".

The state Central Military Commission was the state's decision-making body in military affairs and directed and commanded the armed forces. The state Central Military Commission consisted of the chairman, who was commander in chief of the armed forces, an executive vice chairman, two vice chairmen, and four other members.

The party Central Military Commission, elected by the party Central Committee, exercised de facto, authoritative policy-making and operational control over the military. In addition to the chairman, the party Central Military Commission in 1987 included a permanent vice chairman who was concurrently secretary general, two vice chairmen, and four deputy secretaries general. The leadership of the state and party Central Military Commissions was identical, but the membership of the party Central Military Commission below the top leadership was thought to include regional commanders and service chiefs. Because the PLA has been under party control since its inception, the leadership of the party over the military did not change with the establishment of the state Central Military Commission. Although parallel leadership blurred the distinction between the two groups, the party Central Military Commission retained its traditional, preeminent position in charge of military affairs.

## Ministry of National Defence and NDSTIC

Beneath the two Central Military Commissions were the Ministry of National Defence and the National Defence Science, Technology, and Industry Commission (NDSTIC), which separately took orders from the two Central Military Commissions but had no operational control over the PLA. The Ministry of National Defence was responsible for military modernization and provided administrative support for the PLA. It was responsible for planning, manpower, budget, foreign liaison, and training materials, but it possessed no policy-making or implementation authority.

The NDSTIC—formed in August 1982 by merging the National Defence Science and Technology Commission, National Defence Industries Office, and Office of the Science, Technology, and Armaments Commission of the party Central Military Commission—was responsible for military research and development, weapons procurement, and coordination of the defence and civilian economic sectors.

## Operational Control

In 1987 operational control of the PLA ran from the two Central Military Commissions to the PLA's three general departments: General Staff Department, General Political Department, and General Logistics Department. Below the department level ran parallel chains of command for operational, political, and logistical matters, each with its own separate communications facilities. Military policy originated in the party Political Bureau or the party Central Military Commission, became an operational order at the General Staff Department level, flowed through the military regions, and arrived at a main-force unit. Orders to regional forces also passed through the military district (provincial) level.

## General Staff Department

The General Staff Department carried out staff and operational functions for the PLA and had major responsibility for implementing military modernization plans. Headed by the chief of general staff, the department served as the headquarters for the ground forces and contained directorates for the three other armed services: Air Force, Navy, and Strategic Missile Force.

The General Staff Department included functionally organized subdepartments for artillery, armored units, engineering, operations, training, intelligence, mobilization, surveying, communications, quartermaster services, and politics. Navy Headquarters controlled the North Sea Fleet, East Sea Fleet, and South Sea Fleet. Air Force Headquarters generally exercised control through the commanders of the seven military regions. Nuclear forces were directly subordinate to the General Staff Department. Conventional main, regional, and militia units were controlled administratively by the military region commanders, but the General Staff Department in Beijing could assume direct operational control of any main-force unit at will. Thus, broadly speaking, the General Staff Department exercised operational control of the main forces, and the military region commanders controlled the regional forces and, indirectly, the militia.

## General Political Department

The General Political Department was responsible for ideological indoctrination, political loyalty, morale, personnel records, cultural activities, discipline, and military justice, and it provided the party structure for the PLA. It also published *Jiefangjun Bao* (Liberation Army Daily), the PLA's influential newspaper. The General Political Department director was at the head of a system of political commissars assigned to each echelon in the PLA. One of the primary tasks of the political commissar was the supervision of the party organization through party committees at the battalion level and above or through party branches in companies. Virtually all high-ranking officers in the military were party members. Until the early 1980s, when party membership in the PLA was restricted, an effort was made to have a party or Communist Youth League member in every unit down to the smallest maneuver element. Political commissars were equal in rank and authority to the commander of their echelon in peacetime but theoretically deferred to the commander during war. Commissars assumed many time-consuming chores, such as personnel problems, relations with civilians, and troop entertainment.

## General Logistics Department

The General Logistics Department, headed by a director, was responsible for production, supply, transportation, housing, pay, and medical services. Historically, much of this support came from the civilian populace, and before the establishment of the General Logistics Department it was organized most often by commissars. PLA logistical resources in 1980 were far fewer than those of Western or Soviet forces; in the event of war the Chinese military would be heavily dependent upon the militia and civilians. In 1985 the General Logistics Department was reorganized, its staff cut by 50 percent, and some of its facilities turned over to the civilian sector.

## Streamlining and Reduction in Force

Efforts began in the 1980s to streamline the PLA and organize it into a modern fighting force. The first step in reducing the 4.5-million-member PLA in the early 1980s was to relieve the PLA of some of its nonmilitary duties. The Railway Engineering Corps and the Capital Construction Engineering Corps were civilianized, and in 1983 the PLA internal security and border patrol units were transferred to the People's Armed Police Force.

In 1985 China reorganized its 11 military regions into 7 and began a 2-year program to reduce the force by 1 million. Eight military regions were merged into four—Chengdu, Jinan, Lanzhou, and Nanjing—and three key regions—Beijing, Guangzhou, and Shenyang—remained intact. The PLA accomplished its 1-million-troop cut by streamlining the headquarters staffs of the three general departments, the military regions, and the military districts; reducing the size of the Air Force and the Navy; retiring older, undereducated, or incompetent officers; and transferring county-and city-level people's armed forces departments, which controlled the militia, to local civil authorities. The PLA also reorganized its field armies (main-force armies) into group armies to increase its capability to wage combined-arms warfare. Breaking with the previously triangular organization of military units, the group armies combined formerly independent arms or services into a comprehensive combat unit. Group armies consisted of infantry and mechanized infantry divisions, tank divisions or brigades, and a number of artillery, antichemical, air defence, engineer, signal, reconnaissance, electronic countermeasure, and logistics troops. In the late 1980s, some group armies also had helicopter, air support, or naval units.

In 1987 PLA strength was about 3 million. Ground forces numbered about 2.1 million—the world's largest standing army; the Navy about 350,000—including those assigned to Naval Aviation, Coastal Defence Forces, and Marine Corps; the Air Force about 390,000; and the Strategic Missile Force about 100,000. The PLA was supported by an estimated 4.3 million basic (armed and trained) militia and 6 million ordinary (poorly armed and trained) militia. According to the 1984 Military Service Law, the militia, which was being combined with a newly developed reserve system, and the People's Armed Police Force also formed part of the Chinese armed forces. In 1986 reserve forces were included officially in the organizational system.

## Doctrine, Strategy, and Tactics

From the early 1950s until the mid-1970s, people's war remained China's military doctrine. The PLA's force structure, however, which came to include nuclear weapons as well as artillery, combat aircraft, and tanks, did not reflect the concept of people's war. In the late 1970s, Chinese military leaders began to modify PLA doctrine, strategy, and tactics under the rubric of "people's war under modern conditions."

This updated version of people's war lacked a systematic definition, but it permitted Chinese military leaders to pay tribute to Mao's military and revolutionary legacy while adapting military strategy and tactics to the needs of modern conventional and nuclear warfare. Elaborating on Mao's concept of active defence—tactically offensive action with a defensive strategy—Chinese strategy was designed to defeat a Soviet invasion before it could penetrate deeply into China. Chinese strategists envisaged a forward defence, that is, near the border, to prevent attack on Chinese cities and industrial facilities, particularly in north and northeast China. Such a defence-in-depth would require more positional warfare, much closer to the border, in the initial stages of a conflict. This strategy downplayed the people's war strategy of "luring in deep" in a protracted war, and it took into account the adaptations in strategy and tactics necessitated by technological advances in weaponry. The PLA emphasized military operations using modernized, combined arms tactics for the dual purpose of making the most effective use of current force structure and of preparing the armed forces for more advanced weaponry in the future.

The doctrine of "people's war under modern conditions" also incorporated the use of strategic and tactical nuclear weapons. China's own nuclear forces, which developed a second-strike capability in the early 1980s, provided Beijing with a credible, if minimum, deterrent against Soviet or United States nuclear attack. China repeatedly has vowed never to use nuclear weapons first, but it has promised retaliation against a nuclear attack. Chinese strategists also evinced an interest in tactical nuclear weapons, and the PLA has simulated battlefield use of such weapons in offensive and defensive exercises.

## Education and Training

Reforms in training and education constituted an important part of the military modernization program in the 1980s. Senior officials recognized that improving the military skills and raising the education levels of both officers and troops were necessary prerequisites for the utilization of more advanced weaponry and the conduct of combined-arms operations. The PLA leadership focused education reforms on the military academy system and altered training to emphasize the officer corps, mechanized warfare, and combined arms operations.

## Revitalization of the Military Academy System

Beginning in 1978, the PLA began to revive the military academy system, which the Cultural Revolution had devastated. By 1984 the system had over 100 institutions and consisted of two kinds of schools: command schools and specialized technical training centers. The PLA increased funding for military education, incorporated the study of foreign military experiences into the curriculum, and expanded contacts with foreign military academies. The rejuvenation of the military academies highlighted the emphasis placed on officer training. The PLA stipulated that most new officers should be military academy graduates, set minimum education levels for all officers, and established special classes to help officers meet those standards. Education and military academy training thus became criteria for promotion, in addition to seniority, performance, and experience.

In 1986 the PLA introduced three measures that further strengthened the military academy system. First, at the top level the PLA's Military Academy, Political Academy, and Logistics Academy merged to form the National Defence University, China's senior military training and research institution. Second, a new, three-level training system for command officers was announced, whereby command officers would receive regular training at junior, middle, and higher military command academies. Third, noncommissioned officer (NCO) training entered the military academy system with the establishment of a naval academy for petty officers and an air force NCO academy and the creation of NCO classes in over forty ground force academies.

## Training Reforms

Before the military modernization program began, PLA training was highly politicized and emphasized single-unit infantry troop training. Training reforms started with the depoliticization of training, whereby troops spent 80 percent of their time on military activities and 20 percent on political training. The scope of training then changed to concentrate on training officers capable of directing combined-arms warfare. Improved military education in the rejuvenated military academies provided some of this officer training. In addition, large-scale combined-arms exercises, which served to raise officer capabilities in commanding and coordinating combined-arms operations under combat conditions, occurred on a regular basis.

These exercises stressed defence against attacking tanks, paratroopers, and aircraft and on occasion involved the simulated use of tactical nuclear weapons. The PLA also began using simulation equipment in training and in 1985 held its first completely simulated combat exercise. In 1986 the PLA training system underwent further reforms that complemented changes in military organization. A combined-arms tactical training centre was created for training the newly formed group armies (former field armies) on a rotational basis. The training centre coordinated group army exercises and utilized laser devices and simulation equipment in its training. The PLA also established a systematic training program for new recruits, replacing the old system in which inductees received basic training in their units. Under the new system, before new recruits were assigned to PLA units, they completed four months of training by a training regiment attached to a group army. The training regiments also trained squad leaders.

## Personnel

Defence modernization brought changes to military personnel policies and practices. Personnel reforms emphasized upgrading the quality of recruits, improving conditions of service, altering promotion practices to stress professional competence over seniority or political loyalty, and providing new uniforms and insignia. The 1984 Military Service Law codified some of the changes in personnel policies and set the stage for further changes, such as the restoration of ranks.

## Recruitment

The Military Service Law provided the legal basis for conscription, and it combined compulsory and voluntary service. All citizens between eighteen and twenty-two, regardless of sex, nationality, profession, family background, religion, or level of education, were obliged to perform military service. Almost 10 million men reached conscription age each year, but the PLA chose less than 10 percent of those eligible. A very small number of women were inducted annually. In the 1980s the PLA attempted to upgrade the quality of its inductees by changing recruiting practices. The PLA previously drew its recruits from rural youth of politically acceptable families. But the Military Service Law, the introduction of rural reforms offering greater economic opportunities for rural youth, and the PLA's requirements for higher educational levels caused recruitment to draw more recruits from better educated urban youth. Officers were drawn from military academy graduates; enlisted men and women who completed officer training in officially designated institutions and passed officer fitness tests; graduates of universities and special technical secondary schools; and civilian cadres and technical personnel recruited by nonmilitary units in the PLA. As a result of the new conscription and officer recruitment practices, the level of education in the PLA was much higher than that of the general population.

# Bibliography


Anderson, J., O'Dowd, L. and Wilson, T. M.: *New Borders for a Changing Europe: Cross-border Cooperation and Governance*, London: Frank Cass, 2003.

Barua, Pradeep: *Gentlemen of the Raj: The Indian Army Officer Corps, 1817–1949,* 2003.

Bellamy, C.: *Knights in White Armour: The New Art of War and Peace,* London, Random House, 1997.

Bose, S. C., *The Indian Struggle, 1920-1942,* Bombay, Asia Publishing House, 1964.

Depinder, Singh: *Soldering with Dignity*. Natraj Publishers. 2006.

Donnan, H. and Wilson, T. M.: *Borders: Frontiers of Identity, Nation and State,* Oxford: Berg, 1999.

Guy, Alan J.; Boyden, Peter B.: *Soldiers of the Raj, The Indian Army 1600–1947.* National Army Museum Chelsea, 1997.

Herken, Gregg. *The Winning Weapon: The Atomic Bomb in the Cold War, 1945-1950.* Princeton: Princeton University Press, 1988.

Hoffman, Bruce, *Inside Terrorism*, New York: Columbia University Press, 1998.

Holsti, K.: *The State, War, and the State of War,* Cambridge, Cambridge Univ. Press, 1996.

Imtiaz, A.: *State and Foreign Policy: India's Role in South Asia,* New Delhi, Vikas, 1993.

Jha, Prem Shankar : *India and China : The Battle Between Soft and Hard Power*, Penguin Books India, Delhi, 2010.

Jones, W.H.: *The Government and Politics of Indian Military,* London, Hutchinson, 1971.

Juvale, R.P. : *Military Strategy and Diplomacy*, Cyber Tech Publications, Delhi, 2010.

Kapur, Ashok: *Pakistan's Nuclear Development,* New York: Croom Helm, 1987.

Kelly, John B.: *Britain and the Persian Gulf 1795-1880*, Oxford, Clarendon Press, 1968.

Kunju, N. : *Indo-Pak : Nuclear Cold War*, Reliance, Delhi, 2002.

Lamb, Alastair: *Kashmir: a disputed legacy, 1846-1990*, Oxford University Press, 1991.

Lifton, Robert Jay and Mitchell, Greg. *Hiroshima in America: A Half Century of Denial*. New York: Avon Books, 1995.

Mary, W.: *Military Space Force: the Cultural Dimensions of Authority*, Cambridge, Belknap Press, 1985.

Morris, W.H.: *The Government and Politics of India*, London, Hutchinson, 1971.

Nevile, P.: *Lahore: A Sentimental Journey*. New Delhi: Penguin, 1993.

Raghavan, Srinath: *War and Peace in Modern India: A Strategic History of the Nehru Years*. Ranikhet, India: Permanent Black, 2010.

Rhodes, Richard, *The Making of the Atomic Bomb, New York:* Simon and Schuster, 1988.

Roger, Alexander: *Battle Honours of the British Empire and Commonwealth Land Forces 1662–1991*. Crowood Press. Marlborough. 2003.

Singh, Amarinder : *A Ridge Too Far: War in the Kargil Heights 1999*. Motibagh Palace, Patiala. 2001.

Singh, Jasjit: *Kargil 1999: Pakistan's Fourth War for Kashmir*. South Asia Books. 1999.

Spector, Leonard S., *Going Nuclear*, Cambridge, MA: Ballinger Publishing Company, 1987.

Sumantra Bose, *The Challenge in Kashmir : democracy, self-determination and a just peace*, New Delhi: Sage, 1997.

Sumner, Ian, & Chappell, Mike: *The Indian Army 1914–1947*. Osprey Publishing. Oxford. 2001.

Sutton, J., *Technology and Defence Market Structure*, MIT Press, Delhi, 1998.

Velez-Ibanez, Carlos: *Border Visions and Management*. University of Arizona Press, 1996.

Weeks, John: *World War II Small Arms*, New York: Galahad Books (1979).

Wilson, Thomas M., and Hastings Donnan: *A Companion to Border Studies*. Hoboken, NJ: Wiley-Blackwell, 2012.

Winkler, Allan M. *Life Under A Cloud: American Anxiety About the Atom*. New York: Oxford University Press, 1993.

# Index

❑❑❑

B.R.W. Book